AGAINST THE ODDS
JORDAN'S
DRIVE TO WIN

AGAINST THE ODDS

JORDAN'S
DRIVE TO WIN

Jon Nicholson & Maurice Hamilton

MACMILLAN

First published 1999 by Macmillan
an imprint of Macmillan Publishers Limited
25 Eccleston Place, London SW1W 9NF
and Basingstoke

Associated companies throughout the world

ISBN 0 333 73655 9

Text copyright © Maurice Hamilton 1998
Photographs copyright © Jon Nicholson 1998
(except pages 190, 194, 195, 202, 203, 212
photographs copyright © LAT)

9 8 7 6 5 4 3 2 1

A CIP catalogue record for this book is available
from the British Library

Printed and bound in Italy by New Interlitho

Contents

Introduction

Five years ago, I wrote a book about Jordan Grand Prix. The team was in its third season of Formula 1, mere babes-in-arms when compared with the might of Williams and Ferrari.

The story was about a group of fifty-three people feeling their way around the world on an annual budget which would barely pay the wages bill now. It was a tale of fortitude and persistence which culminated in Jordan finally scoring a couple of championship points at the penultimate race of the season.

It had been a pleasure working with a team which had bravely allowed me to record the painful struggle, warts and all. I made a note to return when, figuratively speaking, Jordan had grown up and was ready to win a Grand Prix.

The team had come close in 1997, finishing second in Argentina and leading in Germany until a puncture had snatched away a certain victory. When Damon Hill was signed for 1998, that first win was as good as guaranteed. The timing seemed perfect. It was agreed that this book could go ahead.

I was looking forward to drawing comparisons between the Jordan of 1993 and a team which had trebled in size and budget. The launch of the new car was an encouraging indicator of how sights had been raised during the previous five years. From a draughty garage at the Silverstone race track, the scene of the unveiling had moved to the Royal Albert Hall. You couldn't ask for better than that. This was going to be a fascinating project.

It would turn out to be the most difficult imaginable. Instead of recording a surging build-up to the heady moment of victory, I had a notebook filled with woe. The launch in London turned out to be the height of optimism. It was downhill from then on as Jordan slid quickly and, it seemed, irrevocably into a morass of increasing anxiety fuelled by a succession of mediocre performances.

Rather than writing grandly about a team on the cusp of greatness, I was dealing with a company in crisis. Instead of sharing and enjoying success, I was witnessing the ravaging effects of failure as the team turned in on itself in the search for a solution.

This dramatic and unexpected switch in emphasis meant the book would be no less significant for that. If anything, the storyline would generate a more emotional twist.

From a coldly commercial standpoint, that was good news. Grand Prix teams rarely subject themselves to scrutiny when winning; never when losing. The effect of failure in such an aggressively competitive sport is something which must be endured behind closed doors. It becomes a family affair as the inevitable domestic squabbles are dealt with in private. And there I was, standing beside the kitchen sink, notebook in hand.

Jordan Grand Prix has changed beyond recognition in certain respects; in others, it is exactly as it was. In the introduction to the previous book, I paid tribute to the team's absence of paranoia in a business where the self-important hesitate if you ask them for the time of day. I was grateful in 1993 for the Jordan management's refusal to usher me away at sensitive times.

That appreciation must be repeated now, but with an even greater sense of respect since much more was at stake. This story was not working out as we had envisaged, but no effort was made to stop it. Indeed, there was no attempt at censorship even though the text was occasionally less than flattering.

It was all very well to wear a marketing hat and claim this tale would be both unique and sad, and therefore justifiable. But that was not the original intention. Just as in 1993, I was desperately hoping for a happy ending, one which would cast a soothing light on the earlier suffering.

There was always hope inside Jordan Grand Prix and, once the reality had set in and corrective treatment applied, it was felt that a finish in the top three would be a possibility before the season was through. Everyone said they would be happy with that.

Thinking about this book, I could only agree. The recording of Jordan's first Grand Prix victory had long since been dismissed as wishful thinking.

Even when that memorable weekend in August began to gather a momentum which suggested something was in the air, the thought of a win in Belgium remained too far-fetched for even the most imaginative script writer.

The one-two finish, when it came, simply defied belief. Furthermore, it had been earned the hard way rather than inherited. Jordan Grand Prix had finally won respect in an intensely selfish arena. There could not have been a better climax and it was a privilege to have been on hand to witness it. The agonizing and heartache suddenly seemed worthwhile. And I'm not just talking about the team.

Maurice Hamilton
Cranleigh, Surrey
October 1998

Reaching the Edge

The music was typically Irish, a combination of

flute and fiddle with other instruments giving the

necessary commercial weight. The voice, as if roughly

shaped by long nights sampling the products of

Gallaher and Guinness, belted out lyrics that seemed

entirely appropriate.

'I'll always be your friend until the end,' he sang. 'We've seen the other side of life.'

The beat was so good you didn't want your party to answer and the telephonist to remove the call from hold. Most Grand Prix teams choose classical music to soothe the frustration of waiting on line. This vibrant backdrop had all the brash but dreamy qualities the world had come to expect of Jordan Grand Prix.

'I'll always be your friend until the end.' Eddie Jordan could have written those words.

The abrupt cessation of the ear-thumping sound brought a sharp return to reality. Back to earth; back to business. In this case, the business of winning Grands Prix. For all the *joie de vivre* and swirling emotion which Eddie Jordan leaves in his wake, there is a sense of purpose driving him forward. In recent years, that ambition had developed a noticeably hard edge.

1998 would be his eighth season as the entrant of a Formula 1 team and yet he did not have a single victory to his name. Time was when it didn't matter that much. Sure, a win would have been very nice, but the team was learning, finding its feet, eyeing the opposition and vowing to give the likes of Williams and Ferrari a run for their money one day.

In 1998, the talking had to stop. The goodwill was about to run out after being used so generously; the media and the fans had allowed affection to subjugate the team's obvious inadequacies. Now it was time for Eddie Jordan to put up and shut up.

Everything was in place. For years, the team's Technical Director, Gary Anderson, had struggled to receive the funding necessary to allow investment in the technical support he needed. Jordan couldn't pay for it because he didn't have a big sponsor. The arrival of Benson and Hedges in 1996 was the first step, the tobacco company appreciating the value of exposure generated by going Formula 1 racing worldwide, particularly with a team such as Jordan Grand Prix. For 1997, the money was increased.

When B&H later committed itself until the end of 2000, Jordan finally had financial security – of a sort. It was not on a par with Ferrari and Marlboro, or McLaren and West, but it was the best Eddie Jordan had ever known. It was enough to give the green light to the purchase of a £2.3m wind tunnel and other elaborate equipment for measuring and translating the performance of the car far better than even the best drivers and technicians could manage by word of mouth.

Then there was the engine. Without adequate power under his right foot, the fastest driver in the best chassis would struggle. A deal was made with Mugen-Honda in Japan. Mugen is run by Hirotoshi Honda, son of the founder of the industry giant, Honda Motor. Mugen-Honda had been largely independent of the main company, using Honda's hardware but effectively doing its own thing. Honda had withdrawn from Formula 1 on the crest of a wave at the end of 1992. Rumour had it that it was thinking of making a comeback. On the quiet. Perhaps through Mugen.

When Eddie Jordan signed up in July 1997, he knew he was walking through the front door of Mugen-Honda and ducking into the back of the Honda Motor Competitions Department. It could only be good news for Jordan Grand Prix. That took care of the engine. The chassis would be the best they had ever made. But who would drive it?

The fact was that Jordan needed a driver with the experience of winning consistently, someone who knew how to take the team down the final mile. Never before had Eddie Jordan employed a driver who had won more than a couple of Grands Prix. That was put right when he signed Damon Hill for 1998. Not only had Hill won twenty-one Grands Prix, he had also been World Champion. More to the point, he had done it with Williams, one of the most seasoned and prag-matic teams in Grand Prix racing. Hill would bring a mixture of speed and experience, the perfect foil for his hard-charging team-mate. Ralf Schumacher would keep Hill honest; Damon would teach the younger brother of his old adversary, Michael Schumacher, a thing or two. This seemed to be the final piece in a jigsaw which Jordan had been struggling to put together for eight years.

When Jordan started out in 1991, the priority was to survive. The Dubliner was coming in on a wing and a prayer, his expansive line of chat making up for the sparseness of the budget. The team scored points in its first season, a notable achievement which seemed to support the view that Jordan was here to stay even though Eddie and his management team were effectively living from one month to the next, working on the basis that everything would be all right on the night. Which it usually was.

But that was the first year. Piles of grandiose plans, hatched by now-defunct teams and festering in the liquidators' files, indicated that the second year would be worse. And it was. Jordan knew the honeymoon was over when he struggled to score just one point in 1992 and the team's finances amounted to a minus more often than a plus.

That bad experience brought a leaner, more efficient unit in 1993 as the team began to turn the corner – albeit slowly. A switch to Peugeot engines in 1995 brought Jordan's first contact with a major engine manufacturer with supposedly serious intentions about Formula 1. Or so they thought. Anderson continued to produce cars which were much admired by rivals in the pit lane. And yet, having moved to the head of the second division, Jordan seemed incapable of making the final step.

In fact, it would require a considerable leap to cross the divide and join the Big Four, Williams, Ferrari, McLaren and Benetton. Recognizing this, Jordan went to work. The result: Mugen-Honda, Benson and Hedges and, finally, Damon Hill.

Adapting the words from the song: Jordan had seen this side of life, now it was time to discover how the other half lived. At the beginning of 1998, he was ready to take off and cross that divide. But it meant his reputation was truly on the edge. That chasm was to prove desperately deep and almost tear his beloved team apart.

Chapter One

Promises, Promises

A week before the start of the first race, Eddie Jordan

got his picture in the paper. There was nothing

unusual about that since newspapers and magazines

were slavishly following a traditional routine by running

previews of the 1998 Grand Prix season – one which,

in the opinion of many observers, promised to be

the best yet.

Nothing unusual about that, either. After a four-month lay-off from racing, speculation frequently runs wild when fuelled by sometimes outrageous optimism. Reality appears to be put on hold as teams, drivers, engine manufacturers and sponsors speak enthusiastically about the future as if attempting to justify the huge sums of money one side has paid to or, more often than not, extracted from the other.

If talking won races, every team with a PR department worth its salt would be champion tomorrow. Eddie Jordan, single-handedly, could put his company ahead in that game. Already, Jordan was neck-and-neck with McLaren and Williams in the race to gain the most column inches before the cars had so much as turned a wheel in serious competition. This was due, in part, to having Damon Hill on board. It was also thanks to the boss and his reputation for providing a useful quote and a tasty story.

Eddie Jordan appeared on the front of the *Sunday Times*. Significantly, Jordan's name was signposting a feature, not in Sport, but in the Business section. No other team principal could boast a single mention there, never mind a full page with a photograph running across six columns. The feature was part of a series featuring the growth of middle-market companies. The writer, David Sumner Smith, had immediately latched on to one of Eddie Jordan's finest assets; within the thirty-word introduction, Sumner Smith had already mentioned 'gift of the gab'.

No success story would be worth the space in print if there had not been a struggle along the way. Eddie Jordan could provide that without having to revert to even the mildest exaggeration. It was too recent for the scars to have healed, and besides, any drama involving money tended to have a traumatizing effect on a man for whom 'the deal' means as much as – if not more than – winning races. Getting there is supposed to be half the fun, but in this case Jordan had his doubts about such easy rhetoric.

The beginnings of Jordan Grand Prix had almost been too good to be true. Having run a team (Eddie Jordan Racing) and won in every category he entered in the junior formulae, Jordan could not resist making the final move to Formula 1 for the start of the 1991 season. He was making his luck to an extent, since if he had waited any longer the rapidly escalating costs of going Formula 1 racing would have put the mission beyond his financial reach. As it was, the newly named Jordan Grand Prix would struggle through on less than £6 million, and that had to include the purchase of engines from Ford. In 1998, Williams was paying £13 million just for the use of Renault engines prepared by Mecachrome. Unless a new team can raise at least £20m today, there is no point in even considering Grand Prix racing. And that sort of budget would guarantee little more than a place on the back few rows of the grid. But in 1991 it was different.

Jordan's arrival was greeted with studied indifference by Formula 1 rivals. How could this new team possibly succeed, given that Jordan had chosen two drivers who, at best, would just about make the reserve list elsewhere? That was an unfair reflection on Bertrand Gachot and Andrea de Cesaris, drivers of mixed experience, each with a different point to prove.

Gachot had enjoyed a spectacular rise through the ranks, his talent matched by a confidence outside the car which, at times, was overwhelming to the point of irritating arrogance. Unfortunately for Gachot, however, his progress in Formula 1 had been less than impressive thanks to the driver from Luxembourg struggling with teams that did not match his expectations. The moment seemed to have passed until he received the call from Jordan. It might have been Gachot's last chance but Jordan knew the twenty-eight-year-old would be worth having for that very reason.

De Cesaris was an entirely different proposition. The Italian held the dubious record of having driven for almost every team in the book. Jordan Grand Prix would be his eighth employer in eleven seasons, his record a trail of incidents rather than prizes. He brought financial support – as did his team-mate – but, unlike Gachot, de Cesaris had exactly the sort of experience the new team needed. Jordan and his Commercial Manager, Ian Phillips, ignored the banter about chequebook racing. When they said they had 'every faith' in their drivers, this was not cosmetic optimism; they meant every word.

De Cesaris's wide-ranging background was necessary because of the demands imposed by prequalifying, a horrendous process brought about by an entry of thirty-four cars for races which could only accommodate twenty-six starters. Jordan needed Andrea's composure during the sixty-minute prequalifying session for minor teams early on the first morning. Fail to be among the first four cars at the end of the hour and your Grand Prix weekend was over. No more practice, no qualifying, no exposure for your sponsors. With the first race held in Phoenix, Arizona, it would be a long way to travel for nothing.

It was ironic, therefore, that de Cesaris missed a gear and selected second when he needed fourth, the resulting mechanical mayhem blowing the engine

and his chances of prequalifying. Gachot got through to the thirty cars allowed to practice and qualify. Not only that, he later took fourteenth place on the grid, the mid-field position as good as anyone could have hoped for.

Equally impressive was the professional turnout by a team with green as its predominant colour. Given Eddie Jordan's proud heritage, one which the Irishman would flaunt at any opportunity, he had gone all-out to secure a sponsorship deal with Pepsi Co. and their 7-Up brand with its green trademark.

Jordan was delighted. No so one or two of the Old Guard, who had been bidding for the Pepsi money in their usual lavish manner only to be undercut by this Irish upstart. Clearly, in the indignant view of the established teams, Jordan did not understand the rules; they claimed he was devaluing the sport. In fact, thanks to lowering his bid, Jordan was raising the stakes by eliminating the comfort zones enjoyed and squandered by his rivals. The deal was only worth a mere $1.1m (peanuts by today's standards) but Jordan loved every minute of its negotiation and the subsequent ripple effect its conclusion sent through the paddock.

The important thing at this stage was keeping up appearances. The simple colour scheme looked superb on a very elegant little car. Thanks to this and Eddie Jordan's open approach – something of a novelty in a frequently paranoid business obsessed with secrecy – the media immediately took to the new arrivals and wished them well. Jordan would reciprocate by providing plenty of copy as the season went on.

Once they had got over the disappointment of de Cesaris's failure to qualify, the team never looked back. Gachot ran as high as seventh in Phoenix before the engine failed. Anderson had started the year expecting his cars to qualify in the middle of the grid. Being outside the top twenty would not be acceptable; being inside the top ten would be a bonus. By the second race he was in the money sooner than expected as his cars lined up tenth and thirteenth on the grid. Round three at Imola saw them eleventh and twelfth and quickly into the top ten during the race. A finish in the points, the ultimate objective which had been reserved for later in the season, suddenly seemed a possibility here and now. Gachot spun away his chances but de Cesaris was into sixth place at half-distance and running strongly. Then a gearbox selector fork broke, a component which had never given a moment's bother during thousands of miles of running. Welcome to the fickle ways of Formula 1.

But the point had been made. Jordan Grand Prix was very serious as it set an exceptional standard for subsequent new teams to measure themselves by. A finish in the points really did seem to be on the cards.

It came halfway through the year as de Cesaris and Gachot finished fourth and fifth in Canada. Not just one driver in the points, but two! An emotional Eddie Jordan didn't know what to do with himself as the green cars swept across the line. For once, he was stuck for words. This was too much to take just five races and three months into the season. It couldn't be this easy. Could it?

Jordan began to believe that it could when de Cesaris finished fourth again at the next race in Mexico and Gachot took points in Britain and Germany. Then Formula 1 began to have its way, even though some of the frustration was completely beyond Jordan's control.

When Gachot set the fastest lap of the Hungarian Grand Prix in mid-August, it would be his last act in a Jordan. Having finally achieved his goal in a competitive Formula 1 car, Gachot threw it all away in a moment of madness. An altercation with a London cab driver over the same piece of road at Hyde Park Corner resulted in Gachot using CS gas to allegedly defend himself. The court took a dim view of this and sent a shocked Gachot to prison. Eddie Jordan, meanwhile, had a seat to fill for the next race at Spa-Francorchamps in Belgium. Given the manner in which everything fell into place, this should have been his finest hour on two counts, but in the end Jordan came away with nothing.

During the closing stages of a race on one of the most spectacular circuits in the world, de Cesaris found himself in second place. There was the thought that Andrea might even win the Belgian Grand Prix as the leader, Ayrton Senna, struggled with a broken gearbox on his McLaren. The water temperature on the Jordan began to rise but that was not as serious as it seemed. The team was more concerned with the blips on the car-to-pits telemetry as the oil pressure began to sag. Eventually, the engine failed with three laps to go.

Having come so close, the team was bitterly disappointed. Eddie Jordan, meanwhile, consoled himself with the thought that he had an ace remaining in his hand.

Casting around for a last-minute replacement to fill Gachot's seat, Jordan had settled on a twenty-two-year-old German driver who had shown promise while driving sports cars for Mercedes-Benz. Michael Schumacher was relatively unknown but Jordan felt he had nothing to lose by giving the extremely confi-

Sponsorship and technology were to increase tenfold over the years, backing from Benson and Hedges helping pay for complex items such as the multifunction steering wheel (top left).

As Eddie Jordan continued to talk up technical and financial support, Richard O'Driscoll (inset and below) took on the job of keeping the finance in check.

Long-term partners. Ian Phillips looked after the commercial dealings while
Marie Jordan was always on hand to listen when Eddie got his wires crossed.

dent young man his chance in Formula 1. It quickly became apparent that this was one of the most fortunate moments in Jordan's career as a talent-spotter and wheeler-dealer. Schumacher was sensational, a complete natural who immediately made himself at home by taking seventh place on the grid at a difficult circuit he had never seen before. His race was short-lived because of clutch trouble, but Eddie Jordan had a winner on his hands. He was quietly chuffed.

Not for long. By the time Jordan reached the next race at Monza two weeks later, he had been out-manoeuvred. The Benetton team had stepped in, punched holes in Jordan's so-called contract with Schumacher and entered the youngster for the Italian Grand Prix. There was nothing Jordan could do about it. This had been a lesson learned the hard way. Welcome, once again, to Formula 1.

The reality of going racing at the highest level was beginning to bite in other areas. The Benetton-Ford team was hardly flavour of the month when the recently installed Technical Director, Tom Walkinshaw, put the block on a plan by Jordan to have the latest Ford engine for 1992. As a result, Jordan would be forced to continue using an engine which was always at least one step behind the specification supplied to Benetton in their capacity as 'works' Ford team.

If Jordan was tired of scraping together payments for what was effectively a 'customer' engine costing £4.3 million, then so was his bank manager. Strenuous efforts were made to reach an accommodation with another engine supplier and an agreement was eventually made with Yamaha for 1992. It was a 'works' deal, meaning Jordan would have a serious technical liaison with a major manufacturer. Eddie Jordan would have exclusive rights to the V12. Better than that, he would not have to pay for it. On paper, it made good sense. In reality, it would be a disaster.

The realization began to dawn at the first race in South Africa in March 1992. One car failed to qualify and the other took twenty-third on the grid, and then finished a distant eleventh. What made such a dismal performance even more embarrassing was the fact that this was on the home patch of Sasol, an oil and lubricant company new to Formula 1 and with which Jordan had entered into a major sponsorship agreement.

Things went from bad to worse. Whereas in 1991 fifth and sixth places became something of a disappointment, in 1992 just one finish in the top six would have been a cause for celebration. Indeed it got to the stage where a finish of any kind was considered an achievement for Sasol Jordan Yamaha.

The engines were not only unreliable, they were also heavy and gutless. All of this was a severe test of the motivation of the drivers as Mauricio Gugelmin and Stefano Modena – both new to the team – reacted in different ways. Whereas Gugelmin, a placid Brazilian, put his head down and plodded on, Modena showed his Italian temperament by either sulking or quickly losing heart if the car was uncompetitive. Which was often. On his day, Modena could be brilliant, but those days were few and far between. After finishing a stunning fifth with thirteen points in the Constructors' Championship at the end of their first year, Jordan went into the last race of 1992 with a large zero on the board. By creeping into sixth place and scoring one solitary point in Australia, Modena managed to avoid a total wipe-out for the team. Jordan Grand Prix was bottom of the points table.

The damage to company pride may have been great but more serious was the havoc that had been wrought with the bank balance. The team was on the brink of collapse – not that you would have known it listening to Eddie Jordan and his infectious brand of optimism. Quietly, however, Jordan had taken steps to sort out the mess by employing Richard O'Driscoll. The former employee of the Allied Irish Bank discovered that the team was technically insolvent. With the full backing of his new boss, O'Driscoll set about cutting costs by 20 per cent through reducing stock levels and tightening purchase control. Eddie Jordan, meanwhile, looked at ways of keeping his team competitive for a minimum outlay.

Sasol were on board for a second year, additional support coming from Barclay cigarettes. The team could just about manage, but in Formula 1 you need to do better than that. There was, for example, insufficient cash in the kitty to allow the introduction of a computer-controlled 'active-ride' suspension system. This was the latest technical toy which was de rigueur for any team worth its salt, Williams making particularly good use of their active-ride system as Nigel Mansell romped home to the championship.

On paper, Jordan struggled once again. But whereas in 1992 they had spent the year stuck in the mire, this time the promise was there for all to see. 'The package has great potential,' said Anderson. 'The problem is, we're not getting a grasp of it.'

The Technical Director had indeed put together a very neat car, which was complemented by a useful engine built by Brian Hart in his modest premises at the back of an industrial estate in Harlow. Hart was every bit an enthusiast and he got on famously with Anderson. The deal was, by Formula 1 engine standards, very reasonable from Jordan's point of view. The downside was that the Hart V10 could not compete with the likes of Renault, but at least it was reliable. The same could not be said for the car, thanks to the late decision to switch to the Hart and the resulting absence of serious pre-season testing. A run of irritating minor problems meant the season was slipping by without Jordan scoring a single point, the huge frustration being aggravated by the obvious potential of the car, not to mention the driver.

Eddie Jordan had taken another of his gambles by signing Rubens Barrichello, a twenty-year-old Brazilian whose impressive results in the junior formulae were offset by the obvious lack of experience. Barrichello was not helped by the constant chopping and changing of team-mates as Ivan Capelli, and then Thierry Boutsen (drivers who were supposed to show Barrichello the way), each succeeded in bringing their distinguished careers to a miserable end. Barrichello celebrated his twenty-first birthday at the Monaco Grand Prix in May, by which time he was the de facto team leader, a huge responsibility thrust on such young shoulders.

Sasol Jordan Hart reached their nadir in September when both cars were eliminated within seconds of the start of the Italian Grand Prix. Not long after this debacle, a rare test session brought an improvement to the specification of the car.

At the same time, Jordan gave Eddie Irvine his Formula 1 debut at the penultimate race of the season in Japan. With no points on the board and a succession of number two drivers having brought money but little else to the team, Jordan felt the precocious Ulsterman was worth a shot. Besides, he had raced in Japan and he was very familiar with Suzuka, one of the most difficult circuits on the calendar. Not only did Irvine fulfil all expectations by qualifying a superb eighth on the grid, his turn of speed helped Barrichello raise his game, the Jordans going on to finish fifth and sixth.

But there was more to this race and to earning desperately needed points. Irvine drove like a veteran as he made full use of his local knowledge to become engaged in a close contest with Damon Hill (having his first Formula 1 season with Williams). Ayrton Senna had just lapped the duo when a heavy shower made the track treacherous. Irvine, who knew precisely how to run this circuit in the wet, felt Senna was being too circumspect in the difficult conditions. So he dared to overtake the great man and unlap himself.

If Senna was outraged over such treatment at the hands of a novice, he was in for an even bigger surprise during the subsequent discussion, when an insouciant

Irvine claimed the world champion had been too slow. Irvine received a thump on the ear for his trouble, and instant publicity worldwide. One way or another it had been a memorable race for Jordan Grand Prix. But it had done very little to move the team forward in the struggle to become a serious force in Formula 1. There was, however, a subtle difference in circumstances as preparations were made for 1994.

For the first time, Anderson knew he would be working with the same drivers and engine supplier. Continuity would be everything for a team with just seven people in the Technical Department. Eddie Jordan had learned many lessons in his three years in Formula 1 but the most important one concerned marshalling of this latent talent into a potent fighting force - and acquiring enough money to make it happen.

On too many occasions Jordan had been let down by footling failures that adequate testing and mileage would have exposed in private rather than the public humiliation of another DNF (Did Not Finish) on the results sheet. The claim that there was not enough money in the kitty was genuine enough, but its novelty value wore out, along with the wheel bearings and other fundamental faults. O'Driscoll's tight financial control was bringing the team back onto an even keel and Jordan was finding more money to keep it afloat. The mood was markedly upbeat as the 1994 car began testing. Finally, it seemed, Jordan Grand Prix was ready to move forward.

In a matter of hours during the first two races, Jordan had scored as many points as it had mustered during the previous two seasons put together. Barrichello finished fourth in Brazil, only to go one better at the next race in Japan, giving Eddie Jordan his first podium finish with third place in the Pacific Grand Prix. By the end of round five in Spain in May, Jordan Grand Prix was nudging the best ever total of thirteen points gathered during the first year. With two races to go in the 1994 season, they had come close to doubling it. Jordan was undoubtedly the most-improved team of the year, fifth place in the Constructors' Championship giving weight to the claim that they were also the Best of the Rest. And there was more to come.

Sasol made way for support from Total Oil as Eddie excitedly announced a liaison with Peugeot for 1995. A proper works-supported deal at last. And, of course, the engines would be free. This was the final piece in the jigsaw – or so Jordan claimed.

Placing a Honda emblem above the Jordan logo on the nose of his car was another of Eddie's major achievements. EJ talks to Yoshi Ebihara, Mugen's programme coordinator, en route to a race.

Catching up with the paperwork during a quiet moment in a Buenos Aires hotel.

At home and away. Damon Hill and one of his mechanics, Paul Bennett, ponder their chances abroad after the preparations have been completed in the Silverstone workshop.

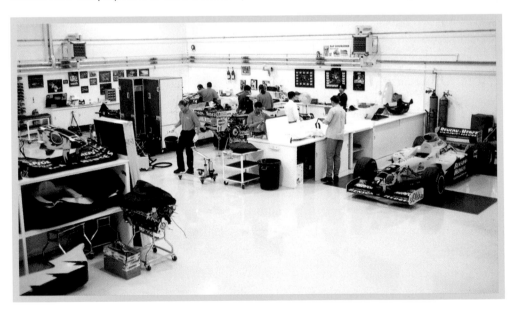

Life is never that simple, but with Eddie Jordan it was difficult not to be upbeat. With one breath, he would play it down; with another, he would remind you that his team had hoped to score twenty points in 1994 and actually came away with twenty-eight. Then, in a moment of typical enthusiasm, he would speak out of the side of his mouth and talk about maybe 'sneaking in a win' in 1995. And why not? Anything seemed possible.

By round fourteen of the 1995 championship, Total Jordan Peugeot had a mere eighteen points. The figure should have been fifty – maybe more. The cars had been qualifying inside the top ten; they were perfectly placed, not to win races, but to regularly collect points. And, time after time, the much-admired little car would roll to a halt with some fault or other. Anderson and his tiny band in the Technical Department were constantly chasing their tails. The search for reliability meant there was no time for development. It was 1993 all over again.

The problems were a typical product of the upheaval brought about by working with a different engine manufacturer and, to a certain extent, a vastly different business culture from the one established so successfully by Anderson and Hart. Because of the compact nature of Hart's operation, Anderson and the engine builder could work by an intuitive and informal method whereby a decision could be reached during a five-minute conversation over the telephone, both men being racers who understood precisely what the other was thinking. Now Anderson had to adapt to the more time-consuming process of a major manufacturer which did not take a step of any importance without having at least one meeting to discuss it.

More time was spent testing than ever before thanks to the establishment of a test team, but that in itself was not the passport to success which many had imagined it to be. Once again, it was a case of adapting to the changing circumstances and making the most of them. At first, Jordan seemed to have a handle on the entire operation when pre-season tests consistently produced very competitive times. Reality set in when the car did not perform very well at the very first race in Brazil, but by mid-1995 the relationship appeared to be working better than before, particularly when Barrichello and Irvine finished second and third in Canada, the first time that two Jordan drivers had reached the podium. Luck had played its part but the Jordan drivers were there at the end to pick up the reward.

They seemed ready to collect more points on circuits which would suit the Jordan-Peugeot. Then the unreliability problems arrived in earnest and Anderson watched thirty points and more fall into the hands of others. There was another lesson here. The team had been carrying out plenty of testing but little of it had been truly productive thanks to Jordan failing to raise their standards and attitude to match the increase in pace and expectation. From the management down, they were unconsciously continuing to think small while aiming to be a major player.

The link with Peugeot was not the widely perceived end to all financial worries. Certainly, the Jordan budget may have been reasonable, but it was not top drawer, a fact underlined at Monza where the Jordans appeared festooned with stickers for tuppenny-ha'penny deals - a colourful hint to Peugeot to open their chequebook a bit wider. But at least the team was not burdened by excessive retainers for their drivers.

Barrichello and Irvine were in their second full season together, and along with Berger and Alesi at Ferrari they were regarded as the most competitive pairing on the grid. Not that it was a partnership in the strict sense of the word since reputations were at stake and Barrichello suffered at Irvine's hands during qualifying in the first two-thirds of the season. Anderson was more concerned about getting his drivers to work for the team rather than for themselves. It was all part of the building process which was necessary as Jordan tried to consider itself as worthy of joining Williams, Benetton and Ferrari. Anderson described the internal growing pains as 'a massive fight'.

1995 had been yet another learning year but – yes, you've guessed – it would come good the following season. It was predicted that the relationship with Peugeot would begin to gel. Barrichello would capitalize on his fourth year with the team, a deal having been done to move Irvine on to Ferrari – to Eddie Jordan's financial advantage, of course. As things would turn out, that would be just about the only good thing to happen to Jordan in 1996.

Another year of promise turned into yet another year of disappointment. This time, however, patience had been exhausted, both inside and outside Jordan Grand Prix. In the past there had always been a reasonable excuse and Eddie Jordan, trading heavily on his popularity, was easily forgiven. In 1996, the team's sixth season in Formula 1, the goodwill had been spent and the verdict was harsh. Jordan was patently not up to the job. People outside the team said it. Worse still, one or two people inside the team said it.

Martin Brundle was signed as Irvine's replacement in the hope that he would make a more productive and sympathetic partnership with Barrichello. Plans were put in motion to expand the Silverstone factory. Then, just before the start of the season, Jordan and Ian Phillips added what appeared to be the final golden touch; netting Benson and Hedges as the team's title sponsor. There could be no excuses now.

The late sponsorship announcement caused the rapid reworking of the team's colours. It was a frantic lead-in to the opening race in Melbourne and, if anything, the pace went into crazy overdrive when Brundle got himself involved in a spectacular accident on the first lap of the Grand Prix. It spoke volumes for the integrity of the Jordan design that Brundle emerged unhurt but the incident appeared to shake him up in every sense.

Eddie Jordan had hoped to call upon Martin's extensive experience to form a useful counterpoint to Barrichello's natural ability which, as yet, had not been fully utilized. The fact that Brundle had struggled onto the back row of the grid gave the first hint that the settling-in process would take longer than expected and matters were not helped when Martin suffered a family bereavement not long after.

Barrichello had retired from the Australian Grand Prix with engine trouble but the disappointment of the first race was quickly dismissed in Brazil when Rubens put the Jordan on the front row for his home event, with Brundle sixth quickest. Rain washed away the hope of a major result on race day as both drivers spun off. The team went downhill from that point on and never recovered.

Barrichello occasionally nudged his way onto the first three rows of the grid but Brundle never got close as he struggled to come to terms with the car. Barrichello scored a few points here and there, but as the season progressed Jordan stood still while McLaren, three years in the doldrums, got its act together and began to outrun the Peugeot-powered cars.

The pressure began to build in Spain where both Jordans retired. Then at the end of June came huge disappointment in France, where the Jordans struggled into eighth and ninth places in front of Peugeot's home audience. By the following race, the British Grand Prix, Anderson had been persuaded to take a break and begin design work on the 1997 car. He reappeared at Monza, six weeks later. The reason for his absence was never satisfactorily explained.

The second half of the season was notable only for Brundle finally coming to terms with both the car and the team – and vice versa – although, by then, the damage had been done and confidence within certain sections of the company had been lost. Peugeot, on the other hand, made impressive strides in both reliability and power, the V10 now considered to be on a par with Renault and Ferrari.

Despite the disappointing results, Benson and Hedges resisted the blandishments of rival teams and chose to remain with Jordan for 1997 and beyond. The arrival of much-needed financial support (in a lump sum, as opposed to having the car decked from stem to stern with numerous small sponsors, a habit which irritated Formula 1's more imperious members) gave the team stability but not necessarily the overnight improvement many outsiders expected.

'B&H are a very good sponsor to have on board,' said Anderson. 'But it's not like flicking a switch and suddenly you see results. It takes time and, unfortunately, this came at a time when the factory was being extended. The drawing office was part of the extension. We needed more people but they could not be employed until the extension was ready and that was not complete until the end of August. So, in a way, it all happened at the wrong time.'

Anderson summed up the season by saying it had been much the same as any other; they had started reasonably well and didn't go anywhere. As ever, the potential was there but the team had yet to find a way of extracting it.

A large part of that task fell to Trevor Foster, recently returned to Jordan (having been Team Manager in the past) to act as General Manager. Using an impressive depth of experience of motor racing in general, and Jordan in particular, Foster slowly but surely introduced systems and equipment to help overcome the shortcomings which had muzzled the team. Despite such a dismal season, the future once again looked bright. But the promise of jam tomorrow could not be tolerated for yet another year. Eddie Jordan had never faced a more critical period. That was the main reason why he took the painful step of opening his chequebook more frequently than before.

An overdue expansion programme was put in place, Jordan allocating £5m for technical equipment and back-up which would enable Anderson to see his usual workmanlike product develop rather than stand still, as it had in previous years.

The team opened its own wind tunnel in Brackley, while seven miles away at the Silverstone HQ a gearbox test rig and, most important, a seven-post chassis test rig were installed, these being state-of-art pieces of kit employed by the likes of Ferrari and Williams. For the first time, Jordan arrived at each race with the car boasting some further development, no matter how small. Better than that, the telecommunication link with the seven-post rig meant that readings taken from the car during the first day of practice could be fed back to the factory, the subsequent analysis on the rig then providing information which would allow the car to be improved for the all-important sixty minutes of qualifying on Saturday afternoon. It was not uncommon to find a Jordan-Peugeot in the first six; the lower reaches of the top ten would be considered a major disappointment. In addition, the good work was continued into the race, Jordan scoring more points than ever before.

The workforce had been expanded to 130. As ever, Anderson could have done with even more people but the budget, reasonable though it was, had to be the limiting factor. Benson and Hedges really went to town with one of the most striking and imaginative colour schemes, the muddy gold of 1996 replaced by a bold yellow, complete with an eye-catching snake on the nose. 'Hissing Sid' (as the snake was affectionately known) proved to be one of the most highly publicized logos of the season. No one quite knew what the snake was for, but that mattered little judging by the unease it spread among tobacco rivals with their staider corporate colour schemes.

As ever, Jordan Grand Prix was forcing the pace. For the first time, the team held an all-singing, all-dancing new-car launch in London. At the time, it appeared to be no more than a colourful stick with which to beat themselves when they failed to deliver, particularly in the light of a controversial choice of drivers.

Rubens Barrichello had decided that the time had come to move on. Martin Brundle's twelve-month tenure at Jordan had hardly been a success, the two sides somehow failing to click. Damon Hill took a look and, making a decision he would regret in private, if not in public, the world champion opted for TWR Arrows in 1997.

That left Jordan in something of a quandary. It had already caused a minor stir by signing Ralf Schumacher on the strength of his victory in the 1996 Formula Nippon Championship in Japan. But Michael's younger brother appeared to have very little else – apart from some attractive backing which might come with the family name. Now the team seemed set on a suicidal course by choosing Giancarlo Fisichella, a young Italian whose experience had been limited to eight outings with the humble Minardi team. Individually, the novices had plenty of promise. Collectively, they did not appear to be what Jordan needed during a season when nothing less than front-running performances were expected. 'We'll see,' said Eddie Jordan. 'But I tell you what. It'll be very interesting. There'll be some fireworks.' Indeed there were.

In Argentina, Schumacher was so desperate to overtake Fisichella that he bundled his team-mate off the road and almost took himself out in the process. But the point was, they were running in the top three at the time. It took some stern words from the boss to bring a touch of law and order, and from that moment on there was much to be said for having two precocious and talented youngsters on the books, particularly when they finished on the podium three times. But once again victory eluded the team. Not for the first time, Eddie Jordan was taking steps to put that right.

We had heard it all before, of course. Several times. A full-page profile in the *Sunday Times* was all very well. But today's news would be tomorrow's fish and chip wrapper if Jordan failed yet again. The bottom line was that failure in 1998 was not an option.

Chapter Two

Dance of my Dreams

The first Jordan Formula 1 car was unveiled in a small

workshop. Twenty-seven journalists turned up to see it.

They sat on plastic chairs arranged in front of a car

which was black and plain. There was no sponsorship

identification because there were no sponsors. The most

significant feature was the fact that there was actually

something to see.

Midnight pass. A tight squeeze as the Jordan 198 is manoeuvred through a back door at the Royal Albert Hall.

Only a few foreign journalists bothered to travel to the nondescript industrial unit in Northamptonshire on a murky November morning because rumour had it that this Irishman and his team was entertaining some wild dream about stepping up to Formula 1. The cynics said it would never happen. And even if by some extraordinary chance it did, Jordan Grand Prix would quickly disappear down a difficult road which had sucked many small teams into mediocrity, followed, almost inevitably, by bankruptcy. Jordan Grand Prix? A waste of space – such as it was.

The backdrop was a whitewashed wall and a roller-shutter door; hardly state of the art in product promotion. Eddie Jordan had been operating from Silverstone since the formation of his team in 1980, and as such he was the longest-standing tenant within the block of units on the edge of the racetrack.

But not for long. Jordan had bought four acres directly opposite the main gate and he had plans for a purpose-built headquarters and factory. He would not be travelling far in the physical sense and yet, seven years later, not only had the team survived, it had come a very long way from that informal launch in November 1990.

Plans for the unveiling of the 1998 Jordan took Eddie Jordan to the opposite end of the promotional spectrum. Indeed, even allowing for his incurable enthusiasm and optimism all those years ago, Jordan would not have believed it possible that his team would be centre stage before 600 guests in the Royal Albert Hall. And yet that was the entry in his diary for Monday 19 January 1998.

The day started early. The boss and his new driver, Damon Hill, had to be on parade in the Albert Hall foyer at 0625 in time for an interview with Independent Radio News, a recording which would be offered to more than 150 local radio stations nationwide. As Damon dived into the cloakroom and changed into his yellow driving suit, a sudden and intense blaze of light in the hallway announced the approach of the first live television interview twenty minutes later. That, at least, was the plan.

The radio interview passed off without a hitch but the link with GMTV's breakfast show went awry thanks to a technical problem. Damon quickly resorted to his mobile phone while the studio ran motor racing footage as a cover for the absence of live pictures, Hill's voice occasionally drowned by increasing background noise as B&H promotional girls arrived in readiness for a briefing. Even though the car was not due to be unveiled for another four hours, the pace was quickening. By 0830, Hill and Jordan had completed fifteen interviews, more than half of them live and split evenly between radio and television. By 0900, they had been joined by

Ralf Schumacher in preparation for further questioning by a Press Association representative seeking to provide copy for PA's wire service and the Internet.

Through the nearby double doors and down some steps, the stage was being set in the midst of the cavernous auditorium. Knowing they were unlikely to fill the entire hall, one end had been secured for the formalities, leaving the rear half free for a dance troupe and supporting entertainment which, if nothing else, would provide a novel twist – in every sense of the expression. In view of these lavish preparations, the new car was almost an afterthought. Almost. For the team, the Jordan Mugen-Honda 198 had occupied their every waking hour since the flag had fallen at the last Grand Prix in October 1997.

In fact, the 198 had been under way long before that. Gary Anderson and his technical team had begun experimenting with various chassis shapes in the wind tunnel the previous May. A month later, certain details such as the gearbox casing had been narrowed down. These were complex items which required a long lead-time in the manufacturing process.

By August the overall concept was taking shape, helped by the supply of the basic engine dimensions from Mugen-Honda. Drawings on the CAD system began in September, the designers getting down to detailed discussion on various engine cover and side pod shapes, particularly now that a mock-up engine had been delivered from Japan.

The first engine proper arrived on 1 December. The immediate task had been to ease the V10 into a 1997 car and carry out track tests which would allow the preliminary sorting out of the new gearbox, coupled with the rear suspension planned for the 198. That would complete much of the basic homework in advance and allow the team to move straight into fine-tuning the new car and its aerodynamics once the launch had taken place. That was the plan. The reality turned out to be quite different.

It had been hoped to complete 1,000 km during tests at Silverstone, a useful distance which would provide the necessary feedback and expose any teething problems with the complex electronics. Teething problems! The package more or less died at birth, the interim car covering no more than 20 km – and hesitant ones at that. The problem was quickly pinpointed but the solution would take much longer to carry out.

Mugen-Honda had previously used a Benetton gearbox control system when working with the Prost team. That option was no longer available following the

When the talking had to begin. Ralf, Eddie and Damon await breakfast television interviews in the Royal Albert Hall (opposite page).

Looks quick from here. The platform party talk up the Jordan 198 (above). Ralf finds some peace and quiet in a cloakroom (right). Giving the sponsors a decent mention: Ralf and Damon prepare for a television interview with important names in the background (below).

split with Prost, Mugen-Honda deciding to allow Pi, the company which supplied Jordan with electronic control systems, to do the necessary work. Jordan went along with the decision in the hope that Pi could cope: the British firm had not been involved with an engine management system before.

It was a mammoth task, and from the outset of the first test session it was clear that the work was not complete. Worse still, it was unlikely to meet the critically tight schedule. A painful decision had to be made. The Pi scheme was dropped, Jordan and Mugen-Honda switching to TAG Electronics, a company which happened to be part of the McLaren group. Never mind any false fears on the part of Mugen-Honda about their technical secrets going to a rival (McLaren used the Mercedes-Benz engine), the bottom line was that TAG could get the job done. But it meant starting from scratch at the eleventh hour. So much for being ahead of the game.

Work continued apace in the factory. Most of the major components were finalized and drawn by mid-December, just as the first bare chassis arrived from Paxford Composites, the specialists trusted with the task of laying up the carbon fibre and moulding the black tub in an oven. Work began immediately on fitting out the chassis. The factory closed for just two days at Christmas and the surprise was that they had managed that. Mind you, a break was necessary, if only to recover from the annual party, a rowdy affair held a few days before Christmas in a large marquee erected on the front lawn.

By 5 January the first Jordan Mugen-Honda was in the race shop, the engine mated to the chassis and ready to receive a myriad of parts and components, topped off finally by the bodywork and wings decorated in the team's corporate hues.

Graphic designers had been at work since October, liaising with the team and sponsors in a bid to arrive at a scheme acceptable to all parties while achieving the ultimate aim of getting the message across. Benson and Hedges and their sponsorship agency, M&C Saatchi, had created a rod for their own backs in 1997 by introducing the snake logo slithering down the nose of the car. Eddie Jordan had been horrified, not least because this creature was occupying valuable advertising space on a prime position. It may have been a gimmick but Jordan was quick to accept that it worked brilliantly when the logo appeared prominently in every publication with an art director worthy of the name.

The problem now was following such ingenuity with an equally eye-catching design for 1998. Agreement had been reached on 2 January. Seventeen days later, the curiosity of the media queuing outside the front door was matched by anxiety within the Royal Albert Hall as the team's key players awaited the initial reaction to their latest scheme.

Eddie Jordan had earned a reputation for beating a path away from the norm. This was a case in point as the double doors opened and the press filed into one of the most impressive buildings yet chosen for the launch of a racing car. Ferrari had rolled out their new car on a foggy morning at the company headquarters in Italy. Williams, the reigning champions, stuffed their latest machine into the corner of an unprepossessing garage at Silverstone, an idea which Jordan had used five years earlier when unveiling his Jordan-Hart 193. Since then he had launched his cars at the factory, a Gallic flavour (accordion music, copious French wine and the odd Tricolour draped here and there) marking the liaison with Peugeot. In 1997, a function room in a London hotel and Irish music signalled the next step. Now this, one of the most famous theatres in the world.

Big and spacious it may have been but the Albert Hall had presented its problems from the moment the Jordan truck had arrived at the side door shortly before midnight. A fierce wind and near-horizontal rain had made the unloading an uncomfortable and difficult process, particularly when the ramp was found to be too high for the truck. A solution was bodged together, the car then being carefully manoeuvred along ramps and onto a temporary stage built specifically for the job at the front of the auditorium. Getting the Jordan thus far was only half the battle. The next mission was to raise it into the murky darkness, high above the stage, an operation which required careful calculations and the use of a substantial hoist. This was for reasons other than a theatrical entrance.

The RAH had been enjoying capacity audiences thanks to Cirque du Soleil performing *Alegria*, a production embracing the excitement and amazing diversity of movement for which the dance troupe had become famous. Not short of ingenuity himself, Eddie Jordan had befriended the troupe leader, Guy Laliberté, a motor racing fan. Laliberté agreed to incorporate his show with the launch of the car. Jordan was delighted, not least because the financial arrangement, including use of the premises, was very favourable. EJ enjoyed mixing with 'stars' from all parts of show business and sport, but he was never happier when he had the best of both worlds thanks to a good deal being born of the association. The actual reveal of the new car was almost a side issue. That was the way one or two members of the media saw it as proceedings got under way.

The introduction followed a familiar format as Steve Rider walked to the rostrum and called forward the key players: Eddie Jordan, Gary Anderson, Hirotoshi Honda and then the drivers, led by the team's new test driver, Pedro de la Rosa, followed by Schumacher and, finally, Hill. As the drivers stepped forward, Jordan not only shook their hands, but also embraced them with a stiff slap on the back. It was genuine enough, a sign of Jordan's innate warmth and friendship. It was difficult to envisage any other Formula 1 team owner openly enjoying such camaraderie on a public platform. Or anywhere else, come to that. Formula 1 takes itself too seriously to allow wholehearted shows of emotion.

Jordan launched into a speech made without notes. In fact, he had earlier pocketed a slip of paper with one or two bullet points scrawled upon it. This was the normal procedure. Even having made the most careful notes beforehand, Jordan was renowned for getting on his two feet and completely ignoring any prompt, a natural flow taking over as he shot from the lip.

Jordan spoke about his choice of drivers, making mention of the fact that their combined fees amounted to more than the team's entire budget during the first season in 1991. He also took the opportunity to introduce a scholarship programme designed to assist promising Japanese drivers make it in Europe. On the face of it, this was an act of some generosity on his part as he promised to help youngsters through the minefield presented by racing abroad. The reality was that this was another deal, part of the agreement which had helped secure the Mugen-Honda engine. It remained to be seen just how effective the team's caring nature would be when, say, the second or third Oriental driver was dispatched to Silverstone.

Jordan quickly moved on to his sponsors, giving lavish praise for Benson and Hedges and a welcome to Pearl Assurance, who would join MasterCard and long-time associates such as Hewlett-Packard, GdeZ and Speedline.

'I'm a bit long-winded as usual,' said Jordan, his candour immediately bringing forgiveness. 'But I must thank the media. Keep clicking the cameras and giving us the column inches! We've got a lot to do this year but I can still promise you the rock 'n' roll!'

It was hard to imagine the likes of Ron Dennis of McLaren rounding off his speech in such a manner. Jordan's words earned warm applause, particularly from the two tiers ranged in a semicircle above the packed auditorium. It was no coincidence that the boxes, with their red velvet and plush fittings, housed sponsors and their guests.

Rider then directed questions to the platform party. The journalists present did not expect any worthwhile answers since the set routine was usually designed specifically to give away very little other than the party line. There was unlikely to be a story here. But that did not take into account that this was Jordan Grand Prix.

Eddie Jordan put the media on the alert when discussing team orders. He said the company policy had always been 'may the best man win' and he could see no reason to change that, even though Hill was a world champion with twenty-one victories and Schumacher a relative novice entering his second season with one third place to his name. Damon was not exactly smiling when Jordan said it. The hacks could smell dissension. Here was a line of questioning to be pursued at a press conference in the early afternoon. In the meantime, there was to be a touch of show business. And, as yet, there was no sign of the car.

Thoughts that it might be behind the backdrop to the temporary stage were dispelled when the screen was raised in order to give a clear view of the rest of the hall. Those who had seen Cirque du Soleil before said the show would be unusual; those who were unfamiliar with this unique blend of dancing and acrobatics could only agree as two thirteen-year-old Mongolian contortionists opened the show by performing an act so complex that it was difficult to tell which limb belonged to whom. 'Those girls would do well in the Formula 1 paddock,' muttered a seasoned cynic. 'They could wriggle out of anything.'

After thirty minutes of truly extraordinary entertainment, it was back to the seemingly more mundane business of men driving racing cars at 200 mph. The screen was lowered into place once more. As music played and a camera rolled, there was the first hint of the new corporate logo as the image of an angry hornet danced on the screen. Then came the gyrating lights and billowing dry ice. Slowly, the car descended on its platform, falling perfectly into place, at an angle, on the stage.

As the mist and the music continued, the audience gradually broke into applause. It was the least you could do. Here's the car. Very nice. Never mind that it represented nine months' work. Forget the fact that the team had been up most of the night. And the night before. And the night before that. Thanks for showing the car. You've done your bit. Now let the media do their job. To the majority of writers and cameramen, one Formula 1 car looks very much like another. Such a thought is heresy to Anderson and his dedicated technical team.

At least fifty photographers crowded round the stage. The key players were called forward once more, taking their place around the car amidst a blitz of flashes and requests to look this way and that. Giselle Davies, Head of Press and

The launch of the Jordan
Mugen-Honda 198 was to
be more spectacular than
its first outing on the track.

PR at Jordan, orchestrated the movements around the stage, ensuring that every photographer got his angle.

Giselle's detailed plan indicated that live interviews were due to take place with ITN lunchtime news, BBC News 24, Capital Radio, BBC 1 lunchtime news and RTE in Dublin. The first was scheduled on stage at 1245. It was only 1230. The programme was running ahead of target, a considerable achievement when the garrulous Eddie Jordan was part of the mix.

As the photographers scurried to the dedicated wire services set up in the Henry Cole Room, the writers took a more leisurely approach as a buffet lunch was served upstairs in the General Scott Room. Under normal circumstances, this would have been a reception area servicing nearby boxes carrying names such as Earl Spencer and Lord Lloyd Webber on the doors. For now it was a temporary press room and watering hole where ideas for tomorrow's papers were taking shape.

But, first, the press conference along the corridor in the Prince of Wales Room at 2 p.m. Jordan, Hill, Schumacher and Anderson took their seats at the top table. After the niceties had been observed, Hill was asked for his thoughts on Jordan's policy of parity for both drivers. Damon left the audience – and the team – in no doubt about his views.

'To win in Formula 1, you have to beat Michael Schumacher, who has the entire team working on his behalf,' said Hill. 'If you have limited resources, you have to direct them in the right way. Ralf is keen to be up front and so am I. To seriously get the best and most competitive performance, you need the attention Michael had at Benetton and now has at Ferrari, and maybe that is to the benefit of everyone in the team.'

Jordan would not be moved. He responded by saying that parity was both fair and productive.

'What Damon has said here is what he said right at the start of our discussions, but what Michael does is Michael's business,' said Jordan. 'At Jordan no individual is greater than the team. Williams do not have a number one but they know it would be stupid not to get one of their drivers to help if the other was in the position to win the title. That's good team tactics.

'I'm not dictatorial,' Jordan continued. 'I gave Ralf assurances about this and both will help each other, in fairness to both. If one has the possibility of winning a race or the championship, the other will help. We have to be reasonable.'

As the daily press scribbled furiously, the specialists moved in to enquire about the possibility of Jordan winning his first race. 'There's every chance,' he said. 'You don't invest the kind of money we have in drivers without hoping to win. But I don't like making forecasts.'

Then, as if slightly numbed by the weight of expectation and the size of the task before him, Jordan mixed his metaphors in the grand manner.

'I don't like making forecasts,' he said again, 'because reality has a brutal axe to its bow.'

There were barely suppressed grins and sideways glances in the audience. Everyone knew what Jordan meant. It was just the way he said it. As ever, he was immediately forgiven.

As the conference broke up, Jordan answered a few more questions, completed another radio interview, and made his way downstairs towards the auditorium. The boxes were empty, discharged champagne bottles and glasses dotted around the red velvet and starched linen. Inside the auditorium, there was a gentle buzz as the final interviews took place and photographers made the most of the semi-deserted stage.

Hill was asked about his chances of winning for Jordan. He somehow found enough enthusiasm to give the impression that this was the first time such a question had been raised. In truth, he had been talking about nothing else for more than eight hours. 'Everything is in place,' he would say. 'I want to win. I believe it's possible.'

The schedule said it should be possible to have the formalities completed by 3.00 p.m. They were. On the stroke of three, officials began to lay the ramp towards the exit door. The car had some serious work to do in Spain. The show was over. For the moment.

'How d'you think it went?' asked Jordan. Before an answer could be given, he revealed the true reason for the question. 'I had to say it.'

'Say what?'

'About team orders. Damon knows. I made a promise to Ralf before Damon came along, and I'm keeping it. I had to make that clear.'

No one doubted his sincerity. It would make a good story for the morning papers. The question was, would it be at the expense of the car and the sponsors? And what about the hornet? Very few people had asked about that.

It would turn out that few had asked because the logo was neither as striking nor as simple as the snake. The hornet was mentioned the following day in the *Daily Express*, the *Daily Mail* and the *Sun*. It did not figure strongly in the photographs. But that was a minor detail for everyone except, perhaps, the creator of the new logo. What was important was the extent of the coverage. It would turn out to be the most generous of the winter season. Television had also served the team well with footage being used by ITN, BBC, RTE, Channel 5 and Sky. For that, Jordan could thank the presence of Damon Hill and the unusual nature of the launch itself.

The potential unrest caused by the question of driver status featured strongly in the tabloids and the *Independent*, but the rest of the national daily papers focused on the team as a whole and the backdrop to the unveiling. The *Independent* carried the most striking photograph, a moody aerial shot taken by the experienced Peter Jay as smoke surrounded the bright yellow car. The *Guardian* went for a similar photographic theme to accompany an excellent feature by Adam Sweeting, a writer who, significantly perhaps, was not a regular on the Formula 1 trail. Sweeting had attended all of the car launches thus far in Britain and he awarded Jordan top marks.

Summing up, he wrote: 'For the publicity that the Albert Hall shindig generated for the car, drivers Damon Hill and Ralf Schumacher and team owner Eddie Jordan, the real winners are the team's major sponsors. Jordan's launch successfully plastered the yellow Benson and Hedges livery across worldwide television. Other sponsors who have paid top dollar to have their names appear on the car, such as Pearl Assurance, MasterCard and Hewlett-Packard, can't have been too unhappy with the results either.'

And neither they were. Round one to Benson and Hedges Jordan Mugen-Honda. But, as the account executives and team personnel enjoyed the coverage, they knew that round one was a preliminary scuffle. Eddie Jordan summed it up.

'When it comes to rock 'n' roll or hype or whatever you want to call it, Jordan are as good as the best. Maybe we are the best. But what we need to do now is become the best technology-wise and I think I have amassed the package that's going to give us that.'

As he spoke, the mechanical part of that package was being rushed back to the factory for final adjustments in readiness for the first serious run in Spain. Only then would Jordan begin to know if his ultimate ambition might be realized. In 1991, having his car move under its own steam without drama was a considerable achievement. Being competitive was a major bonus. In 1998, reality could have a more brutal axe to its bow. So to speak.

Chapter Three

Too Many Negatives

The relationship between Jordan and Peugeot may have ended but the French company quietly lent a hand when it came to gaining further exposure for their former partner. They say there is no love lost in Grand Prix racing. One team helping another is considered to be a sign of weakness in a macho business, but in this instance there was something in it for Peugeot; a reasonable quid pro quo.

Waiting to do his bit. A mechanic uses a spare nose cone as a seat prior to a pit stop during the first race in Australia.

It so happened that Peugeot's latest associate, the Prost team, had chosen to unveil its new car in Spain on the day after the Jordan launch. It was an awkward call for the British journalists since their priority was to cover Jordan, a job which would take most of the day and make it difficult to reach Barcelona on time. Besides, looking at it from a jingoistic tabloid stance, it was difficult to see the British angle in a story about a distinctly Gallic team with a Frenchman and an Italian driving a French chassis and engine.

The feeling was that Barcelona would not be worth either the effort or the expense. That's when Peugeot came up with an air ticket and the clever provision of an open booking which would allow journalists to stay in Barcelona for an extra day when, all being well, Hill would run the Jordan for the first time. Rarely has a French team received such an enthusiastic response as a dozen British hacks signed up for the trip.

But that did not get round the problem of what to say when writing about the Prost-Peugeot. It was fair to assume that readers back home would not be holding their breath to learn about a carbon-fibre gearbox and other technical tweaks on the new car. Somehow, a personality had to be involved. Then someone remembered how Hill had spurned Prost at the last moment in favour of Jordan. Weary eyes lit up at the prospect.

Prost was booked to speak to the British press once the official presentation had finished. It took about three questions before the only subject of interest was raised: was Alain still upset about the manner in which the negotiations with Damon had been curtailed?

The short answer was that he most certainly was. A contract had been agreed, the sponsors informed and everything was ready for signature when a phone call announced that Damon was baling out. Prost was not impressed — and said as much in clear language. Moreover, he doubted Hill's motivation and his hunger to succeed. There was probably a certain amount of sour grapes and mischief-making on Prost's part. But here was a story. And a good one at that.

The launch had been held in a marquee in the paddock at the Circuit de Cataluyna. As the journalists made their way towards the pit complex and the media centre above, Hill was arriving at the paddock gate, hopeful that the new Jordan might appear in time to allow a few laps before the close of play. This was not the moment to relay Prost's words to the Englishman; that could wait until the next day – and, depending on Damon's response, perhaps create another story. Easy, this journalism. And Peugeot was paying for the trip!

Eddie Jordan was footing the bill for the shipment of the 198. Under normal circumstances the car would have travelled by road in the team's transporter, but with time of the essence air freight was the only alternative. The expensive logistics had gradually dawned on him during the press launch; more than once, while at the Royal Albert Hall, he had asked Trevor Foster how he intended to get the car to Spain by the following day. Foster avoided a precise answer, one which would reveal that chartering air freight space to Barcelona is not easy – and neither is it cheap. Jordan had probably guessed as much and didn't want to be told the painful detail.

A two-hour delay in the flight plan appeared to rule out running on the Tuesday afternoon, particularly when the car arrived at the track as late as 4.10 p.m. But that did not take into consideration the keen anticipation surrounding any new car. Besides, this one had run, albeit briefly, in the hands of Schumacher at Silverstone the previous Friday, which meant the basic start-up bugs had been ironed out. By 4.55 p.m. the Jordan was fuelled. By 5.00 p.m. it was running, Hill sliding eagerly into the cockpit for the first time. By 5.10 p.m. the car was on the track.

Hill completed twelve laps without the merest hint of trouble. That was an achievement for any new car (the Prost, hobbled by numerous problems, had failed to negotiate a single lap) and Hill was quietly elated as he stepped from the cockpit. He was grinning from ear to ear. Never had he known a new car to be so impressive on its first outing. That was about as good as it was going to get for the foreseeable future.

The mechanics, lifted by their driver's response, worked until 2 a.m. as they carefully prepared the car for a full day's work and made many of the myriad small adjustments which are part and parcel of any maiden outing. They were back six hours later, ready for breakfast and the track opening at 9.00 a.m.

It was a measure of the importance attached to this car and its potential that Eddie Jordan flew to Barcelona for the day. Normally he would work from his office and rely on telephone and fax reports from the circuit; this time, he wanted to judge for himself, and by a handy coincidence deal with the PR work in the presence of so many journalists from home and abroad.

Dressed in a brown overcoat, brown shoes, grey suit and dark polo neck, Jordan looked like a motor trader on a day out – which, in a manner of speaking, he was. Certainly, he was able to mix easily with the media as they sat down to pasta and red wine at tables outside the team's motorhome. There was nothing more Jordan could add to what had already been said of his team's expectations. And, as everyone knew, there was no point in asking Eddie any technical questions. At least, not unless money was involved.

Hill was the man everyone wanted to talk to. As Damon took his place at the head of the table, his enthusiasm was immediately apparent. That was partly to do with the car's reliable running – there's nothing worse for a driver than being forced to stand on the sidelines all day while a series of footling problems keeps the car in the garage – and mainly with the fact that Hill had not actually driven a Grand Prix car since the final race of the 1997 season, some three months before. Arrows, Hill's previous employer, had kept him to the letter of a contract which had not expired until the end of the year. Given the problems with the electronics on the interim car, this was the first time a runner had been available for the former world champion.

'I certainly got a big buzz out of driving a Formula 1 car again,' admitted Hill. 'Now it's down to the hard work trying to figure out how to develop things.'

At the time, it seemed the logical thing to say. Naturally, the new car would need development. Drivers say, however, that they get a gut feeling about a car, almost from the moment they go through the first corner. Perhaps Hill had already begun to feel uneasy.

Certainly, there was no damning evidence from the lap times. Or, at least, not at face value. The only yardsticks were the latest Benetton and the faltering Prost, both of which ran on Bridgestone tyres, unlike the Jordan on Goodyear. By the end of the test, Hill had lapped in 1m 24.90s: Schumacher, who had taken his turn on the second day, got down to 1m 23.70s. These times compared favourably with a benchmark 1m 22.99s established by Jacques Villeneuve, albeit in a 1997 Williams fitted with the narrow track suspension. All told, it seemed to be a reasonable start.

'Hill joy at fantastic maiden Jordan test' shouted the headline in *Autosport*. It was a different story two weeks later following the team's return to Barcelona. 'Jordan pace disappoints Hill' indicated less promising reading.

The pace, in fact, had been stepped up following the arrival of the new Williams, Heinz-Harald Frentzen being a couple of seconds a lap faster than Hill. Damon chose his words carefully when summing up the second test, which had been hit by poor weather.

Damon, his ear plugs/radio speakers taped in place, thinks about the race and the pit stops to come.

Eddie chats with Ralf: 'One of the nicest guys you could ever have driving for you.' Trudie Edwards (inset) arranges the catering to ensure the feeling of well-being is maintained at the race track.

No pulling back now. Once the testing had begun and the shortcomings of the 198 were revealed, there was nothing for it but for Jordan and Hill to press on.

'We didn't come away terribly happy with the lap times,' he said. 'I've been impressed with the reliability, the engineering and the way the team works, and we've made some good progress with the Mugen-Honda engine, but we weren't competitive.'

That was diplomatic talk for the car being slow. There is not an ideal time to receive such news but this was coming at a particularly busy moment. The first race was only weeks away and there was a very tight schedule, dictated by a mandatory crash test for the car in England, followed by more running in Barcelona.

As soon as the chequered flag indicated the close of play at Barcelona on the Friday afternoon, the mechanics set about stripping the cars (a second having been completed in time for the return visit to Spain) before loading the chassis, gear-boxes and suspension onto a waiting van. An overnight drive by the crew brought the cars to Silverstone, where the team was waiting to completely strip the chassis, crack-test components, remove the fuel tanks and prepare for the crash tests, which would be supervised by the sport's governing body on the Monday. One chassis was subjected to a 15.7 mph side impact; the other to an even more ferocious 26.8 mph head-on collision with a concrete wall. Both chassis passed with flying colours, a claim which could not be made by several teams at that stage.

The cars were rushed back to headquarters and prepared in time to make a flight departure from Luton that night. A team of mechanics flew to Spain on the Monday night and spent Tuesday building up the cars in readiness for the three-day test which was due to start the following morning. They would be back in England by the weekend for a another rebuild, several modifications and a final brief run at Silverstone before shipment to Australia.

The entire programme would be subjected to the usual last-minute panics experienced by every team during the build-up to the first race. MasterCard, for example, wanted a time-consuming change to its logos on the car; Benson and Hedges, a subtle modification to the colour scheme. More important was the manufacture and fitting of new engine covers, a pit-stop rehearsal in the workshop having shown the access panel in the cover to be too small for the refuelling nozzle. That meant that five covers, already made at a cost of £3,000 apiece, had to be scrapped. These things happen. Better to find out now than in Australia. There was just one serious question which would not be answered until the race weekend: how would Jordan Mugen-Honda stack up against competition from Williams, Ferrari, McLaren and Benetton?

The majority of media previews may have been noncommittal concerning Jordan but they were agreed on one thing: McLaren-Mercedes-Benz were the favourites. From the moment the latest car from Woking had first turned a wheel, the lap times had been impressive. Very impressive. To use a motor racing aphorism, the silver-grey car had been quick 'straight out of the box'. The Bridgestone tyres notwithstanding, the engine-chassis package appeared to be brilliantly efficient. All of which brought pressure on Jordan. In recent years, Jordan and McLaren had been vying for position on the championship table, McLaren usually gaining the upper hand by gradual degrees as the year wore on. Now they appeared to be streets ahead, even before the season had started.

The final test at Barcelona was not too bad for Jordan. But neither was it brilliant. Schumacher turned in a 1m 23.68s with plenty of fuel on board, followed by a 1m 22.47s with a lighter load. The McLarens, meanwhile, consistently lapped in the 1m 21s. As the media raved about the McLaren performance, Jordan received a mixed review in *Autosport* even though Ralf was the fastest Goodyear runner.

In a summary of each team, Andrew Benson had this to say about Jordan: 'Drivers [Schumacher and Hill] for now setting their sights considerably lower than the win they hoped for a month ago after disappointing recent results. Car has understeer and is undergoing front suspension redesign. Prospects looked better in Barcelona last week, but rivals say the team and drivers look worried.'

Further inside the magazine, an interview with Damon Hill produced largely negative comments, backed up by Trevor Foster agreeing that the car 'just wasn't quick enough, and we don't know where the time was lost'. A week later, as the teams assembled in Melbourne, the latest issue of *Autosport* carried more of the same from Hill. 'I would say that victory is a long shot,' said Damon. 'Others are much quicker than us on a more consistent basis. There are lots of things to be sorted out and I'm not happy with the balance of the car yet.'

Was this a genuine grievance – or was Hill getting his excuses in first? Either way, it was not what Gary Anderson wanted to read. The Technical Director's discreet silence lasted until the end of practice for the Australian Grand Prix – by which time he had endured enough of the carping.

Jordan's media release in Melbourne noted that Schumacher had taken ninth on the grid, Hill tenth, performances which would hardly set the world on fire, particularly from a team hoping to win its first Grand Prix. Anderson's comments were printed at the bottom of the press bulletin.

The season starts right here. After months of preparation and testing, the team knows true comparisons will begin to emerge as soon as the Australian Grand Prix gets under way.

'If we had been able to get one car in the top six today, I would have been ecstatic,' said Gary. 'So, with cars in ninth and tenth positions, we are not far from where we want to be.'

So far, so good. Then came the rub.

'There have been a fair amount of negative comments recently,' Anderson noted. 'I think that with a more positive attitude and more fight we could be up there in the top six. The fact that both drivers had almost identical times shows they were at the car's potential, but I think that with more work, the potential can be higher.'

It did not take much to read between the lines. Anderson felt that a negative mind-set had taken hold at the top level of the team and this was in danger of filtering through the ranks. Sitting in the early morning sunshine at the back of the Jordan garage on race day, the Ulsterman reflected on the furious activity of the past few months.

'When we ran the first test, both drivers commented that it was quite a nice car to drive,' he said. 'We soon realized that we had an understeer problem. For me, that problem was coming from the tyres because they weren't adequate for Barcelona. When we returned to Barcelona for the second test, the whole emphasis was on fixing this understeer. But we weren't able to fix it because the car's problem is at the rear end; the car is a bit too nervous. The trouble was, the drivers didn't want to hear that and, as a result, we just went slower. You can make the car feel better and yet go slower – and that wasn't my objective. I don't mind what the car feels like – so long as it goes faster.'

Understeer – a tendency for the car to want to go straight on instead of turning in to a corner – is time-consuming in every respect since it causes the driver to lift his foot from the throttle, briefly but with enough effect to reduce the speed out of the corner and down the straight that follows.

'We came back from that test a bit disappointed,' admitted Anderson. 'The next test had to be a bit more forceful and, luckily, McLaren turned up in Barcelona that week and blew everyone's doors off. At long last, we got everyone to be objective about it.

'I spent a lot of time out on the track looking at the car. I could hear the drivers on the radio saying they had a lot of understeer. I would get on the radio and say, "No, you haven't. You can't get into the corner; that's the problem. You can't get the speed into the corner; you haven't confidence in the rear of the car."

' "No, no," they would say. "It's the understeer in the middle of the corner; that's the problem." I said that if we fixed the rear of the car, they would go faster. So, we worked on the rear of the car, the drivers went out and said it was much better. "Oh, by the way," they said, "we've got less understeer as well." What can you say?

'We made some progress; it went a bit better. At Barcelona we were the two fastest Goodyear runners out of the cars that were there. We did some good race runs and some good low-fuel runs. We always knew that McLaren would be strong; we were happy that we were in a reasonable position.'

Anderson admitted that he had been reluctant to make changes to what he called 'significantly different' front suspension on the new car.

'We've got too many people who don't seem to understand anything new,' he said, pointedly. 'Obviously, that's disappointing. It's very difficult when you want to do a development of something and you have to go off the beaten track to get a better solution to the problem. You are talking a couple of tenths of a second a lap here; something that's worth having. But people can get their head round a suspension system they know much easier than one which is different. So, we went back to the one we had run before.

'I think we need to be more committed as a team. We seem to be happy to say that the car's not very good and that we should go back to the factory and redesign it. But how can you do that if you don't know the full extent of the problem? You need to run the car and explore all the avenues if you want to win.

'Anyway,' he said with a smile, 'I think coming here is the best thing. This is the first race. Finally everything is under way and this is where we're at for the moment. So, let's get on with the job and see where we end up.'

The rest of the management, meanwhile, were inside the garage, tucking into a full English breakfast cooked for the team by a crew run by Jordan's Trudie Edwards (wife of Chief Mechanic Tim Edwards) in association with Paul Edwards (no relation), a widely used caterer whose finger was in many pies along the length of the pit lane.

The only fat being chewed was the usual round of gossip which ebbs and flows through the garages as one team discusses the shortcomings of another. The subject this morning was McLaren, fastest in practice by a country mile but bogged down in criticism from several quarters.

There had been much muttering from rivals, led by Ferrari, concerning a special braking system fitted to the McLaren. Ron Dennis, the McLaren chief, said he had successfully sought technical approval for the system from the governing body every step of the way. He was convinced of its legality. But Dennis was also irked by Ferrari's habit of bitching when the going got rough. Seizing the moment at a press conference on the Saturday afternoon, Dennis had spoken of espionage after finding a photographer in the McLaren garage attempting to take close-up pictures of the car. Dennis said the man, under questioning, had admitted he was the brother-in-law of the aerodynamicist with a leading team. Dennis would not name the team. It was widely believed to be Ferrari.

Eddie Jordan almost choked on his toast when he heard the story. 'Ha! That's rich, coming from Ron,' he spluttered. 'I can remember one occasion, at a launch of our new car, catching red-handed a photographer, who did work for a McLaren associate, sending a picture of the car to McLaren — and using our telephone lines to do it! I think Ron needs to be careful if he's going to start making accusations.'

Lying to one side of the breakfast table was a faxed copy of a sports page from the *Daily Mail*. A column by Eddie Irvine had been predictable in its mischief-making. Unfortunately, the Ferrari driver had targeted, among others, Jordan's latest driver.

Irvine wrote: 'Damon had the chance to drive a McLaren, which everyone thinks is going to be the car we all have to beat, and he turned it down because he wanted more money. If Ron Dennis offered me the chance to drive his McLaren, I would have taken it for free. So far as I can see, Damon is just trying to secure his pension.'

Irvine's over-simplification notwithstanding, he was making an uncomfortable point. It was simply another issue which would be best dealt with on the track. Enough of the gossip and speculation. As Anderson said, it was time for everyone to go racing and see where they ended up.

The answer, as far as Ralf Schumacher was concerned, was in a gravel trap on the first lap. A bad start had cost him a few places, putting him among the scrapping also-rans at the back of the field. Jan Magnussen, following the Jordan in his Stewart, claimed Ralf had gone wide slightly at the exit of Turn 4. Seizing what he thought would be his chance, the Dane attempted to dive down the inside of Schumacher under braking for the next corner. Except that there was not enough room. The two cars touched. Exit one Jordan barely thirty seconds into the new season.

Hill steered clear of his team-mate and trouble on the rush to the first corner, finishing the first lap in ninth position. He moved forward one place thanks to a retirement further up the field, and there the Jordan stayed for the rest of the afternoon. It was an undistinguished performance by the man who had won in Melbourne in 1996.

As the team began to pack up, Eddie Jordan drifted away from the pit wall. He tried to put a brave face on the absence of any championship points.

'Not good,' he said quietly, his usual exuberance curtailed for the moment. 'We've a lot of work to do, that's for sure. Damon's two pit stops were disappointing; we lost some time on the first because of a problem with the refuelling catch. But at least we finished the race and that has given us something to work on. Damon's last stint was very positive.'

Jordan's woes were of minor importance in the overall scheme of things after the McLaren team had caused a major furore by controlling and then manipulating the race with the clumsy implementation of team orders. There was widespread outrage, McLaren losing the impact which should have been created by such a dominant performance as their drivers, Mika Hakkinen and David Coulthard, lapped the entire field. Eddie wished he had problems like that.

When Jordan's post-race press release was circulated in the air-conditioned media centre above the pits, Hill's comments were of interest only to the journalists who had previewed the season by predicting that Damon had a reasonable chance of returning to his winning ways. Hill's words were hardly brimful of hope.

'Today's result reflects more the fact that we did not qualify well, rather than we had an average race. I want to go away and look at the telemetry data so that we can work on finding some more speed on the car, but I was encouraged by my performance toward the latter part of the race. I saw Wurz [Benetton] up ahead and pushed to catch up, but then went off – which made me cross with myself. It seems that the key to speed is to get angry, as after that I really picked up.'

That last remark caused a few raised eyebrows, not just in the press room but in the Jordan garage below. Based on his performance throughout the weekend, he ought to have been livid. Clearly, this season was not going to be easy for the Hill–Jordan liaison. It was fair to say that doubts were already creeping in both sides. And there were fifteen races to run.

Chapter Four

Time for Change

Not where he
wants to be. Damon
prepares to start
from ninth place
in Argentina.

Motor racing people flying south to Brazil found an

interesting story in the March edition of British Airways'

High Life magazine. An article on the leading Grand Prix

teams held no revelations for the Formula 1 insiders; the

fun was measuring the 'bullshit factor' on each page.

The team bosses – or most of them, anyway – were profiled in a series of brief sketches, Frank Williams and Eddie Jordan leading the way on the first page. Williams came across with an appropriate blend of gravitas and enthusiasm for what was referred to as 'the most successful Grand Prix team in history'. Jordan, quite simply, was described as 'the rebel of Formula 1'.

Of the two, you warmed immediately to Jordan, even though his comments were interspersed with the usual Irish hyperbole. 'I think that Jordan will be the big surprise in 1998' was the quote that jumped from the page, the unfortunate timing of the story meaning that the interview had been conducted before the Australian Grand Prix. Equally embarrassing was the fact that the magazine would still be in circulation as the teams made their way home from Brazil, Jordan doing no better in São Paulo than it had in Melbourne.

Nevertheless, the story caught Jordan's personality perfectly, an amusing mix of irreverence and desire. Describing his entry to Formula 1 in 1991, Jordan said: 'We were like the hippies of Formula 1. We went to races not knowing where we would find the money to pay for anything and I said: "Let's go, we can sort it out later." At the end of the year we would have these mountains of bills. It was very tough but incredibly enjoyable.'

There was almost a wistful touch to that last statement, as if to emphasize the truism that being bigger and more successful is not necessarily better. It may be more advantageous in the sense that the team is far better financed and equipped than ever before and the boss now has a power boat and the use of a plane. But the attendant pressures have a habit of dulling the sort of carefree spirit which swept the team forward in the early days. Nevertheless, compared to most of his colleagues in the pit lane, Eddie Jordan is part funny man, part force to be reckoned with. The danger, as the 1998 season began to get into its stride, was falling off that very fine line and becoming nothing more than a sad joke.

The subsequent pages in *High Life* carried insights to Tyrrell, Stewart, Sauber and McLaren. While the first three pieces were built around the team principals, the McLaren story focused on Adrian Newey, the Technical Director. It was an astute move since Newey's work would become the subject of reluctant admiration as McLaren picked up where they had left off in Australia and dominated every practice session in Brazil.

Having Hakkinen and Coulthard on the front row of the grid gave McLaren even more pleasure than before since they had achieved it without the aid of the controversial brake-steer system. A protest, predictably led by Ferrari, had prompted the removal of the system pending a judgement by the race stewards. Williams and Jordan, using brake-steer devices which were not as complex as that employed by McLaren, did likewise.

The brake issue was the main subject of discussion – initially, at least – during Jordan's dinner for the British and Irish media on the Friday evening. This had become an annual not-to-be-missed event, if only because its informal, knock-about format summed up a team that refused to take itself too seriously when the time was right.

The atmosphere was aided greatly by the venue, a large churrascaria filled with Brazilian babble as waiters flitted from table to table carving various cooked meats from large joints skewered on swords. In 1993 the Jordan booking in the same restaurant had catered for no more than twenty guests. In 1998 the U-shaped table accommodated forty-three people; a reflection of the growth in both the media circus and interest in the team.

Schumacher and Hill were present, Ralf sitting alongside his manager, Frans Tost, and Jonathan Legard of BBC Radio 5 Live. These occasions are ideal for journalists to get to know team personnel – and vice versa – under relaxed circumstances away from the racetrack. Schumacher, the first to politely make his exit shortly before 10 p.m., had created the right impression. 'Top man,' said Legard. 'Top man. I didn't really know him before.' The evening had served its purpose in that corner of the room.

Hill said goodnight not long after and it was noticeable that his neighbours – mainly the British daily press – were not as effusive as Legard about their dinner companion. A case, perhaps, of overfamiliarity. But then Hill did appear to be preoccupied – as well he might, given the way in which practice was about to go the following day.

For the moment, however, it was time to relax, Anderson in particular breaking new ground with one or two members of the media who had never before had the chance to sample the Ulsterman's easy style. Eddie Jordan, dressed in a crumpled linen jacket and black T-shirt, moved around the table dispersing insults and instant quotes at the appropriate moment.

Ian Phillips, meanwhile, checked on the flow of red wine – 'the best; none of the cheap stuff' was the instruction to the waiter – and reflected on the latest

Down in the canteen. Damon and Ralf make the most of the Jordan office in Buenos Aires not long after practice has finished.

Different priorities. Ralf spends time with the mechanics while Damon prefers a game of table footie with his mates.

On the zapper. The practice times make disappointing reading, whichever channel Hill chooses. Paul Bennett, Gerrard O'Reilly, Darren Beacroft and Nick Burrows, Damon's number one mechanic (right), look unimpressed.

Getting the bad news first hand. Eddie listens to Damon's analysis during practice in Brazil.

development on the commercial side of the team. During the three-week break between the two races, Phillips and Jordan had been to court in New York in pursuit of money owed by a former sponsor, Kremlyovskaya.

From the outset, the Russian vodka manufacturer had appeared suspect. Not for the first time in Formula 1, the warning bells had sounded when a brash new sponsor appeared on the scene and threw money around as if there was no tomorrow. Stories quickly developed, notably the one concerning a vast yacht with a mirrored and deep-pile bedroom which a Kremlyovskaya representative had attempted to make the most of while at anchor in Monte Carlo for the Grand Prix. The best tales surrounded this man's fumbled attempts rather than his success at intimacy.

With rather more certainty, perhaps, the vodka eventually ran dry, leaving Jordan Grand Prix as a creditor to the tune of $1.2m. Jordan won his case in New York, but given the absence of the appellant's available capital it was a matter of principle rather than financial repair.

Phillips had enjoyed the chase. A former journalist, he had always preferred tracking down a good story rather than winning awards for artistic style when writing it. Phillips and Jordan were of a like mind when it came to hooking a sponsor, the difference being that Eddie did not have the patience to deal with the paperwork and tie up the necessary loose ends.

This evening was a small case in point. As Jordan continued to talk freely, gales of laughter coming from wherever he chose to sit, Ian picked up the bill with his MasterCard. At just over $2,000 for the evening – ultimately paid for by Benson and Hedges – it was considered a bargain in terms of relations with the media. The team would need to lean heavily on that goodwill as their week-end went from very good on the Thursday night to bad and, ultimately, to much worse on Sunday afternoon.

It was immediately apparent on Friday morning that the Jordan was not at ease on the bumps of Interlagos, Hill working hard just to keep the car pointing in a straight line. He spun more than once, although the former world champion was not alone, several drivers leaving the road during the course of the day. With Ralf third quickest, almost a second faster than Hill in twelfth place, it was clear that Damon had his work cut out.

By Saturday morning, the stewards had decided that the controversial brake systems were illegal. Eddie Jordan was not particularly bothered, his view being that at least a ruling had finally been made in a grey area. It was left to Ron

Dennis of McLaren to occupy the moral high ground. He had done everything by the book, taken advice from the FIA Technical Department every step of the way during the design stage: and now this, a ruling by three part-time race stewards led by a Mr Nazir Hoosein, a cinema owner from Bombay.

Dennis engendered a certain amount of sympathy in the pit lane although it had to be said that compassion appeared to be in short supply in the Jordan garage, there being little love lost and very little warmth felt towards Dennis and his sometimes patronizing ways. This was a long-standing enmity and had nothing to do with McLaren's continuing dominance – although a massive 1.7-second gap between the two teams on the grid could not have helped.

Even so, Ralf had claimed eighth place, which was reasonable considering the top six was thought to be the ultimate aim at this stage. Schumacher had set the time on the second of four runs, each of the final two being under the best Damon had been able to manage during three runs as he continued to struggle with the car. Had it not been for a white-knuckle ride on his fourth attempt, Hill would have been a miserable sixteenth on the grid. As it was, his brave effort had moved him to eleventh. But he found it difficult to hide his disappointment.

'I'm not having a great weekend,' he said. 'I cannot put my finger on the problem – obviously if I could I would be doing more to fix it. The only thing I can think of is the bumpiness of the track is causing problems and I don't think we are the only ones today who finished further down the grid than we expected.'

You only had to look at Hill's neighbour on the grid to appreciate that final point: Jacques Villeneuve – pole position winner the previous year – was languishing in tenth place in the Williams. But when all was said and done, eleventh place for Hill was scarcely headline news at home, particularly with Coulthard's McLaren on the front row and Eddie Irvine's Ferrari sixth. It was true that the three-hour time difference between São Paulo and London meant early deadlines for the Sunday newspaper correspondents, but it was a sign of Hill's uncomfortable times that none of the British newspaper writers stayed around long enough to talk to the former champion at an informal press conference in the Jordan garage at 5 p.m. McLaren and Coulthard were the headline-makers of the day. Jordan and Hill had been relegated to the margins.

Typically, Eddie Jordan made minor headlines of his own on race morning. His fiftieth birthday was due to fall the following day but the team was unwilling to let the moment pass without recognition of some sort. Jordan was told to be at the front of the garage at 11 a.m. He knew what lay in store and, for once, he was slightly reluctant to be a part of it.

Sitting quietly in the eating area at the back of the garage, Jordan thought about the looming landmark.

'Fifty is fifty, is fifty,' he said with little conviction. 'I don't know what all the fuss is about. I don't feel any different. I was just thinking about it: I've got the team, we're in Formula 1: where could I have had a better chance than this? I'm healthy – God willing – and I'm trying to be as alert and as active as I always was. OK, the speed is not quite there: each year the ten-kilometre runs take fifteen or twenty seconds longer. But that's the only change I see. I'm still enjoying this,' he said, waving a hand around the room. 'Being fifty is just another day. It's no big deal.'

So saying, he got up and walked round the partition, past the temporary offices for the engineers and drivers, weaved his way through the area dedicated to Honda personnel and their engines and walked into the brightly lit main body of the garage where the three yellow cars sat on stands, surrounded by industrious mechanics. The front apron had been cordoned off as ranks of photographers focused on a table which had been made ready with plates and glasses. Bottles of chilled champagne were brought forward, along with a large rectangular cake, covered in yellow icing and topped with a message and the B&H 'stinger' logo. Hill and Schumacher appeared on cue to help with the cake-cutting and raise a glass to the boss. As Jordan made a brief speech and posed happily for the cameras, his earlier reluctance seemed to have been forgotten.

Watching from the side lines, tongue firmly in his cheek, Murray Walker summed it up. 'It's a shame,' grinned the veteran broadcaster, 'that Eddie so obviously hates the publicity.' As things would turn out, it would be the only promotion the team would get on Sunday 29 March 1998. Apart, that is, from an unwelcome few seconds of coverage not long after the race started.

The worry was the dash to, and scramble through, the first two corners, a tight left followed quickly by a right-hander at the bottom of a steep hill. In 1997, there had been all manner of mayhem sparked off by Villeneuve making a poor start and triggering avoiding action among those following. With the Jordans stuck in the mid-field, there was every chance they might become innocent victims of someone else's mistake. In the event, the entire field safely negotiated the first two bends.

Then Ralf spun at the fourth corner. All on his own. He had plenty of time to think about it while making his way back to the pits from the far corner of the track.

'I had quite a good start,' said Ralf. 'But then on turn four I got off the main driving line and I think I got too much dirt on the tyres and I went off. I was hoping for so much from the race as I have had a good weekend here, and really thought I could have won some points. It feels so bad to end like this. I'm very, very disappointed.'

As he spoke, the other Jordan was struggling along in fourteenth place, a poor start having wrecked Hill's already slim hopes of achieving anything worthwhile during the seventy-two-lap race. Indeed, if anything, the situation would deteriorate even further. Not only was Hill lapped twice by the rampant McLarens, the Jordan would be kicked out of tenth place when the post-race scrutineering found the car to be under the minimum weight limit. Five kilograms had been lost due to a water leak but even when that was topped up at the finish – as permitted by the regulations – the car remained three kilograms under. Not enough had been allowed for the usual wear and tear to tyres, brake pads, the central skid pad beneath the car and the consumption of oil (which cannot be topped up). It was a fundamental miscalculation. The only good thing to be said was the team had not lost championship points as a result. Either way, it was an embarrassment. The team management, flying out of São Paulo that night, knew they dared not open the March edition of *High Life*.

As the team's white-collar workers checked in at Guarulhos Airport, the mechanics were checking out of the Hotel Transamerica in preparation for their trip to the airport and a comparatively short hop to Rio de Janeiro. The Argentine Grand Prix was not due to be held until Sunday week and, for once, the Formula 1 race calendar worked in the mechanics' favour. Since the equipment had to be shipped straight to Buenos Aires, there was time for a break before moving into Argentina on the following Monday to begin stripping and preparing the cars. All living expenses would be met. Going home was not an option since a quick calculation had shown Eddie Jordan that having his crew stay in South America was cheaper than flying them back to the UK.

If the mechanics were able to relax, there was some serious talking to be done back at base. Ralf and Damon were called to the Silverstone HQ to discuss the absence of points on the board. It was amicable enough, the meeting lasting

The Jordan pit stops became a
well-drilled operation which paid
dividends as the season went on.

for four hours. But the need for the unofficial summit was regarded as something close to a catastrophe by those watching from outside the team. The next issue of *Motoring News* carried the front-page headline: 'Damon's Team Tackles Crisis'.

Eddie Jordan claimed he did not have time to read the weekly newspaper as he boarded the Buenos Aires flight on the Thursday night. Jordan was travelling First Class. In the past, he had made a habit of buying a Business Class ticket and working an upgrade to First. He did it not so much to save money but to annoy rivals such as Ron Dennis, who had paid the full amount. Rumour had it that Dennis had used his substantial clout to ask that hoi polloi be kept in their place on any flight he was using. When Jordan joined the McLaren boss at the front of the 747 for this trip, there was no doubt that he had parted with the £6,500 necessary to keep such elevated company.

Paying less, but attracting considerably more attention, two blonde girls had boarded the rear section of the aircraft. Casual clothing, cut to emphasize impressive figures, made an unfortunate counterpoint to the British Airways hostesses in their frumpy hats and swishing frocks. One of the girls – Emma Noble – would soon reveal even more as she besported herself in B&H yellow across the nose of a Jordan Mugen-Honda for the benefit of photographers in the pit lane. Eddie Jordan knew the girls – but he didn't let on to his fellow travellers up front as he settled down for the night.

It seemed certain that the sporting headlines would be occupied once again by McLaren, although race previews spoke more in hope than certainty of a surge from the competition thanks to a new tyre from Goodyear. Certainly, when practice got under way, McLaren's advantage was nothing like as sizeable as before, Michael Schumacher and Ferrari making the most of the latest Goodyears on a circuit which, in any case, did not play to the best points on the McLaren-Mercedes-Benz. Jordan was looking good, too. The only problem, when taking into account reputations and sensitive issues, was that Ralf was once again faster than Damon. Even so, Hill was reasonably optimistic at the end of the first day, saying the car felt better than it had in Brazil. Twenty-four hours later, it would be a different story entirely.

As qualifying ended, Hill climbed from the car and yanked off his helmet, spoke to no one as he marched through the garage, strode across the back alleyway and kicked open the door of one of the rooms in the Jordan office, slamming it shut as he went. As the metal partitions shook, the sound of swearing bounced around the whitewashed walls. There was no need to enquire how he felt. Neither was it necessary to ask why.

The list of qualifying times showed Ralf to be fifth fastest, with Damon ninth, more than half a second slower. Hill had made his frustration public by spinning at the last corner of his final lap but, even without that indiscretion, the split times for the lap had shown he had been nowhere near his team-mate's time. As for Ralf, he was quietly chastizing himself for a mistake at the same corner. The difference was, without it, Schumacher would have been fourth fastest. Or perhaps third, just behind his brother. Disappointment over Hill's performance aside, this had been an encouraging run for the Jordan 198. It was also as good as it was going to get.

Eddie Jordan went dancing on the Saturday evening. Bill Jacobs, the Executive Vice-President of MasterCard International, had brought some important guests to Buenos Aires. It was suggested that they should spend their last night in town watching the tango, an idea which received a cool, unofficial response from Eddie. 'What,' he asked, 'do I need to see the tango for?' Or words to that effect.

Jordan, of course, would join the party. It was a decision he would not regret. The MasterCard group, occupying a goodly portion of the night club, was transfixed as this stunning piece of local culture was performed before them. In Buenos Aires, the tango represents the soul of a vibrant city. It is a taste of urban history. It is also a very sensual dance, a point which was not lost on a gob-smacked Eddie Jordan. The excitement of Saturday night merely charged expectations for the following day.

Those hopes were dashed shortly after 1 p.m. on Sunday as both drivers made very poor starts. Schumacher's getaway was particularly disappointing, the German completing the first lap in thirteenth place, four behind his team-mate. Neither driver would make any progress, Ralf retiring eventually when a broken bracket allowed an exhaust pipe to blow – with serious consequences – onto part of the rear suspension, and Hill rounding off his miserable weekend by colliding with Johnny Herbert's Sauber while disputing ninth place. Caught by Louise Goodman and the ITV cameras as he made his way from the garage, Hill did not mince his words. In effect, he said he was not at all happy with the car.

How, then, could he justify the optimistic remarks made after the Jordan's very first run in Spain just over a month before? Hill answered that when asked by Andrew Benson of *Autosport*.

'For me, it was good to be back in a car with a good engine. I'd had a long break and I was quite excited to be back in a car. But you are very quickly down to business and it wasn't long before we realized that there was a huge gap between where we were and the top car, which was the McLaren. However, you have to cleave them off and compare us to the other Goodyear teams. If you look at that, the potential is there – Ralf was only 0.6s slower than Michael during qualifying here. The car is a difficult package at the moment. I need to sit down with Gary and get on top of what we need. Our race pace seems to be poor. Even if in qualifying we can get a lap out of the car, in the races we seem to disappear off the radar.'

Hill and Anderson did have that talk. It went on for ninety minutes and the shortcomings on both sides were discussed, Anderson expressing the view that Damon was perhaps not driving the team on as much as everyone had hoped. That question, too, was raised in the *Autosport* interview.

'It's down to Eddie and Gary to improve the team position,' said Hill. 'I can contribute what I can as a driver with my experience but I can't tell them how it's done. I'm not a designer or a team owner. I can only give my perspective as a driver.'

Hill's opinion would be urgently required as Anderson introduced substantial changes to the car in time for the first race of the European season in Italy. Work, which had started immediately after the Australian Grand Prix, was ready to run. It was a sign of how urgent this had become when the decision was made to use the revisions in the San Marino Grand Prix despite the minimum amount of testing. One of the golden rules of motor racing is to check and double check any new item before committing it to a race. Anderson agreed that it was a gamble.

'We realized that we would not gain anything by doing nothing,' said Anderson. 'We accepted that we had to do something and just get on with it. Both drivers were very happy to do this, so the whole team is behind the changes. We are going to Imola with a car which has had less testing than we would have liked, due to poor weather conditions at our four-day test.'

The deciding factor was that both drivers approved the car in its latest form. The main change was a lengthening of the wheelbase by four inches. In motor racing terms, that was a fundamental alteration, but a typically brave one by Anderson. He was quite prepared to tackle the problem head-on; his knowledge and racing instinct, based on comments from the drivers, told him this would be the way to go. There were other changes too – different brake ducts and rear wing endplates, changes to the air box – all of which would improve the performance of the machinery at Imola.

On a personal level, Ralf took time out to work on his starting technique. Having qualified fifth in Argentina, he had thrown away that hard-earned advantage by making an appalling getaway. On the Saturday before Imola, Schumacher presented himself at Silverstone and spent most of the day preparing for the most critical few seconds of any Grand Prix.

'The work we did covered more than simply the physical start itself to include the psychology behind a good start,' explained Anderson. 'Ralf has tended to become too flustered on the starting grid so we worked on focusing and on relaxing.'

The starting procedure is laid down in the rules and never varies. Once the field has completed a parade lap and all twenty-two cars are in position on the grid, the official starter illuminates five red lights, one after the other. When all five are lit, they can be extinguished any time between four and seven seconds. There are no longer any green lights since the smart drivers tended to release the clutch once the red lights began to fade. When the red lights go out, it's 'race on'.

'The five seconds or so before all the red lights go out can seem like a lifetime and it's important not to get psyched up until the last two seconds,' explained Anderson. 'Having spent the day working on this, Ralf seems far more relaxed about it all.

'From a team point of view, we can help by making sure that the clutch control and electronics do what the driver wants. The main thing is to recognize what you want to do at the start because every track has a different grip level and therefore requires different revs. We worked on finding a base level from which to build at each race. Coming to terms with getting the electronic set-up correct, with getting the psychology correct and working on the driver's reaction times and the physical start itself, meant we had a very productive day.'

The question was: would this preparation and the extensive alterations to the car produce the right results? Imola was the fourth round of the championship. It marked the end of the first quarter of a season which seemed as if it had barely started. If B&H Jordan did not get their act together that weekend, the chances of making an impressive mark in the 1998 statistics would be gone.

Outside the team, speculation was rampant over the identity of the guilty party when it came to laying blame for the state of uncompetitiveness. Some said Hill was not pulling his weight; others, less kindly, said there was nothing there to pull in the first place. Hill's defenders – and there were many – said he was clearly fighting against long odds with a car which was a terrible handful.

So whose fault was that? The buck stopped at Gary Anderson's desk – much as the responsibility for the poor performance by Williams lay at the door of Patrick Head, the team's Technical Director. But Head had won several championships; Anderson had not won any. Had he reached the limit of his experience? Or, as had happened in the past, was he being hampered by the team itself?

Some blamed Eddie Jordan for indecisive leadership. Exasperated team members would speak of meetings where a very delicate point needed to be tackled, only for Jordan to talk around the difficulty without actually confronting it. When it came to leading from the front, Eddie Jordan was not Ron Dennis or Frank Williams. Some in the paddock would say, 'Thank God for that.'

Perhaps, at the end of the day, critics were reading too much into the apparent crisis. These things happen to any team; the car was not working as well as it should and the Technical Department was addressing the problem.

Jordan had been in this situation before. In 1993, the drivers had struggled to make the car work. The wheelbase had been lengthened and suddenly the team was competitive again. The only trouble was, this did not happen until late in the season.

Technically speaking, it is unfair to compare the two cases since the circumstances were quite different. The team had made great strides since then. Everything had changed and yet, as is so often the case in basic concepts of motor racing, nothing had changed at all. The difference was, corrective steps had been taken quickly and efficiently in 1998. Whether or not they were effective remained to be seen. Imola would be a crucial indicator of form. If the car continued to be a handful, B&H Jordan would be in deep trouble.

Chapter Five

Never Mind the Rowlocks

Ralf Schumacher looked completely at home. As the

mechanics sat down to a full English breakfast, he

moved from table to table, a quick quip here, a playful

flick of the wrist there. This was part of the new image

for 1998, a deliberate attempt to improve personal PR

which had been noticeably lacking during his first

Formula 1 season.

Inadequate reflection of potential. The Jordan 198, mirrored in the pit buildings in Spain, did not present a true picture of the effort which was being put in by Jordan Grand Prix.

Being a Grand Prix driver is not just about skills in the cockpit; it is about motivating the rest of the team, ensuring everyone is on your side. Mechanics work long enough hours as it is but they will feel better about going the full nine yards at 3 a.m. if they have a genuine affection for the man who is going to bene-fit from their labours.

Formula 1 mechanics would never dream of taking shortcuts or being sloppy just because the driver appears indifferent and ungrateful. But, if there is a chance of success, or the driver is considered to be a good bloke, they will focus on the small details which sometimes make the difference between a run-of-the-mill result and one which is exceptional. And if the driver makes a mistake, then the mood is likely to be one of cheerful forgiveness rather than mumbled recrimination.

Ralf had been visiting a sports psychologist and Mark Gallagher, a member of Jordan's sponsorship management team, had been one of the first to notice the difference. Gallagher had been quietly amazed by Schumacher when entertaining guests of Hewlett-Packard while in Australia for the first race of the season. In 1997, Schumacher had been the second choice for tasks such as this, Gallagher preferring to use Giancarlo Fisichella, the Italian's sunny disposition making a stark contrast with his team-mate's tendency to the monosyllabic. In Melbourne, however, Ralf was the star of the evening as he gave an informal talk. And it was one thing having a driver present, quite another when he discussed life with his superstar brother. Ralf told his audience that he and Michael had stopped in Sydney for a few days without realizing that their visit coincided with the gay Mardi Gras. 'A number of men were looking at us,' said Ralf. 'And then we realized it wasn't because we were famous racing drivers . . . ' Such dry humour would have been unheard of six months before. This was the start of 'New Man' Ralf, a process he was continuing at Imola as the team settled in for the first day of practice.

His banter with the mechanics was at variance with the actions of his team-mate, a difference which was accentuated by the layout of Jordan's territory in the paddock.

The San Marino Grand Prix marked the start of the European season, the significance of which was measured by the sudden appearance of creature comforts after the make-do of the long-haul trips to Australia and South America. Now that they were within striking distance by road, the European races allowed the teams to move what seemed a sizeable portion of their headquarters to each race-track.

Apart from three vast pantechnicons to carry the cars, engines and equipment, each team could also bring a motorhome. Or two, in the case of Jordan Grand Prix. The rules were quite clear in this matter – as with everything else in Formula 1's strict paddock etiquette. Each team and major engine supplier could bring a motorhome apiece. Mugen-Honda's technicians were happy to use a transporter which had been kitted out with comfortable offices, which allowed Jordan to allocate a second motorhome – a purpose-built Van Hool bus previously used by the Tyrrell team – to Benson and Hedges. The pair of yellow vehicles were parked together, the space between them filled with tables and chairs under two awnings – all to the regulation dimensions, of course.

But there was more to the accommodation than either numbers or size. It was immediately apparent that Jordan Grand Prix had moved upmarket. Gone were the plastic tables and chairs which appeared to have been bought at a garden centre. There was proper metal furniture in black to complement the B&H colour scheme. There were nice touches such as yellow cloth napkins and a china dinner service, each piece carrying the stinger logo. There were pot plants aplenty, adequate lighting, an imposing coffee machine and an air of opulence which was offset by the smell of varnish from top-quality slatted flooring. It was a step up in every sense from the blue and yellow plastic mats of previous years.

A great deal of thought had been put into the presentation and the Jordan enclave was among the most impressive in the Imola paddock. There was a reason, of course; one which went beyond the mere cosmetic. B&H was paying for the privilege of having a paddock base (a figure believed to be adjacent to £100,000 for the use of a motorhome for the season), and in return the bus and its accoutrements would need to be decked out in a thoroughly professional manner. It had cost the team in excess of £30,000 for the trimmings, but one look confirmed that it was money well spent.

Certainly, the feeling of spaciousness and warmth was in contrast to the traditional inhospitable feel at places such as Williams, the reigning champions giving the impression of sulking as they hid behind drab maroon canvas screens. It was true that Williams had little to celebrate given their struggle to keep pace with McLaren, Ferrari and, occasionally, Benetton. But at least they had one or two championship points on the board, which was more than could be said for Jordan.

Nonetheless, this was another race, another chance, and Ralf Schumacher appeared ready for action as he mingled with the crew. The mechanics occupied every table outside the Jordan motorhome. Damon Hill breakfasted with his friend Pete Boutwood on the other side of the fence, the contrast between the approach of the two drivers being accentuated by the fact that the rest of the B&H area was empty, Hill appearing alone and slightly aloof as a result. That was far from the truth but it was another point to Ralf in the unspoken psychological struggle for superiority within the team. If anything, Damon's trouble was that he hardly seemed to notice.

There was much to occupy his thoughts, most notably whether or not the car in its latest guise would be an improvement. He had the answer to that within the first thirty minutes of practice. Indeed, he did not need to broadcast the fact. You could see it in the way he was tackling each corner with confidence, the car no longer darting every which way, its driver a passenger. The opening session lasted for forty-five minutes, and for the first time Hill was quicker than Schumacher. Damon held that advantage until five minutes from the end of the final period, when Ralf went a few tenths of a second faster. As practice came to a close, Hill was on an even quicker lap when he had to back off – ironically because Schumacher had spun at the last corner. No matter. The point had been made. The car was better. Much better.

The mood continued through Saturday morning and into qualifying, Damon taking a very encouraging seventh place on the grid (despite an engine failure on his last run), Ralf managing no better than ninth after taking to the grass on what could have been a better lap. Hill was smiling again as he emerged from the technical debrief later in the afternoon.

'I didn't understand where I was with the car in the first few races of the season,' said Hill. 'It was a bit like being blindfolded and taken to a place in a city where you've never been before. Or like being put in a maze. You make a few wrong turns here and there, slowly trying to piece it together. I'd say that it is slowly improving. I've never really driven the same car twice this season, to be honest. Every time I've tried to cajole a quick lap out of it, it has slapped my wrist. The fundamental problem is that it was a bit twitchy. It was irritating. I've been able to go deeper into the corners, be more adventurous.'

His demeanour was totally different. He was relaxed and willing to talk with anyone passing by. Until now, the tendency had been to divert his eyes. Discussion

As Sam Michael (top, left) and Trevor Foster keep an eye on track activity, Gary Anderson ponders the future for himself and his car. Franz Tost keeps Ralf company as he has a last-minute top-up before the start in Spain, the preparation having been completed during two days of practice.

The sponsors relied heavily on television exposure which, in turn, was generated by success on the track. Jordan's coverage in the first few races was minimal.

surrounded how to cope with his wife's forthcoming birthday; Damon would be testing in Spain on the day. Georgie Hill would understand the downside of a racing driver's life even though she might not like it. But as with any motor racing wife forced to stay at home with the children, she would not appreciate the absence of a present or a bout of apparent forgetfulness on the part of her husband.

If Damon's mood had changed for the better, then the reverse seemed to have happened to Ralf. That was put down to the disappointing grid position, but a press release later in the week quoted Gary Anderson as saying that Ralf 'did not seem in the same frame of mind as he had been for the first three races'.

Whatever could that mean? As mentioned, Ralf had appeared to be in good form on Friday morning but something had upset him since. The fact that no one was prepared to give a clear answer indicated that this was more than a matter of a poor performance during qualifying. Money had to be involved. The suggestion was that Schumacher had been told he would be taking a pay cut; his race performances had not been up to scratch.

He was nowhere to be seen as the tables were laid for dinner on Saturday evening. The team was preparing to entertain members of the ITV crew, the motorhome being a preferred venue to the more formal – not to mention expensive – surroundings of a local restaurant. As the guests began to arrive, Ian Phillips stood by the entrance, bidding a welcome in between exchanging gossip with rival team members as they drifted by.

This marked a sea change for Jordan. In the past, the San Marino Grand Prix had been one of the busiest weekends of the season thanks to the myriad Italian sponsors Jordan and Phillips had taken on board in order to pay the bills. It had become something of a pit lane joke to see the Jordans appear at Imola and Monza like some mobile classified advertising section from a glossy magazine. Every marketable square inch had been sold to some willing punter who could now claim to be part of a Formula 1 team.

That was the drawback, of course. Having stumped up a five-figure sum – a sizeable amount for a small business but a mere drop in the Formula 1 financial ocean – the sponsors wanted a piece of the action. The problem was, each team was allocated a limited number of passes, nowhere near enough to cater for Jordan's army of investors. In 1993 and 1994, when the sponsorship space-sharing was at its peak, the passes, having been used once, could be spirited out of the paddock and redistributed to allow the next wave of guests to gain access. In

1998, such illicit swelling of numbers was no longer possible thanks to an electronic turnstile which read the credit-card style passes at the paddock gate and recorded each and every entry and exit.

Fortunately for Jordan, the high level of security mattered little. The arrival of major sponsorship in the shape of Benson and Hedges meant the end of the two-bit deals, the tobacco company being understandably firm in the wish not to have its corporate colour scheme sullied by stickers advertising anything from a local wine merchant to a pizza parlour. Given half a chance, however, Jordan and Phillips would have been wheeling and dealing, not to earn extra revenue – although that always appealed to Eddie – but simply to experience the thrill of the hustle. But this was 1998. Phillips had never known the Jordan motorhome to be so quiet in Italy. He was bored and it showed as he stood there, loudly exchanging banter with casual passers-by and holding murmured informal discussions with the management from rival teams.

The talk was about money. A recent meeting of FOCA (the Formula One Constructors' Association) had not reached a conclusion about the Concorde Agreement, the document which set out every aspect of how the sport should be run and financed. This was a long-running dispute but its immediate effect was the absence of television-funded income from FOCA at a time when each team was burning money at around $2m each month. For a money-rich sport, it was absurd that most of the teams had cash-flow problems. That was the main bone of contention among the top management at Imola.

Otherwise there was very little to discuss – apart from the prospects for the race, of course. After the false dawn of Argentina – where it had seemed that Ferrari might be in the ascendant – it was business as usual in Italy with the McLaren drivers fighting among themselves for the right to win pole position. No one else was in with a chance. The newspaper journalists, having discussed McLaren at length, looked at the opposite end of the spectrum for teams which had been expected to do well but were now struggling. Jordan and Williams were prime candidates.

On race morning, the *Sunday Telegraph* carried a piece by James Mossop. The introduction said it all: 'Troubled times at the pit lane's rock 'n' rollers, Jordan Grand Prix'. 'The drivers are not performing, the £10-million-a-year sponsors are getting three-penn'orth of value and the principal, Eddie Jordan, talks about pain and concern.'

Even though the figures may have been conservative and the passing of time between writing and publication had seen the drivers pick up speed, the sentiments were accurate enough to send an uncomfortable reminder of the struggle. At the end of three columns of explanation and quotes littered with optimism, the story finished with the thought that 'things can only get better'. They had to. Starting at 2 p.m. on Sunday afternoon.

The hope of finally scoring some points lasted all of thirty seconds. As Hill made a clean start, he tucked in behind Alexander Wurz. The Benetton driver had also made a good getaway, but when he tried to select second gear nothing happened. Accelerating hard from 0 to 100 mph in less than four seconds, Hill was caught out as the Benetton slowed when he least expected it. There was neither the time nor the room to take full avoiding action. The Jordan's nose wing clipped the left rear tyre of the Benetton. There was nothing for it but to head for the pits. A replacement nose saw Hill rejoin at the back of the field, next to last.

It was no consolation having Wurz behind him in twenty-first place. Neither was it time to remind Jordan of the old adage that there's always someone worse off than yourself. The Stewart team's desperate season had just sunk to rock bottom as their drivers collided; a knock-on – in every sense – of the confusion caused by Wurz crawling towards the first corner.

For Jordan, there was hope. Ralf had finally made a decent start and was running in ninth place. As for Damon, his lap times were mighty impressive as he cut through the back of the field. At one stage, the Jordan was the fourth-fastest car on the track – yet another sign that the potential had finally been uncovered.

In the end, there would be nothing substantial to show for the weekend's work, Schumacher struggling home in seventh place after a loss of air valve pressure had limited his speed. Hill, meanwhile, had retired with a similar problem, but not before he had climbed to eighth. Eddie Jordan described the San Marino Grand Prix as frustrating but very positive. There was not a lot else he could say.

He was even more coy on another subject, although this one pleased him no end. The annual Rich List compiled by the *Sunday Times* included one Edmund Jordan for the first time in joint 880th place. Even better, he was shown to be among the top 100 of Ireland's wealthy elite. Jordan Grand Prix was quoted as turning over £29m and Eddie himself was said to be worth 'at least £20m'. For a man of EJ's entrepreneurial background, this was the highest praise. He was quietly thrilled to bits and bursting to talk. Somehow, he managed to contain himself since stories of his supposed wealth would create a negative image which might prove unhelpful when it came to containing the team's budget. Small wonder that he also chose to keep quiet about the arrival of one of his favourite toys in the harbour at Barcelona in readiness for the next race in Spain.

Boats were more than just a status symbol for Jordan, his family making extensive use of them during summer holidays in and around the Mediterranean. Sunseekers were considered to be the mass-production Rolls-Royce of the water, Jordan having started off in a comparatively modest manner with a Portofino 400. This neat offshore cruiser would have turned a few heads in Littlehampton or Cork. Within the harbour at Monaco, however, it had been but a mere rowing boat when dwarfed by such shimmering nautical opulence.

The first hint of a change had come when Eddie placed an urgent call from Spain to the factory. Richard O'Driscoll was summoned from a meeting. Since the accountant was a man of figures, he was the very person to charge with the task of converting 19 metres into something an Irishman might recognize. When told it the answer was close to 62 feet, Jordan sounded happy. Whatever the craft was he was after, it was longer than the boat owned by Arrows chief Tom Walkinshaw. That would do fine. Never mind the rowlocks, just feel the length.

In fact, Jordan had his eye on a Manhattan 62, a major step forward which, in technical parlance, would move him into the Flybridge Motor Yacht class. It would also require a full-time crew member capable of maintaining the boat and moving it to wherever EJ and his family needed to be next. On this occasion, it was more business than pleasure as *Snapper S* tied up in Barcelona in time to provide Eddie and his wife Marie with accommodation for the fifth round of the championship.

Racing in Spain meant a closer involvement than usual with Repsol, the state-owned oil and fuel company which sponsored the team. The trouble here was that Repsol, formerly a prime sponsor of the Ford Escort team, did not seem to understand that Formula 1 had a much higher profile than world championship rallying. Repsol had been a long-time supporter of Carlos Sainz, who, apart from being a brilliant rally champion, was a Spanish sporting hero akin to Alan Shearer, Nick Faldo and Damon Hill rolled into one. With Sainz in their charge, Repsol could call the shots.

In rallying, they had paid $4m and, in return, received exposure over the entire car. It was Ian Phillips's job to disabuse them of the fact that life would not be the

Damon was up to his neck in it
as he struggled to make the car
work and save his reputation...

same in Formula 1. For their $4m, they would be allowed a few stickers on the car, albeit in reasonably prominent positions. This was finally accepted, so much so that Phillips actually sold Repsol even more space on the car.

Phillips' economic sense of diplomacy was at full stretch. It was deemed a sensible move to call upon the services of a soother of fevered brows, someone who knew the Formula 1 sponsorship ropes and could mollify and mollycoddle without going over the top. Phillips had no hesitation in contacting James Gilby, an utterly charming man whose experience in these matters with McLaren, Ford and other motor sport companies was a much more accurate summary of his character than the unfortunate tabloid image created by his former association with Diana, Princess of Wales. The team was happy; the guests were satisfied; the stickers went on the cars.

Removed from the cars were mid-mounted wings – the so-called X-wings – which had been raced for the first time in Argentina in a successful bid to find more downforce. These wings had been introduced by the Tyrrell team in 1997. Since Tyrrell were struggling at the back of the field and appeared to be receiving no obvious advantage from the X-wings, rival designers made a mental note to try them in the wind tunnel when they had a spare moment. That experiment received increased priority as the revised technical regulations – severely reducing downforce – came into effect for 1998. When it was discovered that the X-wings produced a useful increase in downforce, production became inevitable. The fact that the wings spoiled the clean appearance of the car was irrelevant: 'Show me where the regulations say you are not allowed to design an ugly car,' was Eddie Jordan's non-technical summary.

All of this caught the FIA by surprise. When the Tyrrells first brandished the X-wings and no one followed that route, the governing body thought the wings would be a passing phase. When they sprouted on the Jordans, Saubers, Prosts and, Heaven forbid, the Ferraris, action had to be taken. Since the X-wings were perfectly legal, the structure of the rule-changing process was such that any amendment to the technical regulations would require the agreement of the teams. Ferrari, happy to have discovered more downforce in one hit than they were likely to find in an entire season, were bound not to agree. And, even if the technical advantage was not so pronounced, they would fail to agree in any case just to be perverse.

The FIA, however, had a useful get-out clause: a ban could be implemented overnight on the grounds of safety. It was therefore decided that, in the event of an accident, a driver could be struck on the head. The X-wings were outlawed with immediate effect.

Gary Anderson was not alone in being unhappy about the FIA's unilateral decision. Despite the simple appearance of the wings, much effort had gone into design, wind-tunnel research and production. Anderson calculated that four days had been spent in the design office with a further two days in the wind tunnel. In total, 200 man hours had been spent and the bill added up to £50,000. It now amounted to a complete waste of money which could have been avoided had the FIA nipped the problem in the bud twelve months before.

There was another point of contention. McLaren had not run the X-wings and it was assumed that the leaders of the championship had no need of them. While that may have been true to a degree, the fact was that the side pods on the McLaren were shorter than those used by the X-wing exponents. In other words, short of a major side pod redesign, McLaren (and Benetton) could not use the wings even if they had wanted to. It had seemed to be no great loss at the beginning of the season, but it might be a different matter if the competition closed in later on.

For the moment, however, McLaren was once again in a league of its own. Hakkinen, on pole, was 1.5 seconds faster than Michael Schumacher in third place. The competitive edge enjoyed by Ferrari in Argentina seemed to be a thing of the past. It looked to be the same for the Jordan team as it thought about the promise of Imola – and then examined the time sheets which showed that Hill had qualified eighth, with Schumacher eleventh.

The drivers, in fact, were reasonably happy. The competitiveness of the non-McLaren runners was such that 1 second covered eight cars. Damon said the Jordan continued to feel very good; the discrepancy between reality and where they hoped to be on the grid was down to tyres, some of the drivers ahead having run on a softer rubber. This would give an advantage during the one-lap effort of qualifying but it would be a different matter in the race. The rules said that drivers must use the same type of tyre in the race as that chosen for qualifying. The logic, therefore, was that the Jordan drivers would be in better shape on Sunday afternoon with their harder tyres. But who said that logic had a guaranteed place in motor racing, particularly Formula 1? The final reality was that Jordan would experience another average race. Trouble began during the warm-up

on race morning when Hill reported that the car's feel had deteriorated, the sense of balance gone. This was a typical side effect of racing at Barcelona, a circuit which was affected by variation in track temperature, so much so that a car which felt good one day would be difficult the next. Race day promised to be hotter than the previous two. Indeed, even at 9.30 a.m., the track temperature was higher than ever before. It was a bad omen.

Schumacher not only made another poor start, the effect caused him to lose mental momentum as well, and he finished the first lap in seventeenth place after being bundled further down the field as drivers with more confidence and adrenalin took advantage. Damon made a good getaway but then lost his advantage when wrong-footed at Turn 1. He completed the opening lap in tenth place, knowing there was little he could do to improve his position during the next hour and thirty minutes.

The car was average. No more. No less. A process of elimination among those in front moved him to eighth place before a pit stop – followed by a trip across the gravel thanks to being elbowed aside by Heinz-Harald Frentzen – dropped him to ninth. An engine failure with just under one-third distance remaining made the whole thing academic. Schumacher, meanwhile, flogged on to finish two laps behind the winner, Mika Hakkinen. Ralf was classified eleventh. It might as well have been a hundred and eleventh.

The disappointment in and around the Jordan motorhomes was accentuated by rock music thumping from McLaren and Mercedes-Benz a few doors along. And what made it worse for Jordan was the fact that Stewart had broken their duck by finishing an excellent fifth. That left Jordan and Prost with the also-rans, Arrows, Tyrrell and Minardi, as the only teams not to have opened their score as the season headed towards one-third distance.

'I don't want to talk about it,' said Jordan, as he quietly packed up his leather briefcase and headed for the motorhome door. Not even the thought of a Manhattan 62 sitting in the harbour would provide any solace. In truth, it made the situation feel even more embarrassing.

It was difficult to say whether or not Eddie's personal comforts were on Trevor Foster's mind as he reached the airport later that evening. The one thing sure was that he was deep in thought as he stood on his own in the check-in line. Jordan's Race Director had received an interesting offer to join British American Racing (BAR), a new team which had bought Tyrrell and was due to come on stream in

1999. Foster had left Jordan before; he knew about the true colour of the grass on the other side of the fence. But the trouble was he also knew all about EJ and his likely reaction to a domestic difficulty.

The same questions continued to surface. What was going wrong? Who, if anyone, was at fault? The car seemed to be working well. But it simply wasn't quick enough. Did the Mugen-Honda lack power? Did the chassis lack down-force? Maybe a bit of both. If so, what was EJ going to do about it? Not enough, was the answer from certain quarters in the team. It was not a comfortable feeling as all eyes turned towards the next race in Monte Carlo.

The Monaco track was a slightly bizarre anachronism; a one-off played out before the season's most influential audience. The form book was frequently sent flying at Monaco. On the one hand, Jordan could finally get a result. On the other, a failure yet again in such a public arena . . . No one on the team wanted to think about that. Least of all, it seemed, Eddie Jordan, even though the drama was now rapidly heading towards a crisis.

Chapter Six

You're Never There till You're There

Eddie Jordan used his boat in Monaco. But not in the way he had hoped. At £200 per night, the Sunseeker was moored at a jetty barely a stone's throw from the motorhomes parked on the quayside. Going ashore was not the work of a moment as security fencing around the paddock forced a walk to turnstiles at one end, and then a return past Bernie Ecclestone's silver-grey bus and the Ferrari and McLaren headquarters.

Ralf checks the opposition with his engineer Sam Michael (left) and mechanic Patrick Grandidier.

It was a route which, in good times, any high-profiling team owner would have been pleased to make. At the end of each day in Monaco, EJ wished the ground could open up and save the embarrassment of meeting his rivals during a truly appalling weekend. As a result, he spent more time on his boat than intended. There is no hiding place in Monaco. But below deck on *Snapper S* was better than nothing.

Eddie beat a hasty retreat after practice finished on the first day. Interviews were cancelled, save for an appointment with Louise Goodman and the ITV crew as they canvassed Jordan's views on the Stewart team and the difficulties faced by a Formula 1 newcomer in the second year. Jordan quietly wished his problems were as minor as those being experienced by Stewart.

'Does it get any easier?' asked Goodman.

'After a day like today, I think it gets harder,' said Jordan. Then he paused and added wistfully: 'Never think you've made it till you've made it.'

Goodman smiled quietly at the wonderful Irish logic and recognized this as a good point to terminate the interview. No mention was made of the fact that Stewart-Ford, for all its problems, was ahead of Jordan Mugen-Honda on the time sheet.

Hill had not helped his cause by making a silly mistake during the first session and crashing into the barrier at the swimming pool. Then, reducing valuable track time even further, the gearbox had failed later in the day. He was seventeenth fastest, three places ahead of Ralf who had been sidelined by engine trouble. It was a desperate start.

Gary Anderson spent the day hurrying back from an unscheduled visit to Japan. A post-Barcelona meeting at Jordan's HQ had agreed one thing; the Mugen-Honda was not delivering enough power. Anderson decided to speak directly to his counterparts in the Engine Department, his briefcase full of telemetry evidence which backed up what the eye could see; uncomfortable sights such as Ralf's Jordan unable to out-accelerate a Tyrrell powered by a customer Ford engine as they ran nose-to-tail onto the main straight at Barcelona. The discussions were positive, Mugen-Honda being as concerned as anyone else about the shortfall in performance. That, at least, was the official line.

The media, roaming the quayside at Monaco, put a more mischievous slant on the story. It had been known for some time that Honda was thinking of making a comeback to Formula 1. Better than that, it was intending to build the entire car itself. In the six years since Honda's last foray with McLaren, Formula 1 technology had made massive strides forward and it seemed pure folly for Honda to even think about entering such a specialized world to construct its own chassis and then go racing against vastly experienced names such as Ferrari, Williams and McLaren. The answer, of course, would be to buy an existing team. Enter the media hacks, with pencils sharpened.

Jordan, in its present state, was seen as a likely candidate for a buy-out. One point of view was that Eddie Jordan would take the money and run. That, wrote one journalist, was why Anderson had visited Japan.

Autosport took the story a stage further. The British weekly surmised that Anderson was in fact being wooed by Honda to head the technical side of whichever team it bought – and it might not necessarily be Jordan. Anderson may have been in Japan on company business but, claimed the story, he also had a personal agenda.

That was not true; he had been there purely on behalf of his present employer. But such rumour and counter-rumour did not help anyone within Jordan Mugen-Honda, despite strong denials on all sides. The destabilizing nature of such talk was another effect of the lack of results. The expression 'when you're down, you're down' was never more poignant. And there was worse to come.

The traditional structure of the Monaco weekend meant that practice started on Thursday instead of Friday, leaving the second day free for whatever took your fancy. If your team was on the up, there could be no better place to pose and be seen. If life was difficult, however, Friday was a day to be got through.

Eddie was nowhere to be seen as hazy sunshine and a modest breeze brought perfect conditions to the harbour. But at least there was a family presence as the Jordan clan arrived, en masse, at the paddock gate – without suitable passes. This was no surprise to the team management, Eddie having made lavish promises to his mother, his sister, niece and their respective husbands, and then leaving others to sort out the inevitable confusion. After much shuffling of guest and VIP passes the Irish contingent made their entrance. Once camped at a table outside the motorhome for refreshment, they chatted animatedly and watched the world drift through one of the most eye-catching scenes in motor sport.

The view for the Jordan mechanics was less romantic as they worked a few yards away, on the other side of the truck parked directly behind the motorhome. The free day on Friday meant they had plenty of time to prepare the cars for the final practice and qualifying on Saturday. It had also allowed the luxury of an early halt for a few beers and a leisurely meal the previous evening, a welcome change from the rushed dinner and late-night schedule which usually ends the first day of practice.

The absence of garages meant the teams had to resort to working under awnings slung from the sides of the transporters. The area was made as hospitable as possible thanks to details ranging from a hard-wearing carpet laid on the concrete to adequate strip lighting overhead. The main problem was movement outside the team's enclosure as the cramped nature of the paddock frequently brought the place to a halt.

By 4.30 p.m. on Friday, the three cars had been prepared. The final act was to take them to the official scrutineering area at the end of the pit lane, where various dimensions would be checked to ensure complete legality. One look down the narrow access road told the Jordan crew that they would not be going anywhere for the time being.

A van carrying parts for the Prost team was attempting to edge its way through, the passage made difficult by similar vehicles parked alongside the perimeter fence, leaving barely enough room. The van crept forward, nudging past the awnings of Ferrari, then McLaren, and now Jordan. It was a ludicrously tight squeeze, made possible only by Crew Chief Jim Vale pulling back part of the tubular supports – not to save the van from being scratched but to prevent any damage to Jordan's awning – while the mechanics, anxious to get finished for the night, beckoned the van an inch at a time. It was aggravation everyone could have done without. It was an inevitable part of going motor racing at Monaco.

The paradox is that the picture-postcard surroundings actually generate an undercurrent of tension as the teams attempt to go about their business as efficiently as possible. And, almost inevitably in Formula 1, if that doesn't do the trick, there will always be a problem looming from another source.

Damon Hill had filled in part of his time by reading the latest issue of the monthly magazine *F1 Racing*. An interview with Gary Anderson attracted his attention, particularly Gary's answer to the opening question: 'You've criticized Damon Hill this year. Has he improved?'

Anderson explained that, if he had a complaint, it was this.

'Constructive criticism is fine, but destructive criticism isn't. We've got 165 people at Jordan, all working their nuts off. But they need motivation. Instead, they've been reading in the press that the product they're making is not good. I'm not saying that the criticism is unjustified – because the car isn't perfect – but it's been made in the wrong way.'

Then came the sting: 'The really top drivers – the Schumachers, the Sennas – know how to lift an entire team.'

Hill made a note to have a quiet chat with Gary as he scanned the rest of the interview. Speaking about his hopes for 1998, Anderson said he would be happy if Jordan could qualify both cars in the top six. 'I don't see why we can't be on the podium a couple of times.'

It seemed a reasonable remark since this was the very least the team was capable of. Unfortunately, those words would come back to haunt him on Saturday afternoon in Monaco.

Having taken care of her in-laws on Friday, Marie Jordan had the more delicate task of accompanying the Mugen-Honda boss, Mr Hirotoshi Honda, and his wife as they watched qualifying. Marie had met them before, specifically the previous evening as she and Eddie dined in the cliff-top restaurant which overlooks the Principality. The Hondas were fascinated by the breathtaking panorama and the strips of road lights running along the coast like twinkling necklaces on a dark velvet cloth. Now, on Saturday afternoon, Marie and Mr and Mrs Honda were in the Jordan motorhome looking at illuminations of a more serious kind. The lap times on the monitor made very uncomfortable reading.

Why, Mr Honda asked quietly, were the Jordans going so badly? Fourteenth and fifteenth on the grid were the worst qualifying positions so far. And here of all places. Forget the public humiliation. With overtaking being next to impossible, Jordan Mugen-Honda were already resigned to the role of also-ran once the fifty-sixth Monaco Grand Prix got under way on Sunday afternoon.

The picture on the television summed it up. The camera homed in on a delirious Mika Hakkinen as he celebrated pole position, the Finn soon lost amid a hail of back-slapping as the McLaren team converged on their man. Next door, in the Jordan pit, a despondent Ralf Schumacher stood on his own, wanting neither to talk nor to be spoken to. A qualifying time over three seconds slower than Hakkinen made any comment superfluous.

When it came to talking, Eddie Jordan would have his work cut out that evening as the sponsors dined at three different locations. EJ would manage to

The body language says it all as Ralf heads down the pit lane in Monaco (left) and Damon watches his car being extracted from the tyre barrier (above).

Motoring nowhere: the Jordans are hustled through the swimming pool complex at Monaco, but to no avail. Damon and Ralf did not have time to admire the scenery in Monte Carlo as the team's struggle reached an all-time low (opposite).

visit them all, starting with the Delphi guests in the grand surroundings of the Hermitage Hotel, then a short hop through Casino Square to meet Pearl Assurance representatives at the famous Rampoldi's restaurant, and finally a dash down the hill to the harbour and onto a boat hired by Esat Digifone.

By the time EJ returned to his own floating quarters at 1 a.m. he was mentally and physically exhausted. But reasonably satisfied. The evening had gone just as he had expected thanks, mainly, to a typically unorthodox approach.

There had been no excuses offered, no apologies given. 'My mother, God bless her, could have walked round the track faster than our cars!' was a typical quip which set the mood. It was more or less plain sailing from then on.

'This may be an in-house matter for the team to sort out but I haven't been attempting to hide our difficulties from our sponsors,' explained Jordan at the end of his night's work. 'I think one or two of our "friends" in the paddock expect me to be on the rack here, particularly as it's the one place which guarantees a full turn-out of a team's commercial partners. In fact, the sponsors are being unbeliev-able in such difficult circumstances.

'I'd like to think the reason is that I've never misled them from the moment we first met and opened discussions. Even if we think we are going to have a really good season, I've always tried to be consistent when discussing the role the team is going to play. Even though success is the obvious aim – after all, that's what Benson and Hedges Jordan is all about – I've never guaranteed it.

'Our job is to provide sponsors with a platform in the sport while competing as hard as we possibly can. But we can't promise anything. You would be crazy to do such a thing in this business even though the temptation is strong when a substantial deal is in the balance. As a result of being up-front and refusing to make elaborate claims, I've had a very understanding reaction so far.

'In any case, to be perfectly honest, most sponsors have another agenda when they come here! Everyone has a different priority; some want to walk the circuit and take in the atmosphere, others intend to visit either the famous Tip Top bar for a beer or have a flutter in the casino, while the Esat Digifone people are having a truly fabulous time on the boat. The priorities of each sponsor vary and, while the team's performance may not be good, I have been doing as much as I can on the periphery to maximize awareness.

'I think people inside the sport tend to overlook that important point; they will look at the results much harder than most of the guests. For those who make

Formula 1 their business, the results are everything. Sponsors' guests, on the other hand, are just so happy to be here and be a part of a show which we, through familiarity, sometimes take for granted.'

Warming to his theme, Jordan went on:

'The fact is that visitors to a race have a team to support, even if that team is struggling. But, better than that, they are able to meet the drivers, put their arm round Damon and have a photograph taken with Ralf. That sort of thing is mind-blowing. Playing such an active part in supporting a Grand Prix team is the biggest thrill in the world and the actual performance on the track, while being disappointing, is not desperately important.

'OK, guests may think about it more deeply if we carry on like this but, in the meantime, they will say: "Hey, we've had an unbelievable time. Jordan's hospitality was outstanding." That stands to us when things are difficult and will tide us over until we sort the problems. And sort them we must.

'Having said all that, you can understand that it wasn't easy seeing the expectant faces at three dinners in succession. Once again, it was a case of being absolutely straight with everyone. I wasn't going to say I was embarrassed or sorry because everyone knows about the potential pitfalls in this sport. On these occasions, you try to think of things that may be funny when making speech. But I didn't want to go so far as recalling the day when McLaren, who look like dominating this weekend, failed to qualify both their cars at Monaco. But I did point out that two years ago there was an unknown Frenchman – Olivier Panis – who qualified fourteenth and went on to win the race. I felt that was a slightly more positive way of looking at it although, even with me being a total optimist, I wasn't sure if I felt good saying it.'

Eddie's gut feeling was proved correct on race day. Within eighteen laps, Damon was lapped by the rampaging McLarens, Ralf having suffered the same embarrassment a few minutes before as he struggled along in seventeenth place. The yellow cars ran in convoy for most of the race, Ralf eventually retiring with damaged rear suspension after clipping a barrier.

There was no need to ask how Damon was feeling. Hill was usually quite voluble during a race as he talked on the radio, asking for position updates and discussing tactics. On this occasion, the team heard not a single word during the final thirty laps. There was nothing to be said as he struggled home eighth, a full two laps behind the winner, Hakkinen. It was a disaster beyond words.

The mechanics began the weary process of shifting every item of pit gear back to the paddock, where the trucks were waiting to be loaded. That done, they retreated for a quiet meal. Monaco was in full party mood and the thought of mingling in the celebrations did not appeal, not even for a hard-earned beer. Most of the lads went back to their hotel rooms and watched television, eager to be done with this place and get away the following morning. The romance of Monaco? You must be joking.

No one on the team needed reminding that Arrows had brought both cars home in the top six. Two weeks before it had been Stewart breaking their duck. Now this. It meant that Prost, Tyrrell and Minardi remained with Jordan as the only teams not to have scored a single point after six races. The newspapers talked of a crisis at Jordan. Even allowing for media hyperbole, there was no getting away from that painful fact. Eddie Jordan would finally have to address the problem. But how?

There was no time to lose. A two-hour meeting between Jordan, Gary Anderson, his engineers and Trevor Foster had already taken place in the debriefing room in one of the trucks. Among the items agreed was a more influential role for Foster and a further discussion with Anderson when they returned to Silverstone.

That meeting duly took place. It was stormy at times (one witness said a mobile phone had been thrown across the room when the debate was at its height) but the end result was an agreement whereby Anderson would miss the next two races in Canada and France in preference to spending time in the wind tunnel checking and rechecking details in search of the necessary tenths of a second needed to bring the car to a more acceptable level.

It was also agreed that Eddie would consider a new wind-tunnel model. But first he wanted to see the costing involved. This project would be handled mainly by Dr John Davis, an aerodynamics specialist who had joined the team in 1996 after time spent with Lotus and Ligier. The model would examine various ideas and if these areas resembled parts of the McLaren, it would surprise no one since evaluating themes employed by the pace-setter is the name of the game. In Formula 1, pride takes second place to competitiveness.

All told, the mood was positive – for the time being. When Foster reached Montreal a few days later to begin preparations for the Canadian Grand Prix, a phone call from the factory brought his spirits crashing to rock bottom.

It was Foster's opinion that EJ, without consultation, had axed the plans for the model. No reason was given but the suspicion that cost was a deciding factor took an immediate hold. Foster was livid. Never had the offer from BAT looked more appealing to Jordan's Race Director. In fact, Jordan would argue later, he had not given the go-ahead because he had yet to receive the costing. Either way, it seemed a delicate argument when time was so precious.

There was a suspicion in Canada that Jordan had been influenced by Anderson claiming that an improvement had been found already. The model, therefore, would not be necessary. If that was so, then EJ would have jumped at the opportunity to save money.

That was the view from Canada, an opinion which Jordan would later refute. A wind-tunnel model would be a long-term fix. Jordan's argument was that they needed something here and now. It was true that Anderson had offered solutions which, by chance, would be a cheaper alternative. But as time would prove, they would also be successful. Jordan bristled at the very suggestion that he had been heavily influenced by his Technical Director and was afraid to go against him. Jordan rigorously maintained he had nothing but the best interests of the team at heart.

For the moment, however, the atmosphere in the Jordan enclosure at Montreal was as downbeat as it has ever been. Even the normally sanguine Phillips seemed uncharacteristically quiet and low key. If nothing else, Phillips could see the effect this latest piece of news was having on one or two team members.

There was a view that Eddie's renowned parsimony was causing damage at a time when the job needed to be done – whatever it took. If Anderson had indeed found additional downforce, it was difficult to believe that this could be the complete answer. Yet EJ, without examining the detail, was obviously quite prepared to accept that this was the case. Or, at least, that's the way it seemed 3,500 miles away in Montreal.

There was a view that EJ had finally lost his appetite for appearing at the top of the result sheet in preference to a healthy figure at the bottom of the firm's accounts. That was a harsh summary and Jordan would not have countenanced such a suggestion for a single second. But its timing could not have been more uncomfortable in the light of an article in the same magazine which had published Anderson's critical comments about Hill.

The back page of *F1 Racing* each month carried a tongue-in-cheek piece writ-

Graham Hill won the Monaco Grand
Prix five times. Damon came no closer
to giving his father's famous helmet
colours another victory in 1998.

ten in the manner of 'Dear Bill', the sometimes scurrilous column in *Private Eye* purporting to be a chummy letter from Denis Thatcher, the husband of the then Prime Minister, Margaret, to his friend Bill Deedes. The piece in *F1 Racing* was composed by a well-known journalist using the pen name 'The Scrutineer'. In the June issue he wrote to Damon Hill and in passing made mention of Eddie Jordan in a less than flattering light.

'How goes it driving for Eddie Jordan?' joshed The Scrutineer. 'I'm a great fan of EJ on a social level, but was amused to hear a cynical colleague make the point that if Frank Williams and Ron Dennis were down to their last £100, they would spend it on making their cars go faster. Eddie would spend it on having his Sunseeker's bottom scraped. Whatever that might be.

'Well, Damon, I was outraged – and put this chap straight. What a terrible calumny! I believe that EJ is as totally committed as the next man to winning Grands Prix, and any suggestions that he's more interested in being famous than being successful should be treated in the manner they deserve.'

It was supposed to be a joke but the serious subtext had exposed a raw nerve. Had the team been scoring points and finishing on the podium, Jordan would have laughed it off. In fact, the piece would never have been written in the first place. But the disastrous run of results had left EJ wide open. The supposedly casual mention of the Sunseeker neatly found its target below the waterline. Jordan was doing his best to contain his anger.

When he arrived in the paddock on the day practice was due to start, EJ took the opportunity to buttonhole the writer, Alan Henry, as he walked by the Jordan compound. It was done in a jokey fashion but not even Eddie Jordan could disguise his discomfort, particularly when the banter continued and the author showed no sign of remorse.

But at least Jordan was talking to Henry, which was more than could be said for the line of communication between the boss and his Race Director. Foster felt that Jordan knew he would be furious and was therefore keeping a low profile. Eddie's opinion was that because Trevor had not got his way over the model he was not in the mood to talk. Either way, the chilly atmosphere was scarcely productive at a time when Jordan Grand Prix was in need of firm, positive leadership. Instead of rising to this desperate challenge, the mood in the Jordan enclosure hinted at the unthinkable; the team was slowly buckling and might not respond.

This being a fly-away race, the absence of motorhomes and other familiar creature comforts meant the team worked from Portakabins placed at the back of the garage, the area in between being filled with a few tables and chairs overshadowed by piles of trunks and boxes used to ship the cars and spare parts. Food was cooked in a makeshift kitchen and laid out, rather precariously, on upturned packing cases and tables. There was a flimsy awning attached to the rear wall of the garage – not that it did much good when the intermittent but very heavy showers came barrelling in from the nearby St Lawrence River. Given the team's troubles, this was hardly a weekend in Paris.

Seated in one corner, Nigel Northridge took in the scene before him. The Marketing Director of Benson and Hedges had with him Peter Wilson, Chairman of the parent company, Gallaher, and eight senior City analysts who had been involved with the flotation of Gallaher one year before. It was important that the team should put on a good show but Northridge did not need to be told that the situation was grim. He had expressed that very point in no uncertain terms during a lengthy telephone call post-Monaco.

This was another difficulty for the team, and Phillips in particular. Jordan's contract with B&H had one more year to run, with an option. Phillips was keen to tie down that option more securely in case, as the business world rumours suggested, B&H was take over by BAT. If that happened just as British American Racing were arriving on the Formula 1 scene, then the chances of B&H remaining with Jordan would be zero. It didn't take a genius to work out that given Jordan's desperate state, B&H would not be rushing to firm up the option.

Northridge watched quietly as journalists trickled into the area to follow up on the story that Gary Anderson was not present. A press release delivered to the media centre by Giselle Davies had broken the news. Anderson was quoted as saying:

'We've got an intensive wind-tunnel programme for the next ten days, plus a huge amount of data to check to try to unlock the speed from the car and engine. Realistically there are no overnight fixes which can be actioned in time for Montreal and probably not [for the next race in] Magny Cours. I am therefore concentrating on trying to turn the performance around for Silverstone and the second half of the season. There is still plenty to play for, and hopefully a concentrated five weeks now will allow the drivers and team to realize their full potential from the British Grand Prix onwards.'

Fair enough. But now the journalists wanted to know what it really meant. Rumours suggested that Jordan was in discussion with Mike Gascoyne, an aerodynamicist with Tyrrell and likely to become redundant at the end of the year when Tyrrell was taken over fully by BAR, the new outfit which, at this precise moment, looked like being Trevor Foster's employer for 1999. If Gascoyne did join Jordan, where would that leave Anderson? There was no comment to be had from Eddie or anyone else. But the rampant speculation provided yet another turn of the screw. The activity on the track almost seemed irrelevant.

That soon changed when Ralf claimed fifth place on the grid to equal his best qualifying performance thus far in 1998. How had this come about? Goodyear had produced revised rear tyres and these had helped (witness Michael Schumacher's Goodyear-shod Ferrari edging closer to the Bridgestone McLarens on the front row). Tribute was also paid to Mugen-Honda and an upgraded engine which had been used for qualifying. It was also useful to be performing on a circuit which did not require the car to have masses of downforce, an apparent weak spot on the Jordan. Whatever the reason for this upturn, Ralf was understandably delighted with fifth, Damon less so with tenth fastest time after choosing a different set-up for his car.

'The set-up I used seemed to work very well for me,' explained Ralf. 'We really have the opportunity to win points and I really hope I can make a good start and finish in the top six.' Twenty-four hours later, those words would have an uncomfortable ring.

For safety reasons, team personnel are not permitted to stand by the pit wall for the start of each race. Most gather in the garage and watch the television monitors as the Grand Prix gets under way. It was with an all-too-familiar sense of anticlimax and frustration that they saw the yellow car on the third row of the grid stand still while the rest of the field swept forward. Ralf had messed up yet another start thanks to the on-off nature of a clutch which everyone knew was very difficult to operate to perfection.

The team had barely got over that desperate disappointment when hopes soared just as quickly. A multiple collision at the first corner had caused the race to be stopped. Ralf would get a second chance.

He had stalled the engine at the first attempt. Second time round he overcompensated, gave the engine too many revs but got away in a rush. He arrived too quickly at the first corner. The Jordan spun and partly contributed to another collision. This time the race was not stopped, the organizers preferring to run the opening laps under the control of the Safety Car while the wreckage was cleared. Ralf had got going again but the third call on the clutch to do such extreme work proved too much. The Jordan soon ground to a halt and failed to complete a single lap.

Hill, meanwhile, was quite nicely placed. By avoiding the various accidents, he found himself in seventh position as the field formed behind the Safety Car before being released after four slow laps. Having got that far, he managed to maintain position – quite easily, in fact. He recorded impressively competitive lap times as he pursued the Williams drivers, feeling more comfortable with each lap since he knew he was stopping just once whereas a two-stop strategy seemed to be on the cards for a few of the leading drivers – most notably Michael Schumacher.

One way or another, the field had been decimating itself before Hill's very eyes. Hakkinen had not managed to complete the first lap and Coulthard was about to make it a double retirement for McLaren when a broken throttle linkage cost the Scotsman the lead. Schumacher then led briefly before making his first stop.

As he rejoined, the Ferrari driver caused huge controversy by forcing Frentzen's Williams off the road. Whether by accident or design would become the subject of a massive debate, the race stewards meanwhile taking the view that his action had been dangerous and demanded that Schumacher return to the pits for a ten-second stop-go penalty. When the Ferrari dived into the pit lane for the second time, Damon Hill, who had yet to make his first stop, assumed second place, eighteen seconds behind Giancarlo Fisichella's leading Benetton. And still the Jordan kept banging home reasonable lap times. This seemed too good to be true.

Michael Schumacher could hardly believe it either. His stop-go duly completed, he rejoined in third place, three seconds behind – a Jordan! And one driven by his bête noir from seasons past. Schumacher, with the benefit of fresher tyres, quickly closed the gap. Hill, realizing his pit stop was due in a few laps, knew he was fighting for position and that Schumacher would need to stop once more. Given the chance to battle at the front of the field for this first time this season, there was no way Damon was going to miss a bit of cut and thrust with his old mate.

Sweeping onto the home straight on lap thirty-eight, Schumacher moved right – and Hill moved right. Schumacher moved left – and Hill moved left. When Schumacher darted right as they approached the braking area for the pits chicane at more than 190 mph, Hill feinted right once more. Schumacher, now drawing alongside, suddenly swerved away. In doing so, he missed his braking point but staged a recovery by running across the kerb at the exit of the chicane – and kept his new-found second place. Buoyed by the battle and realizing the Ferrari had lost momentum, Hill danced around in Schumacher's mirrors. But Michael had every move covered. Great fun! Or so it seemed.

Damon made his one and only stop two laps later and rejoined in fourth place, three seconds behind the Stewart of Rubens Barrichello – who was due to call at the pits one more time. This was looking good. Not only was Damon on course for the team's first points of the season, a place on the podium seemed almost certain – for about three minutes.

At the end of lap forty-one, the Jordan returned to the pits. The engine had begun to misfire. A sensor had packed up after about thirty laps. In the absence of any messages, the on-board computer caused the engine to run too lean. The exhaust temperature rose steeply but there was no immediate drama as long as air was passing through the car. That changed dramatically during the pit stop. The searing heat quickly melted part of the wiring loom and caused the misfire.

Hill's race was doomed from that moment on. One more lap and he was out, bitter disappointment running through the body language as he climbed from the cockpit and the men in yellow and black went into slow motion, their race over.

Schumacher went on to win. Williams protested his driving and Michael, perhaps as a diversionary tactic, got stuck into Damon.

'If someone wants to kill you he should do it in a different way,' was Schumacher's blunt accusation. 'We are doing 320 kph [200 mph] down there and to move off line three times is simply unacceptable. You can do it once, one side to the other: that's what we usually do. I shall be having words.'

Given some of Schumacher's tactics in the past, it was a classic case of the pot calling the kettle black. Damon, wearing his trademark cap and dressed in T-shirt, light blue denim shirt and chinos, was standing at the back of the garage, swigging from a bottle of water and savouring the taste of having run at the front.

'It was great,' he said. 'It felt fantastic to be up at the front again; I really enjoyed it. Not only that but the lap times were fairly respectable. This was the first time this year that I have been able to race for the top three positions and I was not going to let second or third place go that easily – so I enjoyed some racing with Michael!'

When it was explained that Schumacher did not necessarily share those views and the quotes from the winner's press conference were read out, Hill looked at first surprised, and then serious. He shook his head.

'He overstates the case to try and defend himself,' said Damon. 'He cannot claim anyone drives badly when you look at the things he's been up to in his career. He took Frentzen out completely. He knew he was there. I bet the people on the radio were telling him he was there. I don't think you can put much credibility on what Michael has to say, quite honestly. You have to make your own judgement on the matter.'

One view was that Schumacher had committed a far greater crime during the incident with Frentzen. When it came to Damon Hill, Schumacher's sense of reason appeared to desert him. This was a case in point. Another body of opinion suggested that Hill's final swerve had indeed been dangerous at such high speed. Damon claimed it had been perfectly acceptable.

'Anyway,' said Hill, 'I'm more concerned about the fact that I didn't finish. We really needed the points. I feel . . . well, gutted, to use the popular phrase, so I can't imagine how the rest of the team feels.'

That just about summed it up. Trevor Foster and Ian Phillips found time for some light refreshment as the packing up continued all around them. Foster and Jordan had finally come face to face on the previous day and the confrontation had at least remained civil – just about. Jordan had emphatically denied any wrongdoing or broken promises.

'He'll never change,' said Foster grimly, his views perhaps tainted excessively by the thought that he would be leaving the team. 'I just hope Eddie doesn't claim that today's performance was a turning point and that everything will be all right – because it wasn't and it won't. At least not in the short term.'

Indeed not. As Jordan himself would have said: 'You're never there till you're there.'

Chapter Seven

Making a Point

The figures did not make good reading. Eddie Jordan

squirmed slightly as he watched the lap times juggle

for position on the screen, McLaren and Ferrari rising

to the top, Jordan sinking to the midfield.

'What's going on?' he asked no one in particular.

'I hope we're on the right strategy. There'll have to

be some discussion over this.'

Dressed up and ready
to go. The mechanics
wait for a pit stop.

He was watching the warm-up unfold on race morning in France. Sitting on his own at the front of the motorhome, Jordan had just completed a taping session for his column in a Dublin newspaper. The interview had raised a number of questions which needed answering and the entire process had served to remind him of his present difficulties.

Jordan admitted that the signing of Mike Gascoyne as Chief Designer had been more or less completed. Which prompted the obvious question about how this appointment would sit with Gary Anderson.

'I really don't see any problem with that,' said Jordan. 'It was Gary who conducted the interview, and he seems happy enough. I think they'll complement each other and work very well together.'

Anderson had remained back at base for the second race in succession, his focus being the next round, the British Grand Prix, and the introduction of modifications to the car. In the meantime, the Jordans had recorded their best overall qualifying performance of the season so far as Schumacher and Hill took sixth and seventh places at Magny-Cours, splitting Jacques Villeneuve and Heinz-Harald Frentzen despite marked improvements to the Williams cars.

The increase in Jordan's pace had been mainly due to further developments from Goodyear (a step forward which had taken the Ferraris among the McLarens at the front of the grid) and the much-needed increase in power from the Mugen-Honda qualifying engine. Which indirectly led Jordan to another tricky question which had to be addressed in his column.

The stories concerning a buy-out by Honda refused to go away. Once again, *F1 Racing* was proving to be a thorn in Jordan's side, the latest issue carrying a news item which suggested that negotiations had reached an impasse because Eddie could not be guaranteed a position in the team if Honda took a majority share-holding. In other words, Honda wanted rid of him. Jordan bristled at the very suggestion.

'Even if there had been discussions, there's no way I would even consider such a thing,' he said, thumping his fist on the blue velour armrest. 'I haven't worked all these years to get the team where it is, just to turn around and walk away if someone offered me a lot of money. No way!

'Yes, we have talked to Honda,' he admitted. 'But so have a number of teams. Honda paid what you might call courtesy visits to Jordan, Arrows and

Williams, just to get the lie of the land and understand how much will be involved when they set up their own team – which is how I understand they will operate rather than buying into an existing team. The Jordan name has been linked to Honda because of our association with Mugen-Honda. But there is nothing more than that.

'The fact is that Honda have always maintained that they would manufacture the whole car themselves. You generally find that when the Japanese declare their intentions, very seldom do they change tactics. It's the way they do business. They make a decision and usually it is very difficult to alter it - not that I or anyone else was trying to overturn that decision.

'They realize that Formula 1 in its present guise – what with restrictions on testing and the complex regulations concerning the car – it's more difficult for a new team to get started and come through to join the front runners. We have an outstanding relationship with Mugen-Honda and I'm very happy for it to continue.'

Were these the facts or mere bluster, a smokescreen to cover the discomfort presented by Honda's rumoured demands? Whatever the truth, Jordan's attention was diverted to the television screen showing Hill spinning into the gravel, where he remained stuck fast. Jordan watched the pictures. Then he looked away and remained silent for a moment or two.

'OK, where were we? Yes, Honda. No way am I going to let go all of this,' he said, waving his arm in the general direction of the Jordan garage. 'What would I do if I did?'

During the unofficial debates in Canada as senior management tried to seek a solution to the team's problems, there had been a suggestion that EJ might be better off employing a senior executive to take on the day-to-day running, thus allowing him to play the team's figure head, a role in which he excels. This, after all, would be the reason why Honda – assuming the offer had been made – would want EJ to stand aside because otherwise the public perception would be of the team belonging to Jordan and not to Honda. Such was Eddie's high profile.

Jordan agreed that the idea of a team director had some merit. Then he lapsed into silence once more and studied the screen intently. It was clearly a subject which had occupied his thoughts.

The warm-up ended. The Jordans were eleventh and twelfth, about two seconds away from the McLarens and the Ferraris. 'It looks like they are going to make one more stop than us,' he muttered, as if by way of explanation. 'Or, at least, I hope that's what it means. Otherwise, it's not good. Not good at all.'

As he stood up, his expression brightened.

'Did you hear the commotion in the paddock yesterday?' he grinned. 'There was no need to ask if Italy had scored.'

Jordan was referring to the World Cup match played a couple of hours after qualifying had ended on Saturday afternoon. The Ferrari enclave had been bulging with team members and journalists as they watched the victory enfold, the rowdy reception for each goal injecting much needed life into the sterile paddock.

Magny-Cours, for all its cleanliness and modern efficiency, has about as much atmosphere as an empty car park. Stuck in the middle of France, it is difficult to reach and most of the insufficient accommodation is second-rate. The Jordan management had found a novel solution by renting a houseboat on a tranquil stretch of water. While enjoying an evening barbecue on the river bank, it hardly seemed that this was a Grand Prix weekend. In some ways, that feeling was entirely appropriate.

It was difficult to raise much enthusiasm for a race at Magny-Cours and the journalists present found motivation levels sinking to a dangerously low level when gossip proved to be in short supply. Or, at least, it was until Eddie Irvine opened his mouth.

Growing weary of the condemnation which had been heaped on his team-mate, Irvine was not afraid to voice an opinion about Schumacher's controversial part in the Canadian Grand Prix. Not surprisingly, perhaps, Irvine saw Michael as the innocent party. It was Hill's driving which was at fault.

'The rules say that you can't block – and Hill's third move was a definite block,' said Irvine. 'The rules say that, but the stewards never do anything about it. They won't make a move until someone hurts themselves and then they say that won't do. But it's too late then.

'The fault lies both with the stewards and with Hill. What he did was Formula Ford stuff. In fact, it wouldn't be allowed in Formula Ford! Blocking at 190 mph is incredibly dangerous. If they had touched wheels, one or both of the cars would have been into the pit lane entrance. It doesn't bear thinking about.

That incident was one of the worst I have seen. I think it was just Damon being a prick.'

Irvine's quotes made most editions of the Saturday papers in Britain. Naturally, the Sunday correspondents were not about to let the story die as they struggled to find material. A response was needed.

Hill was having breakfast as the early sunshine warmed the outer row of tables by the Jordan motorhome on Saturday morning. Yes, he had heard about Irvine's comments. He had no hesitation in giving a calm and measured reaction.

'What you've got to realize,' he said, waving a spoon, 'is that Irvine is just a lackey for Michael's misdemeanours. My conscience is totally clear. The issue is not what Irvine has to say. Whatever comment Michael makes, Eddie will back up because he has no choice.

'The point is that Michael went over the chicane in order to get past me – which is not allowed – and strictly speaking he should have let me through again. He never observes the regulations. He does things such as practice starts on the formation lap, when it is made quite clear at every drivers' briefing that practice starts are forbidden. And nothing is done about it. If anyone is going to complain, then that's the issue which needs to be addressed. But, as far as I'm concerned, it's history now. I'm more interested in this weekend. We're in with a good chance.'

Much would depend on Ralf taking full advantage of his position on the third row, alongside Villeneuve and directly behind the two Ferraris as Schumacher and Irvine lined up on the outside of the grid. If he botched his start yet again, the only consolation was that Damon, just over Ralf's left shoulder, would be clear of the congestion.

In fact, Ralf was feeling much more confident thanks to the installation of a different type of clutch, which was more progressive. He had been practising his starts and all of that work was put to good effect when the red lights went out. Unfortunately, it was in vain.

A stalled Stewart five rows back had prompted officials to abort the start, a marginal decision given the absence of immediate danger caused by the stricken car but one which was made much worse when the lighting system failed to respond and the field was released milliseconds before the orange abort lights began to flash. The bottom line was that Ralf and Damon would need to do it all again.

1999 already? Tentative discussions start between Eddie, Ralf and his manager, Willi Weber.
Meanwhile Mark Gallagher (inset) handles an increasing number of calls from angry members
of the Supporters' Club.

Ralf fixes his ear plugs/radio speakers in place, the better to hear comments from Sam Michael when practice begins.

This time the entire field made a clean getaway, both Schumachers being mightily relieved as Ralf held his sixth place and brother Michael, tardy first time round, made a blistering start at the second attempt to shoot into a lead he was destined never to lose.

The Jordans held station and looked very comfortable on the fringe of the top six. Even without overtaking anyone there was the hope that with the usual rate of attrition they could finish fifth and sixth at the end of seventy-one laps. The chances of that happening took a dive as early as lap sixteen when Hill struggled to find gears. Three laps later, he was out thanks to the effects of a leaking seal in the hydraulic system.

Ralf's first stop went according to plan, but as he rejoined a collision with Wurz's Benetton meant a return to the pits for the replacement of a steering arm. Relegated to the back of the field, Schumacher would finish sixteenth and last. The team's only consolation was sixth fastest lap behind the McLarens, Ferraris and Villeneuve's Williams; further confirmation of the handful of championship points which had been there for the taking.

Eight races down, eight to go and no points for Jordan. McLaren had amassed eighty. It was no comfort to know that Prost-Peugeot were in an even worse predicament, hopelessly off the pace in France. It was going to be Jordan's turn next as they prepared to perform in front of the home crowd at Silverstone. Before that, however, the relentless pace would continue from the moment the packing up process began at Magny-Cours.

One car was sent immediately to Danielson, a small circuit in France where conclusions reached in the wind tunnel at Brackley could be confirmed on the track. That visit would last for two days, by which time the test team would be ready to attend the final pre-Grand Prix session at Silverstone.

The three-day test turned out to be significant for reasons other than making ready for one of the most important races of the season. With access at the Grand Prix itself both expensive and restricted, Jordan planned to extract the full commercial benefit from what, in reality, is routine work as the cars thrash round and round the Northamptonshire track, interrupted by sometimes lengthy periods in the pits while adjustments are carried out.

Routine it may be for the team but more than 600 guests were thrilled with privileged access which allowed them to see the cars and drivers on a reasonably informal basis. A special viewing gallery was constructed along one side of the garage, a necessary step as far as Trevor Foster and the team were concerned as they worked through a busy schedule called for by having three cars running at once. The visitors – sponsors' guests and representatives from Jordan's suppliers who would otherwise never get the chance to see the cars in action – took it in turns to come across from the grandstand reserved for Jordan and the marquee beyond.

Two hundred people sat down to lunch each day. Apart from the action on the track, entertainment was provided by games, PlayStations and three chat shows, the final one at 5 p.m. featuring Hill, Schumacher and test driver Pedro de la Rosa.

As a PR venture, the trouble taken was more than worthwhile. As a technical exercise, the three-day test was equally profitable as Ralf set the fastest lap with a car featuring modifications to the side pods and other less obvious areas. Times from testing can be notoriously poor indicators of form (Michael Schumacher, second quickest, had a heavy load of fuel on board when establishing his best lap), but no matter. Such a newsworthy story after the recent trials and tribulations was the perfect tonic as the cars were returned to the factory for a strip down and final preparation.

With the Jordan headquarters sited opposite Silverstone's main entrance, it was only natural that a gentle trickle of Jordan and Damon Hill supporters to the front door should become a time-consuming flow as the week gathered pace and the campsites (one of which was in a neighbouring field) began to fill. The placing of security guards at the front gate from Wednesday was an inevitable side effect of the team's popularity and convenient location.

On the other hand, the close proximity of a civilized space within a stone's throw of the track allowed television companies to sidestep the strict regulations governing filming inside a Grand Prix venue. It became common practice for Jordan drivers and team personnel to be spirited out of the track for interviews by television companies unwilling to pay five-figure sums for the right to enter the hallowed precincts of Bernie Ecclestone's Formula 1 empire.

Another area beyond Ecclestone's extensive financial reach was the Grand Prix Ball, held on the Friday night at nearby Stowe School. A black tie affair, this private enterprise attracted 1,300 guests at £165 per head. For that they received a champagne reception on the lawn, a four-course meal in an elaborate marquee and official entertainment from the Jools Holland Band (Eddie Jordan making a

guest appearance on drums). Unofficial amusement was provided by Damon doing wheelies with a motorbike on the lawn, and a casually attired Eddie Irvine arriving by helicopter to eye up every woman in the place.

While Irvine may have been thinking of himself, Damon was playing his part on behalf of a charity raffle in which the Honda bike (painted in Benson and Hedges yellow and called a Hornet) would be the first prize. In a smart move, Ian Phillips arranged for Nigel Northridge to make the draw with Anthea Turner, the B&H Marketing Director quietly delighted by the exposure gained alongside the former hostess of the National Lottery.

For many, the evening swept by in a glorious haze thanks to the generous application of Finlandia vodka, an official sponsor of the event. By morning, any unofficial headaches in the Jordan enclosure were compounded by headlines jumping off the back pages of the national newspapers. The word was that Damon was going to quit at the end of the year.

The British press had been at work. This being the home event and its attendant importance in print, a throw-away quote from Hill — made some days before in semi-casual conversation — had been elevated to a matter of grave importance. Hill, when asked if he would consider stopping if all of his top-line team options were exhausted, said he would. But that was soon translated into a threat. The implication was that Jordan needed to get their act together if Hill was to take up his second-year option with the team. There was some truth in that too. But retirement was not on his agenda.

In fact, he was thinking of the more immediate future. At an official press conference he said, among other things, that the engines were down on power and Honda ought to do something about it. Jordan and Phillips were stunned when they heard word of this outburst. They were in the middle of negotiations over future engine supply and Honda would not be amused.

Honda were not amused. Hill's comments had some substance but this was neither the time nor the place to say it. It was all very well employing shock tactics — a ruse used to great effect by Ayrton Senna when dealing with Honda in the past — but Damon was considered to have put his size twelve foot in it. In fact, it was so serious that Jordan and Phillips looked upon this as a possible breach of contract; in other words, a handy lever when negotiating a deal with Damon for 1999.

In the meantime, Eddie had enough trouble fending off questions about Hill's future with the team. Now he had to deal with this as well. And at Silverstone, of all places. He seemed to be doing one interview after another.

On race morning, for instance, Eddie was rushed from a breakfast meeting at the paddock motorhome to the factory workshop, where he sat on the side pod of the test car (conveniently adorned with full Benson and Hedges insignia, unlike the race cars at the track which, by law, must run without tobacco branding) and took part in a live interview with Sky TV.

Naturally, he was questioned about the season so far and the team's chances later that day. Diplomatic as ever, Eddie spoke highly of his drivers' efforts. Deep down, he was quietly frustrated with them both for reasons which went beyond mere politics and the press.

Damon had qualified in seventh place and the feeling was it could have been perhaps as high as third or fourth had Hill not been experimenting with different lines through the first corner. The split times showed a continuing improvement in the second and final thirds of every qualifying lap. But Damon kept losing out in the first third. After the hours of testing, and with a mere tenth of a second worth three places on the grid, it seemed a strange time to be trying a different line through Copse Corner.

Nothing was said officially. But you could see the puzzled looks as the team examined the evidence before them. Caught at a bad moment, Gary Anderson was asked if he thought Damon might be leaving the team for British American Racing (another rumour which had been doing the rounds). The Technical Director replied curtly: 'Don't care where he goes, to be honest.'

So much for Eddie's repeated assertion that the team's relationship with Damon had never been better and they were confident he would stay.

The frustration over a failure to get at least one car into the top six was made worse by a disastrous afternoon for Ralf. The day had started on an excellent note, Schumacher recording fourth quickest time in the morning session and declaring himself very happy with the car. It was a fatal thing to say.

In Formula 1, it is necessary to work in the belief that anything that can go wrong will go wrong. There is no room for complacency; no time to sit back and relax. No sooner had Ralf declared himself satisfied than the race stewards wiped the smile from his face. They decreed that he had not paid enough attention to a yellow warning flag, as evinced by his fastest lap at that precise moment.

It was a fundamental error which had a catastrophic knock-on effect. As a

The Benson and Hedges stinger
appears to be goading Damon
into action. After a basic mistake
during the race at Silverstone,
Hill didn't want to know.

punishment, Schumacher's fastest time during qualifying would be disallowed. In other words, he would have to set a quick lap – and then do it all again for the time to count.

The pressure was on. It told straight away when Ralf spun on his first flying lap – and stalled. Now he really was in trouble. A sprint back to the pits meant a short delay while the spare car (ear-marked for Hill) was converted to accept Ralf. In theory, all three cars are the same. In reality, the other two are never quite the same as your own. It's a bit like wearing a comfy pair of slippers and switching to heavy boots which are your size, but worn by someone else.

Schumacher did his best. If he was disappointed with an eventual tenth fastest time, then he was to be deeply depressed when a safety check in the scrutineering bay found that he could not withdraw his knees properly in order to evacuate the cockpit in an emergency. The penalty on this occasion was to have all of his qualifying times scrubbed. Ralf was distraught. Being forced to take twenty-first place on the grid was a complete disaster. Almost. It was little consolation to learn that Olivier Panis had failed the same test and would start his Prost twenty-second and last.

But what made it worse for Trevor Foster was the discovery that rapid work on Irvine's Ferrari before the start of qualifying meant he had been able to pass a test he would otherwise have failed. The officials could check whatever aspect of the car they chose. On this occasion, it had been the cockpit. But how did Ferrari know this would happen? Had they asked? Or had they been tipped off? In a paddock riddled with suspicion, conspiracy theories are born of much less.

Eddie Jordan made brief mention of Ralf's plight before the television interview was complete. Then he walked quickly from the workshop, zipped up his yellow jacket, jumped onto the back of a scooter and set off for the paddock once more.

The jacket was waterproof – which was just as well. Jordan noted that the weather forecasters had been painfully accurate, predictions of wet and windy weather coming to pass as he headed towards the motorhome and his next appointment.

Brian Alexander of BBC Radio 5 Live would be running his morning sports show from the top floor of one of the Jordan buses and Eddie would be a part of the hour-long programme. A fifteen-minute pause for news and a sports round-up halfway through gave Jordan the chance to nip outside for a cup of tea, tape his weekly column and receive a quick assessment of the latest turn of events.

Mark Gallagher reported that the weather was causing havoc with the flying schedules, a serious problem at Silverstone with more than 3,500 movements planned for race day. Most of Jordan's sponsors were being ferried in by some means or other but one of the main casualties would be Jordan himself. A plan to fly MasterCard and Hewlett-Packard directors in from Paris, where they had been making the most of their association with the World Cup, had to be abandoned. That meant Jordan would not be able to accompany them back to Paris for the Brazil-France final that evening. He hid his disappointment well.

Eddie was, to use his words, 'a massive fan of football'. But his team came first. Those elusive championship points seemed further away than ever. But, with this unpredictable weather, you never knew. It may have cost him a trip to one of the greatest sporting occasions in the world. On the other hand, the rain might play into his hands.

In the meantime, there was a pressing problem which needed his attention. Jordan fans were cutting up rough and Eddie's name was mud, a situation unfamiliar to him.

The Jordan supporters club had been an important part of a team which, by its very nature, was fan friendly. When the likes of Benetton had less than 1,000 official supporters, Jordan had close to three times that number. It was a huge success, highlighted by visits to the Belgian Grand Prix and 1,000 members volunteering to pay £20 each for lunch, a factory tour and a day at a Silverstone test session in October. In the end, the team could only accommodate the first 600 applicants, but such a huge response was indicative of the team's popularity and accessibility.

But that was in 1997. For 1998, Jordan decided to expand the service with the help of MasterCard. Access to the credit card company's vast mailing lists and administration service seemed a logical step forward. The membership fee was doubled in return for additional material in the 1998 fan club pack.

Unfortunately, it took time for the new arrangement to work efficiently. The membership plunged to less than 1,000. It was a sign that fans were budget conscious and perhaps suspicious that the personal touch had been lost, the mailing address, for example, having switched from the team headquarters to an anonymous PO box.

Worse than that, however, the fans who had signed up received nothing for their increased fee. By the time of the British Grand Prix, not a single 1998 membership pack had been dispatched. Naturally, the loyal supporters were not happy.

In fact, many of them were very angry indeed and Silverstone had become the focal point for that frustration. Here was an opportunity to have it out, face-to-face. Except that the security guard at the main gate had got in the way. So a man who had driven all the way from Cornwall, with his wife and two tearful children, thumped the guard. And that was just the start of it.

In the middle of such a difficult year, this was additional aggravation the team did not need. The problem had been caused by an unfortunate combination of circumstances, some of which were not directly attributable to either MasterCard or the team but, naturally, the blame fell at Jordan's door. Or on Mark Gallagher's desk, to be precise.

Gallagher had watched with mounting concern as the letters, followed by phone calls, began to gather in momentum and abuse. He had been pressing for action but very little had been done. Now, with the Grand Prix in town, it was too late. Massive harm had been inflicted on the team's reputation and Gallagher needed to incorporate a damage limitation exercise into his schedule of sponsor liaison on one of the most hectic weekends of the year.

A fan club meeting point had been set aside at Chapel Curve. Eddie Jordan had promised to make a visit at 10 a.m. on race morning and he decided to go ahead despite this being at the busiest point of the weekend, the fact that he would be soaked while making the trip on a back of a scooter. And there was the thought that he might be lynched at the front door. Gallagher had already apologized profusely for the organizational cock-up. He said the team took full responsibility but pointed out that Eddie had been running the team and the fan club debacle was not of his personal making. He was willing to come and see the supporters personally – provided they gave him a chance to explain.

That much was agreed and Jordan duly appeared, calming troubled waters in his usual style and receiving warm applause as he did so. The healing process had begun, backed up by generous gestures from MasterCard. In the meantime, Jordan Grand Prix would try to give the fans something more productive to shout about once the race got under way.

The certain promise of rain dominated discussion at the pre-race briefing between the drivers and their engineers. Gary Anderson, making his first appearance in two races, was also present. As was Mike Gascoyne, sporting a Jordan uniform for the first time in his new role as Chief Designer.

Anderson was more relaxed than he had been all season. Having Gascoyne share the workload undoubtedly helped. But his mood was deliberate, the result of a visit to his doctor and the discovery of an ulcer or two which had undoubtedly been induced by the recent stress. With the latest technical modifications in place on the cars, Anderson had spent a few days on board his narrow boat. Once away from the frantic hurly-burly of a motor racing environment, the gentle pace had given the big man the perfect opportunity to review his priorities in life.

'It was lovely,' he said, in his gentle mid-Ulster accent. 'It gave me the chance to see that the politics in the team have become too much. I'm used to having brick walls placed in front of me; I've been able to get through them. But, lately, they seem to be made of reinforced concrete!

'I could spend my time freelancing as a designer, no problem. But, having got this far, I feel a loyalty to the team members. They're a great bunch of guys and I know we can do the job. I've just got to try and ignore the politics.'

Anderson's observations were supported by Gascoyne when asked about the inevitable polarization which comes to any expanding team.

'Um . . . let's put it like this,' said Gascoyne with a wry grin. 'I wasn't here long before I heard one story and minutes later, I was taken to one side and told something else! I expect, as with all these things in any large company, the real story lies somewhere in the middle. My problem is making sure I recognize it when I see it. But, yes, I've discovered already that the politics are quite strong with Jordan. Although, having said that, the potential is tremendous and I've been made very welcome.'

At this stage, there was no evidence of any clash between Anderson and Gascoigne. Gary, for his part, was more concerned about the habits of his boss as Eddie Jordan continued to show his elusive ways, a meeting which had been booked for 9.00 a.m. a few days before having been steadily postponed. Anderson got to see Jordan briefly at 10.30 and quickly outlined six points, all of which were financially related and needed addressing. That was a few days ago. According to Anderson, he was still waiting for an answer.

'Could give you an ulcer, that sort of thing,' he mused. He was joking. But only just.

Jordan did not see it that way. He explained that he had tried to get back to

Anderson on several occasions but he, too, was busy. It may have been an unfortunate set of circumstances during a hectic period but it did little to soothe a relationship which was going through a trying time for both sides.

There were one or two lame jokes about the British weather when final discussion got under way about race strategy. While it was agreed that decisions about the choice of tyres would wait until nearer the off, Ralf and his engineer, Sam Michael, had worked on the principle that there would be nothing to lose when starting from the back. Given the difficulty in overtaking on a dry circuit, never mind one that was streaming wet, there was no point in following the herd when it came to tactics.

It was a sure bet that everyone would start with a full load of fuel in order to allow maximum flexibility in choosing the right moment to make pit stops. With that in mind, the decision was made to start Ralf with a small amount of fuel on board, thus giving him the opportunity to run wherever he wanted on the wet track.

The plan worked perfectly. By the time he was halfway round the first lap, Ralf had overtaken six cars! By the end of the lap, he was fourteenth. Two laps later, he was twelfth. An early pit stop for tyres and more fuel on lap thirteen gave the game away but, by then, the good work had been done. At precisely the same moment, Hill made perhaps his worst mistake of the season and spun out of the race while holding a handy eighth place. Talk about the ups and downs of motor racing.

The conditions had remained treacherous, streams of water crossing the track. It was the same for everyone, of course, and Hill should have known better as he applied the power a moment too soon while accelerating through Brooklands corner at about 50 mph. The rear of the car broke away and Hill made the elementary mistake even worse by allowing the engine to die thanks to his failure to operate an anti-stall device properly. The Honda V10 may have been gutless in his terms, but now it was embarrassingly silent. 'Pathetic' was how Damon described his error. There was very little else to say.

To his credit, Hill did not sulk and go home early. He experienced the mounting tension in the Jordan pit as Ralf continued to do a superb job. The conditions became so bad that the Safety Car had to be employed, those remaining on the track forming behind it and proceeding at a safe speed on a circuit which was awash.

JORDAN'S DRIVE TO WIN

Several leading names had spun off. Ralf was not among them. Not only had he made a brilliant start for once, it was as if his reputation for flying off the road did not exist. He was quick but sure-footed. And he was also in the points. Given the team's appalling luck, this surely had to go wrong. The odds seemed to be stacked against them.

But no. For the final seven laps, Schumacher continued in sixth place, nursing that precious point. Every time he appeared through the murk on the pit straight, it was a bonus, but one which turned the screw even tighter.

When he came past for the last time, it was as if Jordan Grand Prix had won the race. One point! The bogey had been banished. More than that, it had been a sensational drive, Schumacher's sixth place earned on pure merit and not through the charity of others.

Long after the race had finished, a dispute over Michael Schumacher's victory continued thanks to bungled procedures by the race stewards. The previously smouldering conspiracy theory now burst into flames as several members of the Formula 1 paddock became convinced that the authorities were bending over backwards to favour Ferrari.

That was of no consequence down by the B&H motorhome, where Marie Jordan, still dressed against the rain that continued to hang in the air, sipped a glass of champagne. Apart from savouring the moment, she was also enjoying a bit of calm as her four children, Zoe, Michelle, Zak and Kyle, amused themselves elsewhere.

'It's great!' she said through a mixture of delight for the team and the quiet knowledge that her husband might be more at peace with himself than of late. Her pleasure was shared along the paddock, the champagne having been sent by Edmund and Kathleen Irvine as they celebrated their son's sixth podium finish of the season.

That one point could not have been more timely for Jordan. A marquee had been erected on the lawn outside the team's headquarters to accommodate the factory staff, their families and the relatives and friends of the mechanics working at the track.

Arranged by Lindsay Haylett, Eddie's long-suffering personal assistant, the marquee had been open since 11 a.m. in order to accommodate 330 adults and 106 children. Having cheered Ralf home, a barbecue was prepared in time for the World Cup Final shown on six television screens. Eddie Jordan, his cap at a jaunty angle, joined them. Always a man for the big occasion, the boss knew where he wanted to be. Life, however, is not that simple.

Trevor Foster had been frustrated by the sequence of events – some of which were Schumacher's fault, some not – which had led to his problems during qualifying. The time had come for a serious discussion with the boss, Eddie tearing himself away from the celebration for a meeting in his office.

The upshot of the head-to-head was an agreement to give the Race Director power to make more wide-ranging decisions in all areas, reporting directly to Jordan. That was seen in several quarters as a long-overdue move. Provided Eddie was as good as his word, and there seemed no reason why he shouldn't be.

Mark Gallagher had been true to an earlier promise. When the irate family from Cornwall had finally breached security and, in desperation, parked themselves in the reception area of the factory on race morning, Gallagher had interrupted his schedule to dash across and achieve a temporary truce. He had asked the family to return at 6 p.m. on the assurance that the matter would be sorted out then. When Gallagher walked in at the appointed hour with Damon Hill by his side, the mollifying process went into top gear. A word of sympathy and an autograph or two from the former champion did the trick. All was forgiven.

The bridge-building, both in the reception area and, later, in Jordan's office upstairs, had been successful. Having had his productive discussion with Foster, EJ was back in the marquee, enjoying the feeling of relief which infused the mood of the evening.

There was no question about where Jordan wanted to be. 'Who needs to be in Paris on a day like this?' It was a rhetorical question, for which he provided the answer. 'It's only one point. But it seems like we've climbed a mountain to get it. It's a massive relief.'

Chapter Eight

Getting Back to the Habit

You would think the frantic pace of life might have been

reduced in the days following the British Grand Prix. At

Jordan, it went into overdrive. By the time Ian Phillips

reached the sanctuary of the British Airways Executive

Lounge at Gatwick in preparation for a flight to Vienna,

he was ready for a cigarette.

Ralf Schumacher.
Looking elsewhere
for 1999?

Phillips, a serious smoker, had kicked the habit with the help of hypnotherapy. He remained a convert for more than a year, during which time he had felt only the occasional need. But, when he lit up again on a whim, he found the enjoyment to be worth more than the self-imposed sanction.

It may have been coincidental, but the timing of the return more or less matched the gradual discovery that the 1998 season would not be plain sailing. The past week had been a case in point.

Sixth place at Silverstone may have reassured the workforce as they stripped and prepared the cars in preparation for the Austrian Grand Prix but, on the first floor of the team's headquarters, internal politics were proving to be more important than the scoring of a morale-boosting point.

Trevor Foster's new role had yet to be confirmed but, in the absence of Eddie Jordan who had gone off on holiday, the Race Director had become the de facto boss. Word on the grapevine said that Gary Anderson had been talking to Peugeot. Foster knew that the Technical Director had one or two reservations about the restructuring which had been necessary to accommodate Mike Gascoyne. He had reassured Anderson that it would make a perfect partnership, one which would continue to give Gary overall technical control and yet allow him to concentrate on the mechanical side of the cars, an area in which he had few equals in Formula 1.

Nonetheless, the news about Peugeot was worrying. There could be repercussions. Apart from losing a top technical man, there was the danger that he might attempt to take Ralf Schumacher with him.

While the sorting of personnel problems was beyond Phillips' remit, driver negotiations were very much his territory. And it was true that terms had yet to be agreed with either Schumacher or Hill.

Eddie Jordan had taken time on race day at Silverstone to hold talks with Ralf's managers, Willi Weber and Franz Tost, the reasonably informal chat having centred on a reduction in fee but an increase in bonus payments for actually finishing a race. It appeared they were homing in on an agreement with relative ease, but the negotiations were due to become more complex and less relaxed as the weeks went by.

The gap with the Hill camp was much wider. In fact, the discussions had reached a rather silly state. Commercial relationships between the two sides had got off to a bad start earlier in the year when it was discovered that Damon had a

 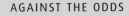

personal deal with a credit card company, one which might be construed as being in breach of Jordan's agreement with MasterCard.

The team felt, rightly or wrongly, that Hill's manager, Michael Breen, had been slow to both reveal the existence of this arrangement and bring it to the necessary temporary conclusion. Then, more serious, Damon had strengthened Jordan's bargaining hand by allegedly breaching his contract even further thanks to the necessary but ill-judged remarks about Honda's shortcomings. Matters seemed to be going from bad to worse. Since the start of the season, there had been niggling on both sides over the use of their respective trademarks on T shirts and paraphernalia. Letters had passed back and forth. During this rather pointless bout of shadow boxing, nothing of serious import had been achieved. But the whole affair contributed to an unnecessary degree of mild tension.

When Phillips poured himself an early morning coffee at Gatwick, he had to admit that the option on Hill's contract remained just that and, for all he knew, Anderson could have left the team, such had been the state of confusion back at the factory. This period in the motor racing year is known as the 'Silly Season' — and not without good reason.

Events continued to move with confusing speed in Austria. Jacques Villeneuve had signed for the fledgeling British American Racing team, a surprising gamble by a reigning World Champion but one which said much about his thoughts on the future prospects of his existing employers, Williams. At least it was a positive story, unlike some which swirled around the paddock as teams and drivers attempted to cover themselves for every eventuality.

While thinking about remaining with Ferrari for a fourth season, Eddie Irvine was also talking to both Williams and Jordan. Benson and Hedges had no objection to Irvine. In fact, the sponsors had actively encouraged Jordan to speak to the Ulsterman since he was seen as a more than suitable fall-back should the Hill negotiations founder. Or, indeed, should Schumacher decide not to stay.

That became a strong possibility when a new story broke the surface and sent ripples in all directions. Irvine had noted that Jean Alesi, currently with the Sauber-Petronas (Ferrari) team, had become very friendly with Michael Schumacher. It was evident that he wanted Irvine's drive but, as in all things associated with Formula 1, the deal was more complicated than that. Michael's plan was to have Ralf take Alesi's seat on the understanding that he would be Number 1 Sauber driver and, more important, Michael would swing it so that his brother

JORDAN'S DRIVE TO WIN

would have exclusive use of the latest Ferrari engines (as opposed to the current arrangement in which the Sauber drivers were given engines which were as much as one year out of date).

That Schumacher-inspired story set the cat among the pigeons, but the Ferrari team disliked it the most. It actually worked in Irvine's favour since a determination by Ferrari to show who was boss saw the management raise their offer to the Irishman. He signed almost immediately, took himself out of the equation and seriously reduced Ralf's options.

Meanwhile, Hill's name was associated with Williams and just about anyone else looking for a driver. The mood within Jordan remained ambivalent. Ralf had done his reputation the world of good thanks to that excellent drive at Silverstone. Conversely, Hill was not being looked upon too kindly after his elementary mistake. And he would do little to correct that image as the Austrian weekend wore on.

The racetrack occupied one of the most majestic locations on the Formula 1 calendar, the A1-Ring nestling under pine-covered peaks which would not have been out of place in *The Sound of Music*. On a clear day, it was picture-postcard stuff, but when the weather pattern shifted it was indeed a moody and thunderous place. On Saturday afternoon, about an hour before qualifying was due to start, the rain arrived with a vengeance.

The teams faced a dilemma as the sixty-minute session began. With each driver limited, as usual, to twelve laps, would it be wise to establish a lap time in case the conditions actually got worse? Or was the sensible option to save those laps until the end when, if the mist continued to lift, the track might begin to dry?

For twenty-five minutes the teams sat it out, no one wishing to make the first move. After thirty minutes, Hill decided to join a Minardi and a Tyrrell on the track and at least put one lap in the bag since it was by no means certain that the drizzle was about to cease. So far, so good.

In the end, those who hesitated were not lost. With fifteen minutes remaining, it was clear that the racing line was drying sufficiently to allow a switch from fully wet weather tyres to the so-called intermediates, a mix between a rain tyre and dry weather rubber. The trick was to wait until the last possible moment to make the move and extract the maximum from the intermediate tyres when the track would be best suited to them.

Hill took to the track sooner than most. He established a time which looked reasonable enough, improved on it further – and was then called back to the pits one lap too soon. As he did so, a flurry of activity on the circuit saw his name plummet to fifteenth place on the starting grid.

Hill was furious – and said so. His remarks made headline news in some Sunday papers, Sky TV adding to the discomfort on race morning by continually running a quote which said the English hero had 'lashed out' at his team.

Right enough, an error had been made by the team when calling him in after only eleven of his allocated twelve laps had been completed. But what really annoyed the management was Damon's failure to mention that the decision to go out – too soon, as had been predicted – had been largely his choice.

As the stories began to get out of hand, Damon took the opportunity to set the record straight when interviewed on the starting grid by James Allen of ITV.

'I'm pretty upset by the reports in the papers,' said Hill. 'Things have been blown out of context. What I said was that we as a team did not do as good a job as we should have. But by "we" I meant me as a driver together with the engineers.'

Trevor Foster concurred. 'We take full responsibility for the fact that Damon did not complete his full allocation of laps,' said the Race Director. 'It was a very confusing qualifying session and we miscalculated the number of laps that Damon had done. In our uncertainty, we took the decision that it was better for him to do one lap too few than one lap too many, because if you do too many laps the driver is disqualified.

'As regards going out and then finishing our laps too early, responsibility for this lies with the whole team, which, as Damon has explained, includes the drivers as well. It is certainly something we have all learned from. Sessions like that are a lottery and the gap between winning and losing is very slim.'

The poor timing of the runs also affected Ralf, who was not much better off as he prepared to start from ninth place. It did not augur well for the race.

In the event, both Schumacher and Hill drove strongly. Hill finished seventh but, unfortunately for him, his efforts were made to look weak by comparison with David Coulthard and Michael Schumacher, both of whom had stormed through the field after various delays to join the winner, Mika Hakkinen, on the podium. And Ralf, too, had taken the sheen off Damon's star with another robust and faultless performance to score two more championship points.

On his way to fifth place, Schumacher had gained Benson and Hedges valuable air time by holding off his brother during a superb battle which lasted for a couple of laps. Blood may be thicker than water, but not when it comes to defending ground on the racetrack. Ralf had not only proved he was far from an easy touch, he had also strengthened his standing in the team on a day when everyone had pulled their weight, the tactics and the pit stops having worked to perfection. It meant a few more points for B&H Jordan. Could they maintain that momentum one week later in Germany?

Running the two races back to back brought additional logistical problems for the team. For Sophie Ashley-Carter, the Race Team Secretary, this was one of the busiest periods of the year.

'Plans for each race are made a year in advance,' explained Sophie. 'But, inevitably, there are a good deal of last-minute alterations which have to be made in the week before each race. Austria and Germany being a double header means doubling up on everything in a short space of time; two sets of flights, two sets of car hire, two sets of phone, fax and modem lines for the motorhomes and so on, finalizing the rooming lists and balance of payments in three hotels in Austria and five in Hockenheim to accommodate all forty-five members of the race team, the drivers, their managers and physiotherapists, and the sponsor and VIP guests. And while you are doing this, you still have to work on finalizing the bookings for the Hungarian Grand Prix and tests in Jerez and Monza.'

The trucks had to carry enough spare parts for both races and drive straight from Austria to Hockenheim. Normally, there would be three sets of everything on board. On this occasion, a total of eight to nine sets of parts had been included in order to see the team through.

And additional complication had been caused by the insertion of the Austrian Grand Prix at this point in the calendar. In the past, the French, British and German Grands Prix had been run consecutively, the organizational bonus being that all three prohibited tobacco advertising. But the Austrian Grand Prix did not. By slotting this race in between Britain and Germany, and then running Austria and Germany a week apart, it meant the team had to cater for a branded and an unbranded race while operating away from home. That affected every-thing, from the use of the Benson and Hedges logos on backdrops in the garage to the advertising on the racing cars, transporters and motorhomes. Double sets of team uniforms had to be carried, along with different sets of flameproof gear

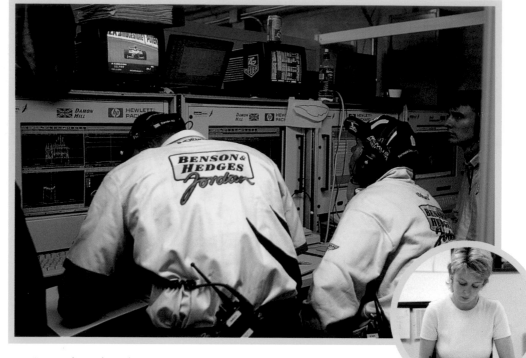

Keeping track on the telemetry. Engineers follow Damon's progress from the back of the garage. Sophie Ashley-Carter (inset) has handled the logistics which got them there. Eddie Jordan discusses tyre choice with Graham Ball of Goodyear while Mike Gascoyne (inset) settles into his new role with Jordan.

Something to celebrate at last. Warwick Pugh (left) and Nick Burrows are cheered by the result at Hockenheim. Marc Donovan congratulates Mike Wroe, the Head of Electronics (left below), as both Jordans finish in the top six for the first time.

for the drivers and the pit crew. 'A giant pain in the arse,' was Phillips' succinct summary.

The trucks left the A1-Ring on the Sunday night, taking twenty-four hours to reach Hockenheim in readiness for the mechanics, who had made the journey by air, to begin work on Tuesday morning. In some ways, the preparation process was actually simplified because the team was operating away from home.

Under normal circumstances, the parts would be removed at the factory, and in some cases sent off to sub-contractors for refurbishment. Once the cars had been reassembled, they would be given a 'shake down', a brief road test at Silverstone to ensure everything was working properly. That entire process could take up to three days. Working 'on the road' meant, by its very nature, that the operation had to be simplified. Tim Edwards, the Chief Mechanic, explains:

'Going directly from one race to the next tends to make life easier in some ways. On the first day at Hockenheim we stripped down the cars and installed the spare gearboxes, suspension and so on. It's not a problem because at this point in the year we have plenty of spares available – unlike the start of the season when the production side are flat out with the knock-on effect of having had to build the new cars.

'Immediately after the Austrian Grand Prix, the engineers brought back some parts such as the steering racks and differentials. These were stripped and checked at the factory and then rushed to Hockenheim. Part of the usual preparation process involves repainting the bodywork in between races but, obviously, we are unable to do all of that on this occasion.'

Edwards need not have worried. With the standard of finish so high, no one outside the sport would have noticed and most of the regular observers would not have checked in any case since an immaculate level of preparation is taken as read. Besides, attention continued to be focused on who might drive the yellow cars in 1999, and come to that just who might be in charge of running them.

Gary Anderson broke away from thinking about the next Jordan Mugen-Honda to travel to Germany and oversee a performance level which was continuing its upward trend. Anderson remained quietly optimistic, but inside he continued to be racked by uncertainty, not to mention the effect of his ulcers and a hernia. The team made much of the fact that they wished him to remain as Technical Director. Anderson was not so sure, a doubt which was supported by rumours suggesting he had held discussions with Tom Walkinshaw. It was known that the

TWR-Arrows boss was in dispute with his current Technical Director, John Barnard. If Anderson was indeed unhappy, the move to TWR would make sense insofar as it would reunite him with his old mate and former associate, Brian Hart, whose engines were currently powering the black cars.

As for Jordan's drivers, Hill seemed to be moving closer to a deal whereas Ralf's stock had risen and he was rightly investigating an approach by, among others, Williams. There was little Eddie Jordan could do but sit tight and hope. Having spent eighteen months knocking the rough edges off his young protégé – and having Ralf do the same to his cars – Jordan was anxious not to lose him just at the point where he seemed ready to mature into a driver of considerable quality as well as speed. All told, things had begun to calm down within the Jordan camp. But that did not take into account the best efforts of the British press.

Friday's practice had been trouble-free. In fact, it had been very good indeed, Damon taking third place. Ralf, less happy about the balance of his car, was ninth. It was a bemused Hill who stood outside the motorhome and watched a posse of photographers jostle for position. 'Just like old times,' he said with a wry grin. 'It's nice to be back in the news again.' He would regret that remark the following morning.

As a small group, including Hill and Phillips, had a quiet breakfast, pictures from Sky TV filled the large screen mounted at one end of the semi-deserted motorhome area. The presenter moved on to discuss the sports news in the morning papers. With the English league about to start, a football transfer story dominated the headlines in every newspaper. Except one.

'And, finally, a motor racing story,' said the presenter, brandishing the back page of the *Independent*. 'The headline says "Damon Hill to take £2m cut". Sounds interesting.'

Interesting? Amazing, more like. There was a moment's silence before Phillips spoke: 'What the effing hell is that all about?' he asked no one in particular. There was a general shrugging of shoulders all round.

The story said that Damon had been told his retainer would drop to £3m if he wished to stay and yet, according to Phillips, the subject of a pay cut had not so much as been mentioned. 'That doesn't mean to say we haven't thought about it!' he joked. 'Sounds a nice idea to me.'

'You can't do that,' grinned Hill. 'I've got a wife and kids to feed, a mortgage to pay. You know how it is . . . '

If there had been a dispute serious enough to warrant the back page lead in a quality newspaper, there was no evidence of it here. Certainly, the thought of a restructuring of fees had crossed the minds of the Jordan management, as it always did when Eddie Jordan was at hand. But it had gone no further. It seemed Jordan was the victim of top spin as one writer attempted to steal a march on his rivals.

'You know what all this means,' muttered Phillips. 'We'll be spending most of the day answering silly questions. It's from the same writer who was alone in claiming earlier in the week that Damon had turned down £5m from Williams.'

'Come easy, go easy. That's me,' smiled Hill. 'I'm a fool to myself sometimes . . . '

His sunny disposition remained for the rest of the day, particularly when he qualified fifth. The only setback was the fact that Ralf was fourth.

The team was understandably ecstatic. After the run of heartache, the hard work was finally paying off. True, the Jordan 198 was working efficiently in the low downforce set up necessary for the long straights of Hockenheim but there was no denying that the latest Honda qualifying engine was playing its part. And both drivers had risen to the occasion. Having got this far, race preparation and tactics would be paramount. The warm-up at 0930 on race morning would assume even greater importance than usual.

Sunday dawned overcast and cool. The sun was beginning to poke through the grey haze as the three cars were made ready, each engine warmed in turn to join the chorus of barking V10s along the pit lane.

With ten minutes to go, comparative silence descended. All that could be heard was the cackle of animated conversation from the massive grandstand stretching the length of the pit straight and strident calls from photographers as they organized a shoot at the McLaren garage next door. With Coulthard and Hakkinen having resigned for another season, the drivers presented themselves with a pit board bearing '1999' and posed before the gallery of lens men pressed against the tape barrier.

'Mika! Mika! Give us a smile, mate. That's it! Lovely. Lovely.'

Hakkinen could be forgiven for being preoccupied. He had won his seventh pole position of the season, with Coulthard starting alongside. Michael Schumacher, after a disastrous practice, was down in ninth place. That was the end of the good news.

Hakkinen needed to make the most of this golden opportunity to extend his championship lead over Schumacher but the Finn knew he would have to fend off a resurgent Jacques Villeneuve, starting from third place in his Williams. And then there were the Jordan drivers, fourth and fifth. Goodness knows what Ralf might do in front of his home crowd. This contest was by no means a foregone conclusion.

Klaxons and horns blasted from the grandstand as Schumacher's yellow Jordan made its way to the end of the pit lane at 0929. Damon waited for the initial crush to subside as the green light appeared and cars streamed onto the track. Then he engaged first gear, turned right, pressed his thumb on the speed limiter button and burbled down the pit lane before giving the Honda V10 an initial burst towards the first corner.

Hockenheim, at 4.2 miles, is one of the longest tracks, and the pits and main straight fell strangely quiet as twenty-one cars headed towards the far end of the banana-shaped circuit, their progress captured in silence on television screens hanging from the ceiling of the garage.

A muffled roar announced their arrival in the vast stadium, of which the pits and paddock were a part. In keeping with the usual procedure, every driver returned to his garage to have the car checked over for leaks or anything untoward. Since the spare Jordan had been allocated to Ralf for his home Grand Prix, he took the opportunity to climb on board and complete three laps, just to make sure everything was working. Hill, meanwhile, stayed put.

'No point in going back out just yet,' Damon said to his engineer, Dino Toso. 'We'll wait for the other cars to take the dust off the track.' He then sat patiently, two mechanics standing by each corner of the car, waiting for the signal to remove heated blankets from the tyres. Another mechanic crouched beneath the rear wing, the tube-like air starter at the ready.

At 0938, Hill pressed the radio button on the steering wheel.

'Go now,' he said quietly. The blankets were off in seconds, the starter engaged, the V10 bursting instantly into harsh song. One minute after Hill had made his departure, Schumacher returned with the spare car, hopped back to his race car and set off once more.

As the back-up car was pushed into the centre space in the garage, yellow shirts descended on it like wasps around a jam jar. They were joined by Honda and Goodyear personnel downloading the onboard computer and, in the case of

Schumacherland. On a day when his brother had a disappointing race for Ferrari, Ralf brought the home crowd a result by finishing in the points.

the tyre technician, literally probing for information. Dark blue smoke swirled from the brake ducts, the acrid smell announcing the fact that his car had been just been *used*.

In no time at all, the computer screen indicated that the session had reached the halfway mark. With just fifteen minutes remaining, television pictures showed the McLaren management by the pit wall, a reminder of other teams operating in their own world but with identical aims to the crew busying themselves at Jordan.

The list of times showed Coulthard to be fastest. Ralf was second, Damon fifth. The Jordans were comfortably on the pace. As both drivers continued to improve, you could feel the gradual building of nervous anticipation.

At 0948, there were thirty-six people in the Jordan garage. Nothing unusual about that. Except each and every person was standing absolutely still, mesmerized by the computer screens. It was as if they were caught in a trance, freeze-framed and scarcely able to believe what they were seeing.

Damon broke the spell when a brief message on the radio announced his return to the pits. His mechanics pounced on the car, a conversation between Hill and Toso reaching the conclusion that small changes to the wing angles front and rear might be worth trying. Meanwhile, at 0952, Ralf set the fastest time. Two minutes later and he had improved even further. By the time the session had ended, only Coulthard had managed to better the Jordan.

As warm-ups go, this had been entirely drama-free, a fact confirmed by Ralf as he trickled down the pit lane and got on the radio to his engineer, Sam Michael.

'The car's OK – no problems at all,' reported Ralf. 'It looks good.' Indeed it did. And, for good measure, Damon was fifth fastest.

Television crews descended on the garage. Eddie Jordan, walking across from the pit wall where he had been watching progress with Anderson, Phillips and the engineers, was ready to talk to anyone with a camera.

'So far, so good,' he said. 'But let's see what the race brings. This is a tough one. We'll have to see what happens.'

In an attempt to make an educated guess at what might happen, the drivers and the engineers met with Anderson and Foster in the briefing room at the back of one of the transporters. The indications were that the McLarens would be in a race of their own. It was reasoned that the only way to get Ralf onto the podium would be to choose a strategy which would allow him to overtake Villeneuve early on and then be towed along by the McLarens. If Jordan stuck to the favoured one-stop routine and started Ralf with a heavy load of fuel, he would never get past the Williams. He would simply finish where he had begun. In fourth place.

That theory was proved when the majority of the front runners finished the race in the first-lap order. Unfortunately, the only exception was Schumacher, R. The order at the end of the opening lap was Hakkinen, Coulthard, Ralf, Villeneuve, Damon, Irvine and Michael Schumacher (soon to overtake his Ferrari team-mate).

The strategy had worked insofar as Ralf had been able to get the jump on Villeneuve at the start. Where it fell down was an unexpectedly slow pace — comparatively speaking — from the McLaren drivers. They were not as fast as anticipated and neither were they tardy enough for Ralf to make a challenge. Yet the fact was he could have lapped faster without them and, as things stood, he would not gain enough of an advantage over Villeneuve and the rest to allow for an additional pit stop.

Thus, when Ralf made his first visit to the pits as early as lap fourteen, he rejoined in ninth place and was effectively stuck there until the cars in front began to make their one and only stop some ten laps later. That would move him to fourth. The joy would be short-lived because, of course, he had one more stop to make. Ralf eventually finished sixth.

If nothing else, the brave tactic had shown Jordan's determination to finish on the podium and not be satisfied with a place in the top six.

Hill, meanwhile, had been running a copybook race, making his one and only stop on lap twenty-three and holding fourth place. There was to be no letting up as Michael Schumacher tried — and failed — to close in on his old adversary.

Here, at least, was proof that frustration and uncertainty in Formula 1 spreads itself around the grid with equal measure. The Ferraris were hopelessly off the pace and no one knew why. There were muttered suspicions about the forced removal of a driver aid which assisted the car while cornering. But it remained pure speculation. Nothing could be proved. Ferrari hotly denied the suggestion. And to rub salt into the wound as Michael struggled home fifth before his adoring public, the McLarens, as expected, finished first and second. And Jordan had now scored enough points to move into fifth place in the Constructors' Championship.

'Who would have believed that?' asked Eddie Jordan, as he faced the cameras once more. 'Three successive races in the points culminating in having two cars finish in the top six. Brilliant!'

He may only have finished fourth, hardly the stuff of legends for someone who had won twenty-one Grands Prix, but Hill was equally elated by his first points in almost a year, the thrill of the chase at the front of the field – and the bonus of finishing in front of both Ferraris.

'That's more like it,' he said. 'It was what I would call a proper motor race, with people to chase and people to try and keep behind me. It's more like the races I have been used to.'

At the end of forty-five laps, Hill had finished just under fifteen seconds behind the winner, Hakkinen. It was obvious that given the scent of a podium he was up to the task. This had been the best result of the season so far for B&H Jordan. Now they had to continue the momentum.

As the two articulated transporters headed back to England for the first time in almost two weeks, the support truck, loaded with garage equipment, set off for the next race in Hungary. Almost immediately, the euphoria began to subside. The tight and twisty Hungaroring, with its call for high downforce, would be a different proposition entirely. A podium finish suddenly seemed as far away as ever. And the chances of a Jordan winning a race were about as unlikely as Ian Phillips giving up smoking for a second time.

Chapter Nine

Better than Expected

The question of whether the winner's trophy finally goes

to the driver or the team was through circumstance not

one which had taxed the Jordan team. For front-runners

such as McLaren and Ferrari, it was a matter of some

importance.

Front row in the supporters' race.
Jordan fans prepare for more
points in Hungary.

In the past, nobody had cared particularly about the final resting place for cups which, by and large, were seen as unnecessary clutter in need of regular cleaning. Niki Lauda, for instance, gave the trophies he had won with Ferrari to a local garage, the deal being that the proprietor could mount a customer-pulling display in return for giving the 1975 World Champion free car washes.

Lauda and others like him may have been devoid of sentiment but the explosion of the memorabilia market in the 1980s suddenly put a value on items which hitherto had been destined for the trash can. It became a problem for the teams as employees with an eye for the main chance began spiriting parts and accessories off the premises.

As demand grew, so did the list of requests from charities for bits and pieces which could be auctioned. Jordan felt there was no option but to adopt a policy of supporting just one good cause during each year. The staff, meanwhile, were allowed to sell items such as the flameproof overalls as a means of earning money for the team's football and karting pursuits. There is always a keen demand for Jordan overalls used by the crew during pit stops but identical to those worn by the drivers: a happy coincidence which did not arrive by accident. The world's economy may continue to fluctuate but the demand for motor sport memorabilia remains high.

Shortly before the British Grand Prix in 1998, in an auction of racing material from a few decades before, a helmet which had belonged to Gilles Villeneuve, the Ferrari driver who was killed during practice for the 1982 Belgian Grand Prix, had fetched £32,000. The trophy presented by Princess Grace to Jochen Rindt after the Lotus driver had snatched victory at the final corner of the 1970 Monaco Grand Prix – one of the most memorable finishes in the history of the sport – had sold for £2,200. A month later, the dealer who made the purchase was asking for a cool £12,500.

That same auction also included various pieces of memorabilia associated with Jim Clark. The Scotsman, who lost his life at Hockenheim in 1968, remains for many one of the greatest drivers the world has ever seen and anything associated with the twice World Champion was worth paying for. One of Clark's Lotus contracts fetched probably far more than its remunerative value in 1963.

Just as interesting was a letter from Clark to Andrew Ferguson, the Operations Manager at Lotus. Apart from disparaging remarks about the reliability of his Lotus Elan road car, Clark also mentioned, almost as an aside, that he would like a room at the Green Man pub for the duration of the British Grand Prix. This was ten days before the event.

How times move on. Rooms within a thirty-mile radius of Silverstone, never mind this hostelry a mile or so down the road, are now booked ten months before the race. The pub has changed too. Gone is the intimate atmosphere created by low ceilings and a pokey little bar. The original drinking parlour has been swamped by extensions and conservatories in which food and refreshment are churned out by frequently uninterested staff as a means of a quick profit for the owners.

Nonetheless, in these fast-moving days, the Green Man serves its purpose. Given the limited choice in the Silverstone area, the pub remains a useful venue of a reasonable standard for the businesses scattered around the racetrack. Eddie Jordan used it for an informal lunch with Gary Anderson in the week following the German Grand Prix.

Eddie had become very concerned about the health of his Technical Director. The best medical advice said that treatment was needed sooner rather than later but, typically, Anderson was focused on his work rather than his physical well-being.

Speaking as old friends rather than employer and employee, Jordan reiterated that not only did he want Anderson to take care of himself, he also wanted him to stay with the team. It was Eddie's view that Gary could design the 1999 car and Mike Gascoyne could use his skills to organize and manage the necessary systems. It would, as had been said before, make a perfect partnership.

Jordan, in conjunction with Foster, had drawn up a management structure which showed Anderson continuing as the technical head. Anderson, in return, wanted certain assurances about the full extent of his role. In the meantime, Gary agreed to undergo a minor stomach operation straightaway and think things through while making his recovery. It would mean his absence from the next two races in Hungary and Belgium.

In fact, with Gascoyne concentrating on further aerodynamic developments in the wind tunnel, neither technical chief would be at the Hungaroring. Not that anyone expected great things from the Jordan 198 on a tight circuit which called for maximum downforce.

Even so, there had been further modifications to the front wing, largely through Gascoyne's work. There was a willingness among the drivers and the mechanics to try this latest development, not only to continue the team's upward trend, but also as a means of discovering the true capabilities of the new recruit.

The jury remained out on Mike Gascoyne. Just how good was this man? The Tyrrells in his charge had generally been efficient cars which handled well, only to be let down by gutless engines. But how much of that technical responsibility had been shared by Gascoyne and his Technical Director, Dr Harvey Postlethwaite? No one knew for sure.

Gascoyne had already made his mark at Jordan with some forthright comments. But his terrierlike self-assurance would not be accepted if he failed to produce. And the best way to measure that would be on the stopwatch. If the results were positive, then a quiet but sometimes cocky confidence would be a small price to pay. It was worth finding out.

As the team prepared for the opening practice session on Friday morning, the mood was noticeably upbeat, a far cry from the brave face which had been necessary in Montreal two months before.

There was quiet optimism even though this would be a difficult race. Seventy-seven laps of the Hungaroring would be demanding both physically and mechanically, particularly if the high temperatures associated with Hungary at this time of year were evident. The feeling was that anything could happen.

It did. Instead of searing sunshine on Friday morning, rain lashed this dusty outpost twelve miles north-east of Budapest. And Ralf Schumacher shunted his car. That was the bad news.

The good news was the damage was not severe and, overall, the Jordan Mugen-Hondas were on the pace. It would give Eddie Jordan something to talk about when he took his turn that afternoon on the so-called 'Friday Five', the mandatory media conference run by the FIA.

Not surprisingly, perhaps, the line of questioning focused, not on the performance of the cars (a good sign in itself), but on the continuing uncertainty surrounding the future of Anderson. Rumours continued to suggest that the Irishman was talking to Tom Walkinshaw. More to the point, he was absent from the racetrack once again. Was he about to leave or had a parting of the ways already taken place?

Despite lingering doubts over just what decision his Technical Director might reach in the days to come, EJ adopted a blustering policy of attack.

'This dialogue about his [Anderson's] future has been going on for four or five years and is now getting to be a little irritating,' said Jordan. 'In this business there are very few high-quality engineers – and Gary Anderson is one of them.

The upward trend continued – even during a wet practice session at the Hungaroring.

Damon with his engineer, Dino Toso (top). The Jordans were not expected to go well in Hungary, but they scored points yet again. Hill discusses his rising fortunes with Colin Jackson as the champion hurdler takes a day off in preparation for the European Games in Budapest.

Virtually the whole of his working life in Formula 1 has been spent with Jordan Grand Prix and I see no reason why that should change.'

That last statement was not quite correct. Anderson had been in Formula 1 since 1973, first as a mechanic with the Brabham team before moving to McLaren, where he became Chief Mechanic and assisted with engineering and design. Between 1980 and 1984, Anderson set up his own company, Anson Racing, and built and raced a Formula 3 car in between carrying out consultancy work. A period in the USA brought work as Chief Engineer with the Galles Indycar team before a return to Europe in 1987 continued the hands-on engineering style he enjoyed so much while working with a championship-winning team in Formula 3000.

Anderson's relationship with Jordan began in 1990. Strictly speaking, Eddie should have qualified it by saying that the majority of Anderson's career as a designer in Formula 1 had been spent with Jordan.

No matter, the point had been made. In fact, it allowed EJ to hint at the underlying cause of the differences which existed between the boss and his technical chief.

'When Jordan Grand Prix arrived on the Formula 1 scene in 1991, we had a total of three engineers,' explained Eddie. 'Although they did a remarkable job, I would hate to contemplate what might happen today if we had to manage with only three engineers. We now have forty people in the technical office, which by our standards is a huge number. It's a business within a business. And still it keeps growing.

'We are continually scouring the market for good people who are fully qualified engineers, experienced in motor racing, free of contract and able to fit our system. Mike Gascoyne happened to be in that position and we are very honoured and pleased that he chose to come to Jordan.

'Mike has been looking at several areas of the team. He is very well organized and that suits our needs. The best way to put it is to say that the Jordan attitude for many years has been "Let's get ripped into it and we'll sort it out afterwards." I think Mike's attitude would be along the lines of "Let's sort things out first — and then get ripped into it." That's maybe what we need and I think Gary and Mike will make a very potent combination indeed.'

Never one to miss an opportunity to talk up his team, Jordan warmed to his theme.

'The last few races have been good,' he said, 'but let's be very clear about this. It has not been easy to come back from the wilderness, which is where we were at Monaco. It was particularly upsetting to be in that lowly position, somewhere we had never really been before. It was obvious that certain drastic measures were necessary.

'Gary took it upon himself to concentrate on the speed of the car and miss a couple of races in the process. One or two journalists read all sorts of things into the fact that he was not at the Grands Prix but the truth was that he was flat out with the Technical Department.

'Now you are witnessing the fruits of their labour and it's not often in Formula 1 that you see such an impressive turnaround in performance during a season. We've had terrific assistance, of course, from Mugen-Honda and Goodyear, both of whom have made excellent progress. We may not be in the running for the championship but I'd like to think this recent phase will be seen at the end of the year as one of the little success stories of 1998.'

Brave talk, indeed. Much would depend on how the team fared during the remainder of the weekend. In the meantime, Jordan had to address the ongoing problem of securing his drivers for 1999. Eddie said he had every hope of finalizing a deal with Hill. Damon agreed by saying he could see no reason why not.

That was all well and good but Hill was not actually doing the talking. In a manner which bemused many drivers and team owners, Hill was continuing his policy of refusing to discuss money directly. He felt that was the province of his adviser, Michael Breen. Some said that was precisely the reason why Hill had lost the drive with Williams at the end of 1996. Naturally, both Hill and Breen vehemently disagreed with that summary of a turn of events which continued to mystify the paddock two years on.

But, if the Hill negotiations were almost there, subject to Breen's demands (considered nit-picking by Phillips – but then he would say that), the discussions with Schumacher seemed further apart than ever. Whereas one month before at Silverstone, it had been Hill who was the worry, now it was Ralf.

Schumacher continued to be tempted by an offer, rumoured to be $6m, from Williams. The problem was, he would not be free to leave, even if he wanted to. Or so Jordan said. The Schumacher camp did not see it that way. In their opinion, the contract with Jordan Grand Prix did not contain an option for 1999. Jordan claimed that it did.

The irony was that Ralf actually wanted to stay. He could see the sense in spending a third year with a team which he had got to know well and felt comfortable with. Cashing in the experience gained, he would be in a position to score points consistently and, subject to a competitive car, finish on the podium.

But he was not happy about the revised terms on offer. Even more, he did not appreciate Eddie's direct methods, which sometimes included open remarks in front of the team's guests and the media. This, of course, was EJ's traditional way of dealing with everyone, no matter who they were. It was Irish, it was brash. But no harm was meant. For a twenty-three-year-old German, however, it was demeaning at times.

Ralf was mulling over the latest development as he sat quietly outside the motorhome with Franz Tost on Friday afternoon.

'I would say that I think Eddie is a very nice man,' said Ralf slowly. 'He's a very nice person.' Then a pause. 'But he is very difficult to deal with. Very difficult.'

It had become clear, for instance, that Schumacher's sudden loss of heart at Imola had been due to EJ implementing an adjustment to the terms of his payment structure. Jordan felt that Schumacher was not performing as he should and this was one way of getting his driver's attention after three retirements in a row.

It did that, all right. But there were those in the team who felt this was not the best tactic for a youngster who, despite a confidence which some observers wrongly construed as arrogance, actually needed a reassuring arm around the shoulder. In actual fact, it was part of his contract and Ralf should not have been surprised.

Jordan and Willi Weber, Ralf's manager, had agreed that it was in Schumacher's best interest to insert a clause which would allow the team to levy a series of fines for misdemeanours which could range from not meeting sponsorship obligations to crashing cars and generally poor performances on the track.

'It was a way of trying to focus his attention,' said Jordan. 'We were trying to get the point across that this is not a piggy bank, an easy means of picking up money. Ralf knew about it. It had been agreed with Willi.'

Ralf was reluctant to discuss the subject, except to admit that it had come up, 'Which, for sure, didn't help me that weekend. But it wasn't a problem.' Coincidence or not, Ralf went on to score his first finish of the season at Imola. Jordan might say it proved his point.

At the time, Ralf was enjoying the benefits of technical revisions made necessary by the struggle through the first three races. In fact, anything was better than the car he had first been presented with.

'I knew straightaway from the first test at Barcelona,' said Ralf. 'You can tell almost immediately whether a car is good or not. Obviously, we were all disappointed. On the other hand, I never had any doubt that we would be able to fix the problem. None at all. I knew what the Jordan team was capable of.

'Don't get me wrong; the car was not terrible. In fact, it was a reasonable car and I didn't really care too much at the time about the problems. The only difficulty was, it took us a bit longer than expected to get the car right. Otherwise, it didn't affect things too much. I have a good relationship with Gary but, for sure, he didn't like it when I said straightaway that the car wasn't very good! But there has been no problem between me and Gary since.

'The worst time for everyone was after Monaco. Everyone was down, including me, because we had performed so badly. But then I qualified fifth for the next race in Canada and things began to lift again. I knew I just had to get on with it. I didn't talk to Michael or anyone like that about it; it was something you have to deal with. You just try to stay calm. Then, suddenly, it all turned around, which was good, although I honestly have to say I didn't expect it so soon.'

Certainly, Schumacher made a good job of hiding any disappointment he may have felt during a year in which he had intended to settle into the job of being a Formula 1 driver. His arrival in Grand Prix racing had been greeted with scepticism. The inference was that he was only there because of his family connection. True, he had won a championship against tough opposition in Japan but his CV had little else of note. In some circles, notably in Germany, he was perceived as being nothing more than a spoiled brat.

His first season had shown flashes of brilliance in between a more consistent pattern of wild incidents. There was no doubt that he was fast, very fast indeed. But Ralf wanted to win his first race today and the World Championship tomorrow. It took time to get the message across that the learning curve was long and steep. And that there was more to this business than a single very quick lap.

'There is just so much to learn when you come into Formula 1,' said Ralf. 'Last year [1997] was all so much that I just concentrated on the racing; I didn't want to do anything else. But, as time goes by and you start to look around, you see what you have to do. You see that this is not just about driving. Therefore I made that side [dealing with sponsors, talking to the media] better this year. Some people think that I had some form of training, but that's not the case. I just had more time to think about it.'

Overnight in Hungary, Ralf had time to consider that Hill appeared to have

AGAINST THE ODDS   **167**

the upper hand this weekend. The trend was due to continue when Saturday's practice got under way, the rain having been banished by blue skies and temperatures heading towards 24°C.

Morning practice, split into two forty-five-minute sessions, would be spent attempting to make the cars handle to the drivers' liking while running set-ups which would be suitable for the seventy-seven-lap race. Friday had been a waste of time when it came to discovering how the cars handled on a dry track. It meant the work load on Saturday morning would be doubled. But it would be the same for everyone. The most professional and quick-witted would come out on top as the cars left the pits at 09.00 sharp.

The time table of events in the Jordan garage looked like this:

0900. Hill and Schumacher complete one lap each before returning for a routine check.

Hill completes another four laps before consulting with Dino Toso about continuing understeer. The rear roll bar is stiffened and a set of new tyres fitted.

Schumacher's engineer, Sam Michael, also suggests this would be a good moment to compare the two types of Goodyear dry-weather tyres available: the so-called 'prime' and the softer 'option'.

0920. Trevor Foster, stationed at the pit wall and overseeing the operation while keeping an eye on the opposition, reports that Fisichella has stopped his Benetton at the chicane. 'There could be a yellow flag,' he warns. 'Don't go out just yet.'

0930. The track clear, both cars venture out and return to the garage again. Schumacher has thumped a kerb: complains he has too much understeer. Phil Howell, the number two mechanic on Ralf's car, grabs a slim torch and rolls beneath the rear of the Jordan, inspecting for damage.

Hill reports that the turn-in to the corners is better but the back of the car feels nervous and the understeer remains. 'We've not got a good balance yet,' he says to Toso as the engineer studiously jots down each alteration to the car and every worthwhile observation from the driver.

The list of times shows Mika Hakkinen fastest for McLaren with Michael Schumacher second quickest. Hill is fourth.

Suddenly, the television pictures show Coulthard spinning his McLaren, followed not long after by Frentzen's Williams. Spectacular it may be for the spectators but this sort of thing is not welcome in the drivers' respective garages.

There is work to be got through and the last thing any team wants at this stage is to have one or, heaven forbid, both of their cars sitting idle by the trackside. There is no chance of retrieving abandoned cars until the session is over and, with the use of spare cars not permitted until qualifying later in the day, a driving mistake simply will not be tolerated.

As the precious minutes tick away, pictures of stranded drivers, rather than please their rivals sitting safely in their garages, merely add to the pressure. They know they must drive quickly in order to explore the car to the full. But they daren't cross that very fine line between a dramatic moment when the car teeters on the edge and the disastrous consequences when it refuses to come back.

Each Jordan driver has a screen which drops into place from an overhead gantry. Using a remote control, Hill flicks from the television picture to a Hewlett-Packard channel showing a telemetry readout. By placing the trace of his fastest lap above Ralf's best effort, Hill can see that, although the quicker of the two drivers, he is losing out to his team-mate at Turn 4, a fast left-hander. Toso points this out. Hill says nothing, but any information is worth having.

With ten minutes remaining, both drivers rejoin. Throughout the session, Foster is receiving a constant flow of information from a mechanic stationed at the end of the pit lane and reporting when any driver goes out with a fresh set of tyres. It is a method used by every team so that a proper judgement can be made when lap times are compared.

0937. Hill is third fastest; Schumacher sixth. Hill says the understeer is still there but the back of the car feels more stable. Schumacher simply says that the car is better. After quick adjustments, mainly to the front and rear wing settings, both drivers attempt to squeeze in one more flying lap before the session ends.

The pace has increased elsewhere but Ralf moves up to fifth place. Hill stays third.

On their return, the drivers are fairly happy. Hill says he now has a reasonable aerodynamic balance and he wants to concentrate on making the car ride the bumps without losing too much traction. Schumacher says a decision to remove some of the angle on the rear wing has helped.

The garage is now a furious mass of activity. Both drivers climb from their cars, remove their helmets and find quiet corners in which to study the telemetry printouts with their engineers. Ian Phillips, meanwhile, is ready to inject a different kind of figurework to the proceedings.

AGAINST THE ODDS **169**

Damon takes Melinda Messenger's
advice and goes for it with back-up
from Race Director Trevor Foster (top)
and Crew Chief Jim Vale.

Once the pit lane is clear, Phillips goes to the back of the garage and brings forward Melinda Messenger. The model, surprisingly petite in some respects, is more fully dressed than normal when on a photo call. Wearing a suit of yellow Sparco Jordan overalls, she walks to the pit wall and poses with a signal board which urges Damon to 'GO FOR IT'.

That's all very well, but the photographers are keen to have Melinda reveal more of her assets. This poses a dilemma as the zip is lowered and part of the Benson and Hedges logo on the front of the overalls is lost to cleavage. No matter. The message will get across.

The mechanics have no time to look. The thirty-minute break is gone in a flash and Ralf is the first to leave the pit lane on the stroke of 1015.

Eight minutes later, he is back. Now the rear of the car feels nervous. Ralf wants to know how Damon is doing.

1024. Hill's car, its engine silent, is pulled into the garage. His breathing slightly laboured after a hard run, Hill says that the rear of his car feels 'lazy' and they need to think about a solution. Meanwhile, Foster reports that Frentzen has moved into third place. He was using the softer 'option' tyre and then, significantly perhaps, returned to the pits after just one quick lap.

1030. A moment of light relief as the Jordan crew see Tora Takagi spin to a halt, the camera then catching Tyrrell's Technical Director, Harvey Postlethwaite, mouthing choice words of disgust to anyone who will listen.

1035. Hill has moved back to fourth place, his time having been established while using old tyres. Damon reports that the balance of the car feels better now. 'It's given me a better front end,' he says. 'But I'm not so happy when the car is loaded up [going through a corner].'

Hakkinen is quickest, then Coulthard, Villeneuve and Hill. Ralf is seventh.

Hill wants to try a revision to the front roll bar. Rather than fit a new set of tyres as well, he asks if there is time to make a comparison while running the same set of older tyres before making the switch to fresh rubber. Toso confirms that will be in order.

1042. Hill sweeps onto the pit apron and has his thumb on the radio button immediately. Even though he was slowed by traffic on that lap, he learned enough to establish that the change to the front bar stopped the car's tendency to roll too much in the fast corners – 'which is what I wanted,' says Damon. 'Right, put the new tyres on.'

1045. As Hill prepares to leave, Schumacher returns, damage to the nose wings and the vertical barge boards mounted behind the front suspension providing evidence of a trip across a kerb and into the gravel while pushing hard on a new set of tyres.

1048. Hill is going for it. With each lap divided into three sectors, the first two split times of his latest lap are shown in green, indicating a personal best for the day so far. Then the television camera catches Damon running wide at the penultimate corner. He carries on. His muffled and slightly jagged voice comes on the radio as he races towards the end of the lap.

'Can I do one more timed lap on these tyres?' he shouts. 'Is there time?'

'Yes,' says Toso. 'Keep going.'

1051. In the midst of the bustle on the track, the camera catches a glimpse of Ralf driving out of another gravel trap. He dives into the pit lane for a quick adjustment to the front wing.

1053. Hill returns. 'Don't think the hard ["prime"] tyres will work. Can I try another set of "options"?'

'No,' says Toso 'because you have only three sets left and you will need them for the race.'

For qualifying, the warm-up and the race, each driver will be limited to seven sets of dry-weather tyres. The same type of tyre must be used throughout, the drivers and engineers making the choice between 'prime' and 'option' based largely on the evidence gathered during the practice session that is about to finish. During qualifying, each driver is likely to use four sets of tyres, leaving three fresh sets for the race in case a two-stop tactic is chosen.

1100. The session ends with the McLarens quickest, followed by Michael Schumacher, Fisichella and Villeneuve. Damon is sixth ('I'm not happy that we have found the best balance yet') and Ralf eighth ('Too much understeer still and we seem to lack grip').

It is clear that qualifying, due to start in two hours' time, will not be plain sailing for Jordan. Two months before, sixth and eighth would have been quite nice. But the expectation has risen to such an extent that at least one top six place is expected. Even on a circuit where the 198 is not supposed to do well.

The trouble with the Hungaroring, apart from the twists and turns, is that the circuit does not receive heavy use from competition traffic during the year. As a result, the track gets faster as more rubber is laid down. On that basis, the best lap times of qualifying will be at the end of the sixty-minute session rather than the beginning.

For twenty minutes, no one stirs. Not even a Minardi or a Tyrrell. Coulthard is the first of the big names to appear. Followed by Hill. Damon's lap is a tenth of a second slower than the McLaren. Not bad for an opening skirmish. But everyone knows there is more to come.

At the half-hour mark, the pace has picked up and Hill has dropped to sixth, with Ralf seventh. Then Damon finds a second and a half and shoots to third place, behind the omnipresent McLarens. Hill's time is made to look sad when Michael Schumacher slashes almost a second from it to take provisional pole, a move which stirs the McLarens into action once more. Almost before he knows it, Damon is down to fifth, with Ralf ninth. Now the heat is on.

With less than ten minutes remaining, a very busy track sees the McLarens assert their superiority with times which are more than two seconds faster than Hill's first attempt. But Damon has one run left. As the qualifying session enters the final five minutes, Hill puts together a controlled but aggressive lap. His name shoots to fourth on the list of times, just behind the McLarens and Schumacher's Ferrari.

As Damon heads back to the pits, the Jordan crew are watching the screens intently as Villeneuve makes his last run. A personal best for the Williams driver in one sector spells trouble for Hill. In the end, he falls short of Damon's best time by more than a tenth of a second. Villeneuve has to settle for sixth (behind Irvine's Ferrari), with Ralf claiming a disappointing tenth place after a continuing struggle with understeer and problems with slower cars. Nonetheless, Schumacher is the first to congratulate his team-mate on a job well done.

'A Jordan fourth on the grid! Who would have believed that a few months ago?' beams Eddie Jordan.

'Fantastic!' says Hill as he emerges from the back of the garage to an unaccustomed welcome from a gathering of the media. Wiping his brow with a towel and plonking the Hill trademark cap on his head, Damon makes sure everyone receives due credit.

'A great team effort,' he says. 'It shows how far we have pulled ourselves up since Argentina and Monaco which, when you think about it, were similar circuits to this and where we suffered on the twists and turns. I'd like to think of finishing on the podium tomorrow, but I have to be realistic. I know how tough this race can be and if I can finish fourth, that will be a result as far as I am concerned.'

Hill knows what he is talking about when it comes to assessing his chances. He won his first Formula 1 race at the Hungaroring in 1993 and he has finished either first or second in every Hungarian Grand Prix since. As he says, there's not much chance of continuing such an impressive record. But you never know.

Certainly, fourth place was enough to keep the momentum going as the mechanics set about stripping down and preparing the cars for Sunday. Damon's crew finish by 7.30 p.m., Ralf's team completing their work an hour later. 'It's fairly typical of what happens in motor racing,' said Jim Vale, the Team Manager. 'When everything's going well, it's easy. You finish nice and early. It's when you're struggling that changes are continually being made to the car. On a bad night, you can be working until very late. Everyone is tired and there's always the thought in the background that you're not going to do that well in the race. That's when it gets really hard. But this is OK.'

After dinner at the motorhome and the shuttle back to the Radisson Hotel in two hired minibuses, there was time for a Guinness or two in Becketts, the Irish pub which had hosted a team dinner on Thursday evening. It would have taken a true optimist then to forecast fourth place on the grid. Even now, one or two crew members could hardly believe the turnaround. But, given Damon's previous form in Hungary, you never could tell what might happen in the race.

Before he could begin to think about a decent result, however, Hill would need to make a good start. It would be easier said than done, given that his grid position was on the right-hand side of the track. Not only was this off the racing line, it was also extremely dusty. Even the best coordinated start by the driver could result in hopeless wheelspin and a lack of traction.

Damon sought to put matters right during the warm-up on Sunday morning. He had been allotted the spare car and, following the usual procedure, Hill completed a few laps in this chassis, just to ensure everything was in working order. Running an old set of tyres, Damon came out of the final corner on his last lap in the spare car and, rather than keep left, he moved right, aimed for his grid position – and slammed on the brakes. The Jordan neatly left two strips of rubber, enough to provide at least some grip at the start.

The plan worked well. Too well, in fact. When the red lights went out, Hill made a storming start and moved left, intending to duck behind Schumacher. Except Michael made a hesitant getaway, forcing Hill to back off momentarily. By the time he had regained momentum, not only had Schumacher pulled away, Irvine had taken advantage and pushed the Jordan down to fifth.

There Damon stayed until Irvine suffered a rare mechanical failure and retired. Hill maintained fourth through the first pit stops, but more through the fault of a poor performance by Villeneuve's crew than the quality of the Jordan. It was reasonable in race trim – but not as good as the Williams. When Damon had disappeared into the pits and Villeneuve had enjoyed a clear track for a few laps, he had lapped almost a second faster. Villeneuve proved the point once more during the second round of stops, the Williams crew getting him away in time to move ahead of the Jordan.

Damon assumed fourth once again when Hakkinen's front-running McLaren ran into trouble but the three points for Jordan came under threat when Frentzen closed in during the final laps. Hill held him off, setting his fastest lap in the process and gaining yet more championship points for Jordan. Ralf finished ninth, Foster being particularly unimpressed when Schumacher appeared to go onto automatic pilot when stuck behind the Arrows drivers for laps without end.

'He seemed to fall into the "this is Formula 1 and you can't overtake" syndrome,' said Foster. 'I've had to have a word with him. Ninth is no good to anyone. But I'm pleased with Damon's performance. To qualify fourth and finish fourth is good on such a difficult circuit. It shows we're still competitive.'

Damon was delighted. The mood elsewhere was ambivalent. True, Damon had been running the softer 'option' tyres whereas the harder 'prime' (as used by Villeneuve) might have been the better choice. But his drive nevertheless seemed to lack sparkle for most of its duration.

'It was a tough race,' said Damon.

'Aren't they meant to be?' muttered one crew member as the clearing up process began.

That may have been a harsh judgement. But it was a sign that ambitions within the team had finally reached the level anticipated when the season started eleven races and five months before. Jordan Grand Prix were not about to win a race. But a nice cup for a podium finish had to be the next step.

'Who gets to keep the trophy if we do?' mused Phillips. 'Dunno. We haven't a policy. Haven't had much need, really.'

That was about to change in a manner that would simply defy belief.

Chapter Ten

Trouble with the Schumachers

'If I wasn't so inept at the English language, Phillips,

you'd be unemployable!'

Ian Phillips grinned. Even though there was little

truth in either part of the statement, he knew precisely

what his boss was getting at. Words may be Eddie

Jordan's fast-flowing currency but he leaves the routine

paperwork to his Commercial Director.

Damon: Happy
to stay put?

It is Phillips's job to get the drift of what Jordan has to say and make sure it is placed, when necessary, on the record and in the appropriate manner.

EJ has no time for such niceties. As his opening remark hinted, even if he did get down to physically committing his words to print, he would, in his haste, dot the 't's' and cross the 'i's'. Mind you, give EJ a column of figures and it would be a different matter entirely.

As it happened, money was indirectly at the root of Jordan's outburst. The only surprise was that he was so cheerful in the face of the latest turn of events. A double-page spread in the front section of *Autosport* on Thursday 27 August was devoted to Jordan Grand Prix and it did not appear to make good reading from the team's point of view.

The so-called 'Top Story' – often a euphemism for a minor event which is blown out of all proportion in the absence of decent hard news – had, on this occasion, latched on to a development which had escalated all on its own and without any assistance from an editor desperate to sell his magazine.

Having come close to amicably agreeing a deal with Ralf Schumacher in July, Jordan now faced a writ from its driver, claiming the team was preventing him from leaving. They were still speaking, of course. But, in this day and age, the legal manoeuvring was part and parcel of the game. It was also interesting fodder for the media.

Schumacher said Jordan had written to Williams and BAR – with which Ralf had been in discussion – claiming Jordan Grand Prix had a binding contract on Schumacher for 1999. Their assertion was based on a new deal which had allegedly been drawn up between the team and Weber Management in July and confirmed by an exchange of faxes. In the week following the Hungarian Grand Prix, a QC had confirmed the legality of the faxed documents.

Schumacher said he had not agreed to the new deal. In fact, he claimed to know little about it. It seemed, therefore, that the argument at this stage was between Ralf and his manager, Willi Weber. Hence Jordan's relaxed mood as the team arrived in Belgium for the thirteenth round of the championship. There was, however, a downside to all of this.

In a bid to fill two pages with a story which was worth perhaps at column at the most, *Autosport* had unearthed every old chestnut they could find. In a panel entitled 'Comings and Goings', with a subheading 'Eddie Jordan has had a tough time hanging on to his rising F1 stars', there was a list of the drivers who had apparently slipped through Jordan's fingers, the suggestion being that Ralf would be the latest.

Michael Schumacher was the first and the most notable mention, his loss after just one race (see Chapter 1) a point Jordan did not wish to be reminded of. But as for the rest – Eddie Irvine at the end of 1995, Giancarlo Fisichella in 1997 – Jordan was adamant that the moves were to everyone's benefit and had nothing to do with carelessness on his part.

It was Jordan who had helped to engineer Irvine's switch to Ferrari: the court case over Fisichella was simply to establish that Jordan received its due payment from the Italian's new employers, Benetton. It was no coincidence that in each case Jordan had been advantaged financially. Indeed, it was a crude interpretation of that point which would cause deep offence.

The smile was wiped off Eddie's face when his attention was drawn to an article covering the Schumacher case in *Motoring News*. A bald quote from Michael Schumacher said simply: 'Williams is the best for Ralf because they will do everything to get on top again whereas Jordan is known to always be thinking about money.'

Talk about a dagger through the wallet. Eddie was incensed. He sent a message to Michael, saying he wished to have a word. When Schumacher did not respond, he adopted Plan B.

By a happy coincidence, Thursday night in Belgium had been set aside for three members of the British press. Stan Piecha (the *Sun*), Bob McKenzie (the *Express*) and Ray Matts (the *Daily Mail*) had offered to buy Jordan, Phillips and Foster dinner. This was an annual affair, but a rare event in Formula 1. It could be seen as a sign of the esteem in which EJ was held as well as of the fact that both he and Phillips would be good company at the table. Ron Dennis and other team principals were hardly swamped with similar invitations.

In return for such generosity, Eddie decided to provide his hosts with a juicy story, one which would serve both sides admirably. He realized full well that the journalists, knowing they were sharing a minor scoop, would file it the following day.

When Jordan arrived at his motorhome on Saturday morning, his first request was for the sports pages of the British dailies. Faxed copies duly arrived. The headline in the *Sun* – 'ANGRY ED RAPS "CASH MAD" SCHU' – gave a pretty clear indication of what was to come. EJ was quoted in the fourth paragraph.

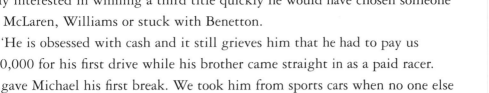

'Michael Schumacher gives the impression that he races for the love of it but he is the biggest money-grabber of the lot. He's doing a great job at Ferrari but he went there only because they offered him £20 million a year. If he had been really interested in winning a third title quickly he would have chosen someone like McLaren, Williams or stuck with Benetton.

'He is obsessed with cash and it still grieves him that he had to pay us £150,000 for his first drive while his brother came straight in as a paid racer. We gave Michael his first break. We took him from sports cars when no one else would take a chance. But, after one race, he left us in the lurch because he was offered a better deal by Benetton. If it hadn't been for the Jordan team, you could argue he may never have made it into Formula 1.'

As the story got into its stride, Jordan stepped up the attack.

'What right has Michael to accuse us of being money-grabbers?' he asked. 'I find it extremely offensive and rich coming from a guy who has taken so much money out of the sport. I feel I have been kicked in the teeth. It is a personal attack by someone we helped and I always respected. I thought about ignoring it but for the sake of the team, I can't let that sort of outburst go totally unanswered.

'We are as ambitious as any team and to fulfil that ambition we spend what it takes. We don't have the same huge budgets as some teams so we run a tight ship. But we are not penny-pinchers. Part of the problem we now face with Ralf is as a result of Michael's involvement.'

Using his platform to full advantage, Jordan concluded by saying:

'I don't remember a team in modern times turning itself around quite so dramatically in a season as we have. We had a terrible start but have come out of the doldrums to score points in the last four races. Turning things around is costly and would not have been possible if we were a bunch of penny-pinchers – whatever some people think.'

Jordan may have been stung by Schumacher's words but this remedial treatment brought a smile to his face.

'Michael's going to love this!' he said, tapping the pages with his finger. 'You'll never guess what happened last night. I was in the same restaurant and who should be at the table right beside me – I mean, right alongside – but Michael. He couldn't escape. I took the opportunity to have a quiet little chat; gave him full chapter and verse on my feelings on this matter.

'He went to great lengths to make the point that he had been misquoted. If that was the case, then I said he should issue a public denial. I think he had been giving it some thought; you know, thinking about where he had come from and how he and his brother had got to where they are today. The Schumacher boys have not done badly out of Jordan and on that basis I said I didn't expect him to openly slag us off.

'If he says Ralf should go to Williams, I've no problem with that. But I object strongly when he starts taking personal swipes at me and the team. When it comes to driver transfers and deals associated with them, I'm quite up front about it.

'That source of income is occasionally part of my annual budget. I allow for the fact that I will find somewhere to make money, because that is the nature of what I do. I'm a trader. I have to trade to make money to help keep the team alive. It's always been my philosophy. I don't object to being called a trader, or a hustler or whatever. But I do object to being called a money-grabber.

'Anyway,' he said, after a short pause, 'Michael's got the message. Whatever Ralf may be thinking about his future, he's got to prove he's worth it on the track. I've always said he's quick. But I can tell you that Damon's up for it this weekend. I don't think he's been this relaxed or confident all year. We're in pretty good shape.'

Jordan was basing his optimism on Friday's practice times, which showed Hill fourth fastest. Ralf was ninth, team members noting that he was spending just as much time on his mobile phone (discussing the purchase of boats and planes thanks to his anticipated increase in spending power) as he was with his engineer, Sam Michael, talking about Belgium 1998. 'Don't know where Ralf is at the moment,' mused Trevor Foster. 'But he's certainly not at Spa . . . '

Hill undoubtedly was. Damon was relishing a circuit which captured the imagination of drivers and spectators alike. Spa-Francorchamps was as different from the Hungaroring as it was possible to be: 'from the ridiculous to the sublime' was the popular adaptation of the familiar saying.

Spa was proof that circuits did not need to be a bland collection of chicanes and near-identical corners linked by short straights. Part of the secret lay in its rich history and its use of public roads sweeping through the Haut Fagnes region in the Ardennes. The original track, measuring almost nine miles, had linked the towns and villages of Francorchamps, Malmedy and Stavelot. Spa, some six miles from Francorchamps, had lent its name because the organizing club was based there and the town was well known thanks to its natural spring water.

Spa-Francorchamps hosted the Belgian Grand Prix for the first time in 1925. The circuit was rough and dangerous, and while the bumps might have been smoothed over the years, the risk element remained high. Deemed too perilous for modern Formula 1, it was axed from the calendar in 1971 and remained absent until 1983.

In a first-class piece of modernization, the old circuit, which was roughly triangular in shape, had been virtually cut in half. A link between two legs of the original triangle made full use of the plunging topography and maintained the essential character of the place. The drivers loved it and that enthusiasm was still evident fifteen years on. In fact, it was accentuated by the gradual loss of corners of character on race tracks elsewhere.

Spa had retained a place known as Eau Rouge. This was more than just a corner since it was located at the bottom of a steep hill, where it turned left, crossed a bridge and then swung right, climbing steeply as it did so. As the cars crested the rise, the track then curved left. With an entry speed of 180 mph, this was not a place for the faint-hearted. Mistakes at this point would be heavily punished.

Jacques Villeneuve provided a graphic illustration on Friday and lived to tell the tale. Attempting to take Eau Rouge without lifting his foot from the throttle, the French-Canadian proved that such bravado was not possible in the latest breed of Formula 1 car with its narrower, grooved tyres. The telemetry showed that he had reached 186 mph on the entry when the back of the car briefly stepped out of line. Villeneuve caught the slide but that put him slightly off line as he rocketed through the right-hand curve and started to climb the hill. The Williams drifted further than he wished. He almost made it. But not quite.

The rear tyres suddenly lost adhesion. This time, for good. The Williams spun across the crest of the hill and went in backwards at very high speed. Fortunately, four rows of tyres placed in front of the barrier did their work, absorbing the impact and spitting the Williams into the small gravel run-off area, where it came to rest a steaming wreck. Villeneuve hopped from the cockpit.

Despite Jacques's casual response – 'It's the best accident I've had in Formula 1 so far!' – the accident served as a reminder of how Spa can bite back. For most drivers, however, such an incident would be quickly dismissed and filed under: 'It won't happen to me. I won't make a mistake like that.'

Flat out. Phil Howell emerges
from beneath Schumacher's car
in the garage at Spa.

Certainly, it had not affected Damon Hill. But then he had the advantage of knowing that his Jordan was working well and did not need the almost desperate measures taken by Villeneuve as he searched for a quick time with the difficult Williams. On Saturday morning observers at Eau Rouge said Damon was the neatest and the most committed. The Jordan looked sure-footed and fast.

That was reflected in his demeanour each time he returned to the pits for further consultation with Dino Toso. Instead of desperately looking for clues and making fundamental changes in the hope of lighting upon a half-decent set-up, Hill and his engineer were fine-tuning. Instead of groping for a reasonable compromise, they were gently feeling their way towards perfection.

As the car was pushed backwards into the garage, Hill almost disappeared from sight, his dark blue helmet poking from within the deep confines of the cockpit and just about visible as his timing screen was lowered from above, air and power lines dropped from the overhead gantry and mechanics swarmed over the Jordan at every quarter.

Toso, clipboard at the ready, stood in front of the car to wait for a comment. Hill closed his eyes, the latest lap running through his mind in fast-forward. Then he put his thumb on the radio button and described how the car was under-steering slightly here, trying to oversteer there, struggling a little for grip somewhere else. But nothing too serious.

Toso had noted that Damon was only 3 kph slower in a straight line than the fastest man, Hakkinen. The readings were taken at the top of the long hill which led from Eau Rouge to Les Combes, a place where weaknesses in power curves were exposed and engines ran out of breath. This was proof positive of the good work done by Mugen-Honda. With the minimum of fuss and fanfare, the engine manufacturer had produced four updates in quick session, each noticeably better than the last. And there had not been a single failure at the race track. Such was the strength of their research and development, Mugen-Honda could simply say: 'Here's the latest engine. You can use it for qualifying. It'll be OK.' And, invari-ably, it would, the V10 singing its heart out while running at the absolute maximum, in this case approximately 16,000 rpm.

Competitive straight-line speeds meant Hill and Toso could experiment further with the wing settings, trading drag for improved handling in the corners. They continued to speak in a calm and orderly way. Yet there was a detectable tremor, one which said, 'This is what it's all about!'

JORDAN'S DRIVE TO WIN

'Yep,' said Hill. 'It feels good. Not undriveable by any means.'

From Damon, this was praise indeed. Such bold talk would have been unheard of three months before. No one was saying as much, but there was the distinct feeling that Jordan could be a force during qualifying later in the afternoon. McLaren seemed unassailable. But as for the rest . . . with Damon in this sort of form, you never could tell.

Rather than follow the usual procedure of waiting until the final thirty minutes of qualifying, when the track was likely to be at its quickest, Hill, Michael Schumacher and Hakkinen went out almost straight away, the presence of dark clouds prompting a lap in the dry just in case it rained. Hill was third quickest. It was a good start but everyone knew there was more to come, provided it stayed dry.

The rain held off. More laps were completed, Hill dropping to fourth place behind the McLarens and M. Schumacher. With ten minutes remaining, the timing screen indicated that each of the leading runners had enough laps left for one more effort. And as if to heighten the drama, Coulthard, Hakkinen, Schumacher and Hill left the pits almost at the same time.

It was clear that the McLaren drivers would be fighting among themselves for the right to pole position. Jordan's concern focused on the Ferrari driver, not because he might improve further but because he could stop Damon from beating him.

Hill was anxious to complete a fast 'out' lap but Schumacher was content to take his time, thus forcing Damon to drop back if he wanted a clear lap. That would not have been a drama for Damon had the clock not been ticking its way through the final minute of qualifying. If he could set off on his last lap before the chequered flag fell, then the subsequent time would count. But if Damon held back for too long, he might arrive at the start line too late. Perhaps that was Schumacher's intention.

Hill made it with twelve seconds to spare. But he wasn't free of Schumacher just yet. It was obvious that the Ferrari team would keep Michael informed about Hill's progress. Should Damon look to be on a fast lap then, if he was so minded, Schumacher could save his third place by holding him up through the final corner. Accidentally, of course. That was a chance Damon would have to take.

Schumacher had already lost a tenth of a second or two with a locked brake at the first corner. When the monitor showed Hill to be quicker on the first of three sectors, the news was relayed to the Ferrari driver. How was he going to react?

AGAINST THE ODDS

On the middle sector, Damon lost out to Schuey by a couple of tenths of a second. That was probably a blessing because it would have thrown Ferrari off the scent.

Schumacher pressed on and completed his lap. But Damon went quicker still. As he crossed the line, the legend 'Car 9. D. Hill' sprang from fourth to third on the screen. The Jordan pit erupted. The order was McLaren, McLaren, Jordan, Ferrari, Ferrari. Who would have believed that? And, as a final touch, Ralf was eighth. But judging by his preoccupied expression, he might as well have been somewhere else.

Hill was ecstatic. He beamed from ear to ear as he accompanied Hakkinen (who, to add to the drama of the moment, had snatched pole on his last lap) and Coulthard to the media centre. It was a long time since Damon had followed this routine, one which was very familiar to him in his days with Williams.

'I'm very, very happy,' said Damon, stating the obvious. 'This is absolutely brilliant. The team has worked so hard and Eddie has had to spend loads of money to get the car working! But this is what happens. You get there. We've made a tremendous improvement since the start of the season. I've worked very well this weekend with my engineer, Dino, and every step we made on the car seemed to be going in the right direction. It was very, very good.

'I beat the Ferraris by only a small amount but it was good fun. Michael is the acknowledged expert around Spa, so there is a certain satisfaction to be had by out-qualifying him.'

You could see the glint in Hill's eye as he said it. Not only had he taken on Spa-Francorchamps and won, he had beaten Michael Schumacher in the process. This was a moment to savour. The race would have to wait.

'Right now, I'm not thinking about tomorrow,' said Damon. 'We'll just celebrate what we've done today for the moment. Then we'll get down to talking about the race. Can we beat the McLarens? You never know. You just can't say.'

At the time, that seemed like good PR. Damon had to say it. Of course he did. And why not? Good luck to Jordan and Hill. Nice team and all that. But no one really believed it possible.

Chapter Eleven

Can this be True?

There were two ways of looking at the incessant drizzle on race morning. It would make Spa-Francorchamps even more dangerous than before; on the other hand, pit-lane intelligence said the McLaren drivers would struggle with their Bridgestone wets. It was typical sporting paradox. Do you curse the weather, say it would have been better in the sunshine and simply acquiesce? Or do you put your head down and accept that there can only be gain through a bit of pain? Damon Hill was definitely ready for the latter.

A moment to cherish for ever.
Hill on the top level of the
podium at Spa.

His first priority, however, was to find a pair of overshoes which would cover his driving boots. The forecasters said the rain would give way to fine weather. But what did they know?

The circuit straddled a deep valley which often seemed to have a microclimate of its own. The sun might be shining on the start/finish area but the track at the top of the hill could be soaking wet. As an Irishman once said: 'The most accurate weather forecast in these parts is the question "What's it doing now?" '

The rain looked to be set for the day and Hill knew his flameproof black suede Mizuno driving boots required protection. As it was, he had to have the soles wiped before climbing into his race car for the warm-up. The spare chassis had been allocated to him but since the garages at Spa only allowed two cars per bay, the backup was housed next door. Damon's first job was to slip into the T-car and have the mirrors adjusted to his liking. Then he climbed out and nipped round the front of the garage towards his regular car, the foot-wiping ensuring the soles of his boots would not slip from the pedals when the warm-up got under way.

In some respects, this was venturing into the unknown. Part of Friday's practice had been held in damp conditions and lessons had been learned from that. But now the track had changed yet again, thanks to the drizzle which was turning to rain. There would only be thirty minutes in which to try different tyres (the intermediates, plus a hard and a softer wet compound), run full wet settings or perhaps experiment with a compromise in case the race was run on a drying track. So much to do and so little time.

As Hill was strapped in, his eagle eye caught Michael Schumacher's Ferrari making its way towards the pit-lane exit.

Hill came on the radio: 'Looks like he's got a lot of wing on.' Toso nodded, but said nothing.

To the inexperienced eye, the rear wings on the various cars looked more or less identical. To engineers and drivers dealing in barely noticeable angles and degrees, and with flaps measuring in some instances no more than a fraction of an inch, there were huge differences both in appearance and performance value.

In Schumacher's case, he was running more wing than usual to generate additional downforce in the slippery conditions. But that was Ferrari's game plan. The secret was to work through your own schedule and not be diverted by the actions of others. Either way, grid positions didn't mean much for the moment. Everyone was starting afresh.

Both Jordan drivers were told to carry out radio checks throughout the entire lap, a routine which took on more importance than usual given the length of the circuit, the occasional weak signal and the need to know precisely where the driver was and what his problem might be. With each lap measuring 4.3 miles, the timing of pit stops would be crucial. The last thing you wanted was your driver missing the call and having to complete another lap, perhaps on the wrong tyres or with a minimum amount of fuel on board. Little did the Jordan crew realize, but this would assume an absolutely vital importance later in the afternoon.

As Ralf began to edge from the garage, Sam Michael gave him a reminder about the radio. A slightly clipped 'Yes' indicated that the driver had not forgotten. To make his point as he joined the queue waiting to leave, Schumacher said: 'I'm at the end of the pit lane now. Can you hear me?'

'Yeah,' said Michael in his droll Australian accent, 'and when the green light comes on, you can leave the pits.' A brief chuckle from Ralf indicated the point had been made. That was the end of the light entertainment. For the next half-hour, the tone would be deadly serious.

Both drivers were back, as planned, after one lap.

'Can't see anything,' said Schumacher. 'The spray from the car in front . . . ' and his voice tailed off. There was no need to say any more as the rain intensified.

Hill, meanwhile, was out of his car in preparation for a lap in the backup. This signalled the start of a minor pantomime as he ran next door, followed by crew members, some carrying the dripping wheels and tyres taken from his race car. When he returned after a single lap, the process went into reverse. It may have looked mildly chaotic in such cramped confines but it was carefully orchestrated, each man knowing precisely what he was doing without the need for instruction.

As Hill settled into the cockpit once more, he informed Toso that the clutch on the spare car was 'a bit dodgy'. Dino, half-Dutch, half-Italian, quietly side-stepped the quaint English terminology which Damon's father would have used as a matter of course when racing at Spa thirty years before. The message was understood and duly noted.

Each time a Jordan returned to the garage, the engine cover was removed, and along with rest of the bodywork and front wings wiped free from the black streaks of rainwater, oil and rubber. The mechanics working on each car listened

on the radio to the conversation between driver and engineer and were ready to act simply on a nod from the man with the clipboard. New set of tyres here, a change of wing angle there. The job would be done swiftly and without fuss. When the car left the garage, the floor area where it had stood was immediately mopped and dried. Again, hardly a word was spoken.

Ralf's car was cared for by a team of three: Andy Stevenson (the number one), Phil Howell and Patrick Grandidier. Damon's car was under the charge of Nick Burrows, assisted by Darren Beacroft and Dave Perrott. The spare car was looked after by Matt Deane, Ian Mitchell and Darren Burton.

The tyre logistics came under the auspices of the truck crews, led by Gerrard O'Reilly and assisted by Dave Coates, Warwick Pugh and Lee Pettifer. There were other crew members hidden behind the rear screen studying the telemetry read-outs, people such as Mike Wroe, James Key and Marc Donovan, but the mechanics, overseen by Crew Chief Tim Edwards and Team Manager Jim Vale, were on stage at the front. And after Hill's impressive performance during qualifying, every move was being recorded by a battery of camera crews noticeably larger than of late. Behind them, on the pit wall, were Ian Phillips, Eddie Jordan, Trevor Foster and Mike Gascoyne, the last two in particular assessing developments along the pit lane.

At the end of the warm-up, Schumacher was fifth fastest, Hill sixth. The performance of the cars seemed satisfying enough. There had been a point during the season when the Jordan had not been competitive in the wet, but things were different now – enormous strides had been made with the car. It mattered little whether it rained or stayed dry; the team felt quietly confident they could cope. The only problem was predicting the weather for the race and attempting to second-guess their rivals. The calculations and speculative work continued deep into the four hours before the start of the race.

Foster, Gascoigne, the drivers and their engineers disappeared into the briefing room at the back of the truck. Things had moved on since the days when tactical discussions were held in the motorhome as sponsors, guests, press and sundry characters squeezed past the narrow table in the middle of the room. Now they had an area devoted to themselves; peace in which to debate every nuance.

They talked about filling the cars to the brim, allowing plenty of scope for a late first stop in case the conditions changed. But that was a conservative option. In Ralf's case, it was decided to choose the same aggressive tactic which had

A Jordan leads a Grand Prix! Hill
shows Mika Hakkinen and
Michael Schumacher the way
through La Source at the restart.

worked well at Silverstone: starting with a small amount of fuel and pushing hard in the first quarter, hopefully making up places as he did so. If necessary, he could stop three times. Starting eighth, there was everything to play for.

Damon, starting from third, had more to lose. The calculations showed that one stop would be too slow, given the penalty of the extra weight of fuel. Two stops seemed to be the best bet, with a slightly longer first stint to keep the options open.

'We talked through the various situations,' said Foster. 'We asked questions: "What happens if this arises . . . What would we do in such and such a situation?" We discussed it from every angle. You get everyone to have their say. You want to get everything out because in the end it's important to have unanimity. You've got to get everyone's agreement beforehand. If you trying to do it during the race, it can be a nightmare.

'We thought we were in with a very good chance of scoring points. We come to every race believing that, of course, but on this occasion we knew we were looking reasonable. A podium finish? A possibility, yes. But to be honest, that would have been a bonus. We simply wanted to keep adding to our points. We knew how difficult this race was going to be . . . particularly at Spa . . . in the wet. You have to be prepared for anything.'

Prescient words. As the Jordan management gathered in the garage and watched the start on the television screens, they saw the yellow car on the second row more or less stand still and become engulfed by red as the Ferraris and Villeneuve's Williams moved forward.

In the space of five seconds, Hill had destroyed his weekend's work thus far. The clutch had snatched slightly and Damon had given the Mugen-Honda too many revs. As his rear wheels spun on the wet track he was helpless. So much for a brilliant qualifying and third place on the grid. He was seventh by the time the leaders reached the first corner. The team looked on, disappointment etched on their faces.

Fuck it! All that talk, all those hopes, all those plans. Now we have it all to do . . .

But wait a minute! The television screen was delivering pictures which were becoming more horrific by the second. Coulthard had lost control at the exit of the first corner. The McLaren had shot straight across the road, gone nose-first into a concrete wall and bounced back into the path of the pursuing pack. A multiple accident might have been inevitable from that moment on, but this was the ultimate worst-case scenario. The television showed wheels and bodywork flying in all directions, car after car piling into the mayhem. There was no alternative but to stop the race.

One driver after another miraculously stepped from wreckage strewn halfway down the hill towards Eau Rouge, each team desperately attempting to assess the damage.

Foster had seen Hill disappear from camera shot, and he looked unscathed. But with so much debris flying around, you never knew. Schumacher had pulled onto the grass on the left and stopped just before the main area of carnage. Foster's immediate thought was that the nose must have been damaged – at the very least.

The radio went into overdrive.

'Where are you, Damon? Damon! What's happening? Did you hit anything?'

'Ralf! What's wrong? Is there any damage? Can you get going again?'

The situation was not helped by the poor radio coverage on certain parts of the circuit. In the meantime, Foster ordered the crew on the spare car to stand by in case it was needed. If Ralf's car was damaged, then the T-car, set up for Damon, would have to be converted to suit.

Gradually, the picture began to emerge. The team could hardly believe what they were hearing. Neither driver had any damage to report.

Damon had sidestepped the wayward McLaren and Irvine's spinning Ferrari. Ralf, cool as you like, had seen the accident begin to unfold and decided to pull to one side and wait until it was over. As he did so, at least half a dozen cars whistled past on his right and contributed to a repair bill which would exceed £3 million. Large as it was, the cost involved mattered little when placed alongside the fact that no one had been badly hurt. Grand Prix racing had never been luckier.

As the cars made their way back to the start–finish area, Foster was issuing instructions while keeping his eye on the monitor (waiting for news of the restart time) and running through the regulations in his mind. The rules said that this would be a fresh start with the race running the original distance. Hill and Schumacher resumed their third and eighth places, the huge gaps behind Ralf telling the true tale of the destruction wrought on the midfield.

In the end, four drivers did not make the restart. While the rest were climbing into spare cars and making their way to the grid, the Jordan technicians were taking advantage of the lull to reassess tactics.

The rain had eased. Both drivers had started on full wet tyres but it seemed that a switch to intermediates would be the way to go if the weather continued to improve. That led to further discussion about the cars: did the drivers wish to adjust their set-ups in readiness for the track drying out? It was very difficult to know. This, after all, was Spa: a weather forecaster's nightmare.

In the end, Hill chose to switch to dry settings, Ralf preferring to run with more downforce which would suit wet conditions, the variation in choice emphasizing the difficulty. The only certainty was that Damon was being given an opportunity to make up for his bodged start. This was an unexpected second chance.

He grabbed it with both hands. Throttle and clutch perfectly synchronized, he shot forward, powering away from the Ferraris, overtaking Coulthard (in the spare McLaren) and then running alongside – and past! – Hakkinen. As the field entered the first corner, a Jordan led the Grand Prix! But for how long?

Damon had the advantage of a clear track. Hakkinen might have just spun himself out of the race but Michael Schumacher had quickly sliced his way past Irvine and was setting after Hill. Schumacher's every dramatic movement suggested that the lead would soon be his. Damon resisted for seven laps.

On the eighth, Schumacher tucked in behind the Jordan as they swept through Blanchimont, a flat-out left-hander. It took nerves of steel to do that in the dry, never mind in the wet when vision was seriously impaired. The Ferrari then darted from the ball of spray and raced alongside. Hill made life as difficult as he could, but in the light of their contretemps in Canada wisely chose to yield the position.

No disrespect to Damon whatsoever, but there was an inevitability about such a remarkable move. After all, this was Schumacher and this was Spa – in the wet. Nobody would stop him. As far as Jordan was concerned, second place would do very nicely, thanks very much.

Ralf, meanwhile, had jumped to seventh place on the first lap but could go no further, stuck as he was a few car lengths behind Frentzen, then, a couple of laps later, behind Alesi and Villeneuve as they made mistakes and dropped into the Jordan's clutches. Overtaking, however, was next to impossible in worsening conditions. In fact, they had become bad enough to warrant thinking about a change to full wet tyres. Ralf was due to stop early, and this would be the perfect opportunity to give him a tyre advantage.

He was scheduled to dive into the pits on lap fourteen but they brought him in at the end of lap eleven, losing just one place in the process. Better still, he rejoined on a clear track. Eddie Jordan and his crew studied the lap times with interest.

On lap thirteen, Damon went round in 2m 08.1s, Ralf recording 2m 09.3s. Next time, Damon had dropped back to 2m 11.5s. Ralf was fractionally quicker. On lap fifteen, Ralf was the fastest man on the track; faster, even, than his legendary brother and a full three seconds quicker than Damon. The full wet tyres were coming into their own.

The message was noted along the length of the pit lane. At the end of the next lap, five cars in front of Ralf came into the pits. When they resumed, with Michael leading Damon by twenty-four seconds, Ralf had catapulted to third! And as if to prove the point about intermediate tyres no longer being up to the job, Villeneuve, who had not come in, spun into the barrier.

At the end of lap twenty-four, Schumacher led Hill by a massive thirty-seven seconds. The Ferrari driver was in a different league. Jordan were not too bothered about that since they were running second and third. The fourth man, Jean Alesi, was five seconds further down a road which was becoming even more hazardous than before. The race had barely passed half-distance; there was still a long way to go. But not for Michael Schumacher.

Coulthard had spun yet again on the first lap and Schumacher was about to lap him. This would be an interesting situation. With Hakkinen out of the race, Schumacher was in a position to score maximum points and move into the lead of the championship for the first time this season. The only thing standing in his way appeared to be Hakkinen's team-mate, since one false move by Coulthard could take Schumacher out and maintain the status quo on the points table.

In a bid to avoid accusations of foul play, Coulthard was instructed by his team to let Schumacher through. Coulthard, who could not see in his mirrors beyond the wall of spray being kicked up by the McLaren any more than Schumacher could see through it, asked for the Ferrari driver's whereabouts. When told he was directly behind, the Scotsman hugged the right-hand side of the track and did not accelerate as hard as usual.

Even if the wisdom of a reduction in pace in such conditions was question-able, Coulthard's positioning on the track could not be faulted. Moving across to the left and off the racing line would have brought accusations of weaving and dangerous driving in poor visibility. As it was, Schumacher did not see the McLaren until a millisecond before he slammed into the back of it at 137 mph and tore off his right front wheel.

The Ferrari made a curious sight as it sped along on three wheels, the McLaren, with its rear wing missing, following at a discreet distance. All hell broke lose in the pit lane as Schumacher erupted from the cockpit and went off in search of Coulthard, the German having to be physically restrained when they finally met in the McLaren garage. As Schumacher, clearly in an emotional state, accused the Scotsman of trying to kill him, this little domestic drama made riveting viewing for the Jordan boys next door. But the truth was, they didn't know which way to turn. In the midst of the excitement, the pair of Jordan-Mugen Hondas had moved into first and second places!

Eddie Jordan had watched the fuzzy pictures on the monitor mounted on the pit wall. It had been a frightening moment as the front of the Ferrari appeared to explode in a shower of metal and carbon fibre. Jordan knew instantly that Damon would take the lead any second. But he showed no emotion whatsoever. He was numbed both by the pictures of the collision and its dramatic effect on his team. Could he really win this race? Don't even think about it. Don't even mention it.

The final pit stops were due soon. Ralf was summoned at the end of lap twenty-seven, the change of tyres (another set of full wets) and refuelling going without a hitch. Damon had a few laps in hand before a stop would be necessary. But yet another horrific incident was about to force the issue.

Blinded by spray, Giancarlo Fisichella tanked straight into a Minardi on the approach to the so-called Bus Stop, a rather clumsy chicane designed to slow cars through the final curve leading onto the pit straight. Fisichella was very fortunate to escape injury as the Benetton's front wheels and suspension flew past his head. When the tobogganing wreckage came to a halt in the middle of the track, it was pretty obvious that the Safety Car would soon be employed. This could change everything.

If Damon was due to stop, then now was the time. In fact, it had to be at the end of this very lap. The Safety Car would pick up the leader and the rest of the field would form behind them. Jordan needed to get Damon in and out of the pits immediately without either losing the lead or getting caught behind the Safety Car on his way in. If the latter happened, he could leave the procession and make his stop, but he would then be forced to rejoin at the back of the field. The question was, where was he at this precise moment?

The telemetry at the back of the garage indicated that he was halfway round the lap and in contact. Just about. Toso got on the radio.

'Damon! Pit now! Pit now!'

The radio check during the warm-up had showed the signal to be weak at turn eleven, which was situated deep in the valley between Pouhon and Fagnes. And that's where he was. Had the message been received? If he went past the pits at the end of this lap, he could kiss victory goodbye.

There was silence for a moment or two. Then, as Hill made his way along the return leg, through Blanchimont, contact was established. Seconds later he was rushing towards the pit-lane entrance. But the drama was not yet over.

The tyre change and refuelling went smoothly enough but Damon had asked for an adjustment to the front wing. Having started with a dry set-up, he was paying the price in the extreme wet conditions. Lowering the angle of the front wing would help. But this presupposed that a fundamental change to the structure of the nose wing had already been made while waiting for the restart. In fact, as they were about to find out, the point had been overlooked in the confusion.

As the refuelling and wheel-changing were completed, Paul Bennett simply needed to insert a key in the front wing sideplate and give it a turn. But with the wing already at its lowest setting, he found the key would go not budge. One further desperate twist of the wrist meant the key became stuck. Now it would not come out.

With the car off its jacks and ready to go, Crew Chief Tim Edwards knew they could not risk leaving the key in place for fear of, at worst, damaging the right-front tyre. As Bennett continued to struggle, Edwards simply yanked him away. And with him came the key.

In a burst of sound, Hill accelerated away and rejoined just as Ralf, still in second place, was streaking along the pit straight. The Jordans were still in charge.

The advent of the Safety Car had effectively brought a new race. Ralf, lapping faster than Damon because of the more suitable set-up on his car, had reduced the gap to fourteen seconds prior to Fisichella's crash. Alesi had been a further nine seconds behind, with Frentzen another twenty seconds adrift of the Sauber. Now they were bunched together behind the Safety Car. If Foster thought he had

Finally . . . finally! Damon went through changing conditions throughout the weekend to bring an unbelievable result.

First contact (opposite page). Eddie Jordan fights for the winner's attention as Damon greets (right to left) Tim Edwards, Ged Robb, Wayne Greedy, Warwick Pugh (hidden) and Paul Bennett immediately after climbing from his car in parc ferme.

troubles before, they were nothing on the dilemma which faced him with eleven very long laps to go.

'This was not something we'd actually discussed!' he joked later. 'If I'd said during the pre-race briefing, "OK, boys, this is an imaginary situation. Ten laps from the end, we're first and second, the Safety Car is out. What do we do?", they would've had me certified.

'We had talked about various team orders. If, say, it had turned dry and Ralf was on a three-stop strategy, then obviously he would be running quicker. If he caught Damon then Damon would be asked to move over because he was on a different strategy. That was agreed.

'But when you have them running one–two with about eight laps to go, Michael is out of the equation and there are sixteen points on the table – and bear in mind, we've only scored ten points in total so far this season – then the last thing you want is your drivers taking each other off and the team ends up with nothing. We'd look complete idiots if that happened.

'Ralf was the quicker of the two at this stage but the fact was, he was only directly behind Damon because of the Safety Car. The team needed the result and Damon had done all the work during qualifying and the race so far.

'So I told Ralf to hold station behind Damon until further notice. I said: "If Alesi becomes a serious threat and Damon is not going quickly enough, then I'll tell Damon to move over and let you go." Ralf didn't answer at first. Finally, he said, "OK".'

Clearly, Ralf was not happy. Neither was Sam Michael, who had been urging his man to go as hard as he could immediately after his pit stop, Ralf's engineer sensing that this was the moment when they could legitimately move into the lead as Damon continued his struggle with the car and then made his stop.

Foster fully understood the frustration but he had the advantage of being able to take one step back without the close involvement each engineer enjoyed with his particular driver. Foster had the wider picture in mind. And it was not necessarily a comforting sight at this precise moment.

There may have been just eight drivers in the crocodile behind the Safety Car, but the most threatening from Jordan's point of view were Alesi and Frentzen. Alesi's talent in the wet was second only to Michael Schumacher. The volatile but hugely talented French Sicilian would grab any chance to give Sauber their first win.

Frentzen, after a very disappointing two seasons with Williams, would see

JORDAN'S DRIVE TO WIN

this as the perfect opportunity to show his worth at a time when he was looking for a drive for 1999.

From Damon's point of view, he had Ralf swerving around in his mirrors, warming his tyres and preparing for a final push towards what could easily be the first win for himself and for Jordan. And, as Eddie knew only too well, the legal argument over Ralf's contract and his wish to leave might prompt him to do who knows what. Talk about an explosive cocktail.

As they came towards the end of lap thirty-two, the Safety Car extinguished its flashing lights, a sign that the track was now clear and the driver, Oliver Gavin, would pull into the pit lane at the first opportunity. The race would officially restart as the cars crossed the line to commence lap thirty-two. The first corner, where the build-up of spray would not be so severe, would be critical.

Hill's car slid sideways as he came through the Bus Stop and prepared for the restart, Schumacher closing in with Alesi darting every which way. By the time they crossed the line and aimed for the first corner, La Source, Damon had composed himself. The depleted field stuttered through La Source without incident. As Hill accelerated safely towards Eau Rouge, he knew the latest crisis had passed. But with more than forty miles to run in atrocious conditions, this race was far from over.

With so much at stake, each lap seemed to last for ever. There was nothing the team could do now but think about what might go wrong; a puncture, wet electrics, transmission trouble, low oil pressure, a failure of the electronics, driver error, a foolish lunge by Alesi, an unexpected river of water across the track, a spin into the gravel. You name it. Everyone on the team had been in the game long enough to know that motor racing has the capacity to inflict the most terrible cruelty. No one was more aware of that than Eddie Jordan himself.

Throughout this incredible race, which had been running for more than two hours if you included the first start and subsequent delay, Jordan could scarcely believe what was happening. He sat, almost mesmerized, on the raised platform at the pit wall, watching the television pictures, checking positions and lap times, discussing tactics with Foster, worrying with increasing intensity as the laps slowly slipped by and the dream of a lifetime beckoned.

First and second! No! No! I've already said: 'Don't even mention it!' The disappointment would be crushing if it all went wrong. As they entered the final laps, the only consolation was that the order had settled down. Ralf was a few car lengths behind Damon. Alesi, after an initial push, had settled for third. Frentzen had never been a threat. But don't think about it yet. Don't think about anything. Meanwhile, Hill's concentration was close to overload.

The rain had eased slightly but the track was particularly treacherous at the scene of Fisichella's crash. With a lethal mixture of oil and water spread across the road at the very point where it turned, and acceleration was required, Hill had to treat the throttle pedal as if there was an egg beneath it. Elsewhere, the road was no longer awash, although it remained very wet at Stavelot and on the long climb towards the Bus Stop. And, by now, Hill had become familiar with the exact location of the streams of water draining the surrounding hills.

'One of the worst bits was at the top of Eau Rouge – at the point where Villeneuve lost it during practice,' said Hill. 'There's a slight kink and the water runs down the hill towards you and then crosses the road. So, you go round the corner and suddenly drive into a stream. There is no alternative but to cross it. The water is just pouring down that hill; half a mile of rainwater is being collected and channelled towards the apex of that corner. Even when it's not raining, the drainage is still coming off the hillside.

'You learn to spot the worst-drained parts of circuit and the areas where the water always seems to collect. There is also a bit after Pouhon, at the point where you head towards Fagnes. That does get quite deep at times because it's collecting from the hill you've just come down and the road levels out.

'When you hit water, the first thing you feel is the steering go light. The next thing, the 750 bhp surging through the rear wheels is looking for grip. You're supposed to be flat out at that part of the circuit and if there's no grip, then you've got 750 bhp going all over the place. Not nice.'

Hill also had to pay attention to the kerbs and stay away from them if he could. Irvine's parked Ferrari at the exit of Pouhon was a reminder of how one wheel on the gloss paint of a kerb could spin the car into the gravel. In Irvine's case, it had cost him a likely third place.

In fact, the circuit was littered with abandoned cars. Which was good news and bad news for Hill. Good, because he wouldn't be troubled by back-markers. Bad, because there were not enough cars on the road to help disperse the water.

'That was the worst thing,' said Hill. 'At first I wondered where everyone was, and why even though it was no longer raining as hard as before there was no sign of the line being cleared of water. Then it dawned on me that there were only a handful of cars still running and they were not that far behind me. It required total concentration and, of course, with Ralf and Alesi in close attendance, I couldn't exactly hang about.'

The mechanics stood absolutely still as they followed the image of the two yellow cars on the television screen. The few who could not bear to watch wandered aimlessly. Giselle Davies's mobile rang. It was a request for an interview with Eddie. The first of many. *But let's win this race first!*

As the cars splashed past to start the last lap, Ralf was one second behind Damon. Coulthard, who had rejoined after a long delay to repair the back of his car, was positioned between Ralf and Alesi. That, at least, was some comfort.

But there were still 4.3 miles to go on the most demanding circuit on the calendar. And the rain was continuing to fall. Apart from one small error when he locked his brakes and ran across the grass at the Bus Stop, Damon had not put a foot wrong. Ralf had been absolutely faultless. Don't make a mistake now, boys. Please!

Stomachs knotted, fingers chewed to the quick, the men in yellow watched the murky scene on the little TV monitors.

Two Jordans still in front as they reached the top of the hill at Les Combes. Through the long right at Rivage and down the hill, past the scene of Schumacher's demise - tough shit, Michael, but thanks anyway - and into the very fast left-hander at Pouhon. On to Fagnes and into the right at Stavelot. Now the long climb through Banchimont, heading towards the Bus Stop for one last time.

Keep going! Keep going! Don't stop now for God's sake!

Finally . . . finally! First one Jordan and then the other, fishtailing into sight and under the chequered flag. The entire crew, now crowded at the pit wall, went berserk as Damon and Ralf swept past. Fists, hands, hats, yellow arms, black gloves, Union Flags, Irish flags. It was a sea of colour and delirious mayhem.

On the hundred and twenty-seventh attempt, and after almost eight often tempestuous seasons, Jordan had finally won a Grand Prix. Deservedly so. Better than that, they had finished first and second. No 'ifs and buts'. This was the perfect result. Eddie Jordan, the master talker, was too stunned to speak. It was simply unbelievable.

Chapter Twelve

This is for You

In the midst of the emotion swirling around the Jordan

pit, Andy Stevenson searched for his opposite number

on Damon's car. Nick Burrows was doing the same even

though he knew that Stevenson, as Ralf's number one,

had lost – in a manner of speaking. Burrows did not

wish to crow. But there was no need to worry.

Stevenson was as delighted as anyone with the result.

They met and embraced with an understanding which

**Dave Perrott and
Tim Edwards (right)
help make Damon
comfortable.**

could only belong to those who had been in this from

the very beginning.

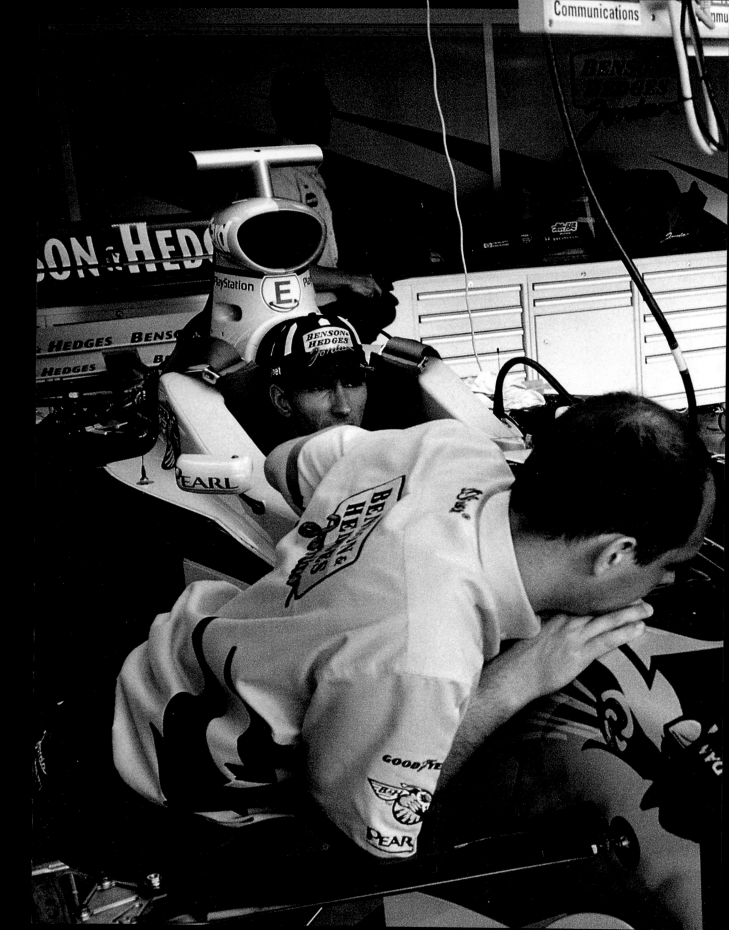

Burrows and Stevenson, along with Phil Howell and Dave Perrott, had worked with Eddie Jordan since before the start of his Formula 1 campaign. They had travelled the long and difficult road together, dismissing the blandishments of other teams, carrying on in the belief that this day would finally come. The niceties of whose car had crossed the line first was totally irrelevant. It was Jordan Grand Prix which had won. That's what really mattered.

Stevenson had joined in December 1987 and worked with Eddie through Formula 3 and into Formula 3000. In those days you could count the entire team on both hands. And that included the drivers. Burrows and Howell had signed on a few months later, with Perrott making the move to Jordan the following year. When the flag fell at Spa, this unspoken bond brought them together in more than the physical sense as crew members collided in sheer delight.

As the initial pandemonium began to die down, a second wave hit the team. Mechanics, engineers, managers and drivers from rivals on all sides came forward with heartfelt congratulations. Most of them had won before. They knew exactly what it had taken; fully understood the effort which had been expended. The long hours, the frustration, the disappointment, the fatigue that is heightened when nothing goes right. Jordan Grand Prix had finally earned its colours. It had arrived. Big time.

Some of the mechanics were very familiar to the Jordan boys. Others were purely nodding acquaintances whom they only knew vaguely. But it was such quiet but genuine appreciation which brought a tear to many a hardened eye. Jordan had done more than finish first. It had won respect, a quality which is not dispensed lightly in Formula 1.

The general public was waiting to show similar appreciation. Among the crowd was a coachload of fans from the Jordan Supporters' Club, plus seventy staff members from the Jordan factory who had chosen this of all races for their annual trip to Europe. The podium presentation was going to hold a significance beyond anything they had witnessed before, or were likely to see again. But first Eddie himself had to find his way to the rostrum.

The location of the pit lane relative to the control tower at Spa was unique thanks to the former being before the La Source hairpin and the latter positioned on the downhill run to Eau Rouge. It was necessary to bundle the platform party – the first three finishers and the winning constructor, namely one E. Jordan – into a minibus for the journey to the podium.

The drivers were on board, but in the excitement it took EJ a few minutes to establish his whereabouts. Once pointed in the right direction, he did a joyous mix of an Irish jig and a childlike frolic while skipping towards the van, where Damon beckoned his boss with open arms.

The welcome inside was mixed. Hill was ecstatic. Alesi (an old friend of EJ thanks to having won the Formula 3000 championship with Jordan – at this very circuit!) warmly embraced his former mentor. Ralf mumbled congratulations. And then looked away, his face like stone.

Jordan did not need to ask what was amiss. In the time the brief journey allowed, he pointed out that while appreciating his driver's deep disappointment, it was necessary for Ralf to understand that the team came first. No one was bigger than Jordan Grand Prix. Team orders were inevitable. He explained that if it had been the other way round, with Ralf ahead of Damon, then he would have told Hill to stay put. Ralf's day would come.

The problem for Schumacher was that it had not come on Sunday 30 August 1998. He had desperately wanted to win Jordan's first Grand Prix, and for some time now he had had a feeling that he could do it at Spa. There could be no better place to score a maiden victory for both himself and the team. Spa-Francorchamps, although in Belgium, was close to his home town of Kerpen, not far inside the German border. It was not so much the team orders which had annoyed him, it was the fact that he had actually come so close to winning this milestone event. And now the moment had gone for ever.

The frustration was still evident as he stood, po-faced, amid the semi-hysteria on the podium. On a day when Ralf's brother had tossed away a certain ten points, Damon rubbed it in by climbing onto the top step and aping Michael's trademark leap in the air. That dramatic picture would make the front pages of all the British quality daily newspapers on Monday morning.

Sport would have its brief place in the sun although, as ever, the relentless undercurrent of world politics would always be present. Jordan was aware of it as he stood on the podium and looked up at the colours being raised; the Union flag for Damon, the black, yellow and red of Germany for Ralf and the French tricolour for Alesi. In keeping with the rules, 'God Save the Queen' was played for the winning driver. Then, according to the regulations, the organizers would play the national anthem of the winning constructor.

Jordan had always maintained that his team, although based in Britain, was

Eddie clutches one of three trophies awarded to his team and drinks in the heady moment on the podium.

as Irish as a glass of Guinness. He fully expected to hear 'Amhrán na BhFiann'. A flicker of consternation crossed his brow when the Irish national anthem wasn't played. There would be questions asked about this. But that would have to wait.

When Eddie received his trophy, he made a point of moving to the front of the rostrum and picking out as many employees as he could among the sea of faces below. In each case, he pointed at them, and then to the trophy. 'This is for you,' he mouthed. There was hardly a dry eye in the house.

Once the ceremony was over, the drivers were hustled into the television studio for the unilateral broadcast and then to the media centre, where they received a standing ovation, an event as rare as the victory itself.

Eddie, meanwhile, was handed a mobile phone. Bernie Ecclestone was on the other end. The Formula 1 supremo, as is his wont, had left the circuit before the finish, but typically he had kept in touch with everything that was happening in his domain. 'Jesus, Jordan,' whispered Ecclestone, 'you'll be unbearable now!'

Ecclestone was quietly delighted. Along with most of the paddock, he had a soft spot for Jordan. But from a business point of view, this result was good for Formula 1. The championship battle remained wide open; there had been spectacular but injury-free crashes; and there had been a new winner, a popular one too. The Belgian Grand Prix would make world headlines. Bernie liked that.

Jordan was whisked to the motorhome where Giselle was standing by with telephone interviews and a list of requests from waiting television crews. EJ's first job was to ask the mechanics to stop what they were doing and come down from the garage to enjoy a glass of champagne. When everyone was present, Eddie grabbed a microphone (which Davies had quickly organized for just such an eventuality) and thanked the team with a short but very sincere speech. Then the champagne flowed like never before.

In the midst of this, the drivers returned, their press conference over. Ralf pushed his way through the waiting media to his motorhome. Damon was immediately engulfed by cameras and microphones.

An hour or so later, when there was a brief lull, EJ took the opportunity to seek out Ralf and reassure him. To his surprise, Eddie found that Michael had dropped in to see his brother. This was a nice gesture – or so EJ believed – given that Ralf had finished second and Jordan (the team which had given Michael his first Formula 1 drive at this very circuit) had won its first Grand Prix.

Michael offered his congratulations. Then he asked why his brother had not been allowed to win the race. After all, he said, Ralf had been quicker than Damon in the closing stages.

EJ could not believe what he was hearing. Once he had recovered his composure, he gently explained that the team came first, and besides, Michael was hardly the one to talk about the best man winning when, on at least one occasion, Eddie Irvine had given up the chance of his first victory for the sake of his teammate. OK, Eddie was the number two and Ralf had joint status with Damon. Next time, it might be Ralf's turn. Nevertheless, it ill behoved Michael to tell Eddie how to run his team. 'I mean,' spluttered Jordan afterwards, 'can you imagine me going to Ron Dennis or Jean Todt and telling them how to run their race? No way.'

It brought a sour note to an otherwise superb day. One which was not yet over.

EJ looked at his watch. It was 7.15 p.m. Under normal circumstances, he would be halfway home by now. But these weren't normal circumstances by any means. Most of the team had been forced to leave the champagne and rush to Brussels airport. Now Eddie had to do the same.

Changing quickly from his uniform into dark slacks and a black polo shirt, then grabbing his briefcase, he made a dash to the car park where Phillips was waiting with the hire car. Once onto the nearby motorway they became ensnared in traffic. There was no chance of catching the last flight now.

As they wondered what to do next, a fellow motorist spotted EJ and got out of his car to offer congratulations. That started it. Within minutes, they were surrounded, the passengers from a nearby coach decanting to join in the impromptu celebration. It was very nice indeed. But it did not answer the question of how Jordan was going to get back to the UK.

'By then, I was ready to go home,' said EJ. 'Throughout the weekend and the race, you are so bound up in what you're doing that you haven't time to stop. Marie was supposed to fly to Belgium that morning with Brian Richardson, the Chairman of Coventry City, but the bad weather meant the helicopter couldn't make it. All I wanted to do now was get back and share the moment with my family. After all, Marie had been through this every bit of the way. It would mean as much to her as it did to me. I just wanted to go home.'

Picking up his mobile phone, he called Brian de Zille, an entrepreneur who had made his money by establishing and eventually selling the Sweater Shop chain. The 'GdeZ' emblem on the rear of each Jordan is in recognition of de Zille's sponsorship. Brian and Eddie had been friends since Jordan raced in Formula 3 and, separate to the sponsorship deal, Brian allowed Eddie the use of one of his aircraft when required. And now it was needed more than ever before. EJ said he knew he was asking a great favour but, given the circumstances, would de Zille mind sending someone to collect him? De Zille, who relishes the organizational challenge of such an operation, had no hesitation in dispatching an HS 125 to the small airport at Liège.

The next problem would be landing at Kidlington since the estimated arrival time would be after the airport was due to close. On the phone once more, EJ spoke to Lindsay Haylett and asked his PA to see what could be done. Working her charm to the full, Lindsay explained the situation to the man in charge at Oxford airport and persuaded him to have the landing lights turned on specially. Talk about a fitting welcome home. It had been that sort of day.

By the time Jordan reached his house in Oxford, the place was awash with champagne and friends. The phone was ringing nonstop. The fax machine had run out of paper. The full import of the day had yet to sink in. It was only when Eddie sat down to watch the race highlights on ITV that the confirmation finally arrived. There it was. The Belgian Grand Prix had been won by – a Jordan!

The winning car had since been through post-race scrutineering, the final hurdle which, in the past, had been known to wipe the smile from the victor's face. Officials had checked the car's dimensions, taken a sample of fuel and downloaded part of the on-board computer program to ensure that illegal electronic devices such as traction control had not been employed. Both Jordans were given a clean bill of health and returned to the team's garage, where the filthy bodywork was washed down in preparation for loading onto one of the three waiting transporters.

As darkness closed in, the garage lights accentuated the bright yellow paint scheme as the two immaculate cars sat side by side, silent now, their weekend's work done. They made an impressive sight, the more so because no other team in the pit lane could boast having two unmarked cars at the end of such a dramatic day. The ravages of the race had been such that most competitors were loading cars which had been either severely damaged or reduced to a heap of broken parts.

Coulthard's race car had finished the day with just one wheel attached. The chassis had been hit on every quarter. Arrows had suffered three write-offs during the course of the weekend. Ferrari had two damaged cars. It was the same at Benetton, a story which was repeated along the length of the pit lane. With the two Jordans sitting in mint condition and the spare car untouched, here was a sign that the team's luck had finally turned.

In fact, it had ridden with Damon during the race. It was only after the wheels were removed from his car following the second pit stop that two cracks were discovered in a rear rim. They had probably been caused by a brief clash of wheels while lapping Prost; it was the only incident Damon could think of which might account for such potentially serious damage. As it was, the pressure in the tyre had dropped from 19 to 12 psi. He was very fortunate indeed not to have suffered a flat tyre, the last thing you need on such a long circuit.

Such a lucky escape contributed to the light mood in the garage. The packing up was completed with no trouble at all. On a bad day, the humping of heavy kit merely added to the pervasive feeling of tiredness. Tonight, it was as if even the most awkward item was floating on air.

As the team's side screens, complete with sponsor identification, were removed to expose the wire mesh dividing walls in the garages, Jordan's neighbours were revealed; McLaren on one side, Prost on the other. It was a reminder of how insular your world can become as you focus exclusively on your cars and drivers. Yet, just a few metres away, rivals are going through the same mixture of stress and emotion, more so in the case of McLaren as the championship fight with Ferrari headed towards its climax.

For tonight, however, Jordan Grand Prix was King of the World. The garage was gradually emptied, the cars loaded last. The detritus of the weekend was brushed into a corner: Discarded black gloves with their yellow Jordan insignia on the back; empty tins of Armor All polish and AP Racing brake fluid; a grubby copy of *F1 Racing* magazine tossed to one side – possibly, as someone observed, the best place for it in the light of the aggravation caused by the stinging editorials a few months before.

Monaco and Canada seemed a very long time ago, a different experience to the surging euphoria which had enveloped the garage at Spa. The two race trucks had been due to leave at 8 p.m. and aim for an overnight halt at Lille before making the final run to Calais the following morning, the smaller truck heading south to Monza for a three-day test later that week. Those plans had been turned on their

Andy Stevenson, Ralf's number one mechanic, waited a long time for his team to score that first win. Lindsay Haylett (inset) had to use all her charm to get her boss home on the night of the Belgian Grand Prix. Damon's trademark hat hangs over a radio headset in the battery-charging bank at the back of the garage.

Ready to bring them back to Blighty. The two immaculate articulated trucks lined up at the back of the garages (opposite page).

head. A skeleton staff of twelve mechanics had remained behind to assist with the loading. The truck crews would join them and stay the night. There was talk of some drink being taken.

It was shortly after 10 p.m. when Gerrard O'Reilly and Dave Coates eased the articulated transporters through the semi-deserted paddock which had once been a scene of heaving humanity and scurrilous gossip. Now it was dark, tatty and abandoned, its role in the 1998 Formula 1 World Championship now complete.

At the bottom of the hill they joined the former racetrack which had become a public road once more. Turning right, the vast vehicles crossed the bridge at Eau Rouge and began the steep climb considerably slower than the two cars they were carrying had managed on forty-four occasions that afternoon.

Into the pitch black, the yellow trucks churned their way up the hill. At the top, instead of turning right at Les Combes and aiming for Rivage, Pouhon and the rest, they swung left and trundled gently down the old racetrack, passing the occasional flickering light from a farmhouse as they went. After a mile or so the welcoming glow of Plain Vent, a restaurant set back on a small hillside, signalled the end of the hard work.

Inside, Giselle Davies, Mark Gallagher, Richard Surface (Chief Executive of Pearl Assurance) and a few colleagues had started the ball rolling. On the table sat the massive cut-glass trophies. Three of them, no less. One for the winner, one for second place, and one for the team. They were the first tangible evidence that this had not been a dream. Jordan Grand Prix really had won the Belgian Grand Prix.

The first priority was either a beer or a glass of wine. And then food at the finish of a long and dramatic day. But the emotion was not yet over. As the mechanics finished their steak and chips and settled into comfortable settees, they had one common regret; Gary Anderson had not been present to see his car win its first Grand Prix.

A mobile phone was pressed into service for a call to Northamptonshire. Anderson could barely speak.

'He's choked, completely choked,' murmured Andy Stevenson as he cradled a glass of red and thought fondly of the man whose cars he had taken apart and put together thousands of times during the past eight years. There could be no doubting the affection for Anderson on the factory floor. The big Ulsterman was one of the boys. A former mechanic himself, he was not averse to picking up a spanner and getting stuck in. That, some would say, was precisely Anderson's problem as

 JORDAN'S DRIVE TO WIN

the team grew and the Technical Director's responsibility perforce became more managerial rather than practical. It was his refusal to give up the role he enjoyed most which was causing the present difficulty. But at Spa that night the mechanics would have none of it.

'I'm a big fan of Gary,' said Stevenson. 'He'd be on the shop floor at six thirty in the morning, leading the way. Completing the first car on time is always a rush, and on several occasions we'd never have got it finished without him. I don't know many designers who could work to a budget the way Gary has had to and yet get the job done. Maybe this car wasn't working at first. But he made it right.'

That said, it was clear that the mechanics present had a growing respect for Mike Gascoyne. This was a difficult time for the new recruit. The media had already made the easy connection by pointing out that Jordan's run of new-found reliability had coincided with Gascoyne's arrival. Therefore, taking that view to the next stage, the win was down to him.

If anything, Gascoyne was mildly embarrassed by it. He insisted that he had merely tied up a few loose ends, worked on the age-old theory that you won't score points if the car doesn't finish. He stood in the background and said the car was not his, but Anderson's.

There was a growing number in the team who felt Gascoyne was selling himself short. Before the start of the race, Foster had mentioned that Mike had made some small but very significant changes to the car. The bottom line for many was summed up by one of the mechanics: 'Anyway, he seems a good bloke. He talks to you – which is more than designers on some teams will do.'

There was no shortage of talk in the Plain Vent as the wine – a very fine vintage paid for by Richard Surface – flowed until 2 a.m. Some, notably the truck crews, had retired before midnight. There was work to be done on Monday morning.

The stillness of the night was occasionally broken by the sound of a car horn as a motorist, seeing the two huge pantechnicons parked by the verge, would signal his approval. That was the prelude to a fanfare which lasted all the way home.

The trucks left at 7 a.m., a gentle downhill start through the hamlet of Burnenville and on to Malmèdy, where they joined the motorway and headed west towards Liège, Charleroi and Mons. As the mighty Scania V8s stoked up 540 bhp and churned their way through the gears to a pre-set cruising speed of 90 kph (57 mph), the chorus began.

The majority were British-registered cars, making their way home from Spa and enjoying the benefit of the extra day caused by the Bank Holiday in the UK. But there were Belgians too, and the occasional French and German motor racing fan speeding by. Multinational they may have been but they were united in their response. The sight of the B&H Jordan trucks brought the need to express pleasure at the remarkable result the day before. Thumbs up, flags waved, Jordan fan club gear and Damon Hill hats brandished from every window. One hardy soul even stood up on the front passenger seat of a BMW, stuck his head through the sun roof and took a picture as they breezed past. Everyone, it seemed, wanted to share the joy of this win.

It was the same at Brussels airport as British Airways staff fell over backwards to welcome team members, special treatment being given to the winner's trophy as Richard Surface carried it on board. The morning newspapers from home were full of Jordan's success, the gratifying part being that the Schumacher-Coulthard row had not relegated Damon's victory to the margins.

There was the rostrum shot, Hill in full flight, sponsorship insignia to the fore, most notably – and appropriately in view of the previous night's hospitality – the Pearl Assurance logo on his belt. Jordan may have lacked exposure during the previous twelve races but Spa had more than made up for that. 'They've never had so much for so little,' Jordan had grinned to a group of smiling sponsors the night before. 'The price will be going up!' He was laughing. But he wasn't joking.

He could afford to say that now, of course. In fact, he could get away with anything in the current climate. Jordan awoke on Monday morning to requests for more interviews, starting at seven forty-five. By lunchtime, he was talked out. An escape with Marie to the Leatherne Bottle pub near Henley brought some respite. But even there punters on the river recognized the cheery bespectacled face and shouted their congratulations. This win, it seemed, had touched everyone.

If the result of the Belgian Grand Prix would soon be superseded in the minds of the British public by some other heart-warming sporting endeavour on a far-off field, the events of 30 August would live with the staff of Jordan Grand Prix for ever. Tuesday – the first day back to the office and workshop – would be equally memorable. There would be no work done as they celebrated the work which had been done. 'The place,' as Mark Gallagher noted, 'just went absolutely crazy.'

Everyone had a tale to tell of where they had been when the Jordans crossed the line, who they spoke to first, how they had marked the moment. Richard O'Driscoll's story was typical.

'I was supposed to go out for a quick nine holes of golf after the race with my wife,' said the accountant. 'I watched the television – and couldn't believe what was happening. We opened a bottle of champagne, but the result hadn't sunk in. The babysitter arrived to find me sitting in a chair, my jaw hanging open, a glass of champagne in my hand. I couldn't speak. The babysitter wondered what the hell was going on. It was three on a Sunday afternoon and I was supposed to be going off for a quiet game of golf . . . '

The lucky seventy had returned from Belgium carrying priceless memories and pounding headaches in equal amounts. But their happy discomfort was nothing compared to a couple of the Irish contingent in the care of Tony Laszlo, the team member responsible for chaperoning the Supporters' Club. Laszlo was as exhausted as he looked.

'Boy, can they drink,' he said with a shake of the head. 'One of them was at the bar until five. Then he had his breakfast, and went to bed. Serious – or what?'

The usual form on the first day back after each race was an address by Trevor Foster in front of the workforce. This had not always been an easy task given some of the results the race director had been forced to discuss. Monaco, for example. One car finishing two laps down, the other retired. A battle between Jordan and Minardi to avoid being the first team to be lapped by the leaders. On that occasion, Foster had to lift chins from the workshop floor.

'I told everyone that despite the result, I had absolutely no question in my mind that anyone working for Jordan Grand Prix could go to any team – be it McLaren, Williams or whomever – and hold their head up high and do the job. I said they were just as good as anyone else and they must never doubt that. The only way I knew to get the results we wanted was to put our heads down and try even harder. I was sure we were capable of it.'

Here was the proof. On the first Tuesday in September the workforce gathered in the race shop. The front doors of the headquarters were locked, the reception vacated, the answer machine turned on. Eddie Jordan emerged from the first-floor offices and began to make his way across the balcony leading to the staircase. He was carrying the trophy.

In a completely spontaneous response, the entire place erupted. 'One-two! One-two!' came the roar. They were delirious. Jordan, in all his years, had never witnessed anything like it. Emotion was thick in the air as he began to speak.

'I've heard EJ make many speeches,' said Gallagher, 'some, shall we say, better than others. But this one was absolutely perfect. It wasn't too long, he didn't ramble or become overly sentimental. And yet it was from the heart. He meant every word of it. A few people had lumps in their throats, I can tell you.'

The response, as Jordan himself might have said, was massive. Then Foster took his turn.

Foster said the applause shouldn't just be for EJ; it should be for every single person in the factory because they all deserved it. But the weekend had meant more than simply finishing first and second. The team had earned a lot of respect from rivals. Jordan had done everything right – or as good as anyone could ask under the circumstances. The entire team had performed; every department had done their bit and that had been recognized, not just within Jordan Grand Prix, but outside as well.

'That,' said Foster, 'means more to me than anything. It's no longer a case of people saying: "Ah yes, it's Jordan, a good bunch of blokes, we don't mind them having a few points now and then." The fact is we did a better job than everyone else in very difficult conditions. We've proved we're as good as they are.'

Just like he had been saying all along, in fact.

The high lasted all day, the Green Man pub coping with a lunchtime invasion. There was work to be done, of course, but this was Jordan's day of days. A message from Damon Hill summed it up perfectly.

'Make the most of this win,' he urged. 'It's very, very special. The second win, the third and so on; these are very nice, of course they are. But they're not the first. There isn't the same feeling. Never will be. The next time you will feel like this is when you win the championship. That's the next big one. So enjoy the first win. It's unique. You'll never experience its like again.'

Chapter Thirteen

The Meaning of Life

There was some work done on Tuesday 1 September after all. If the collective headache brought about by an excess of excitement and alcohol was not enough, Ralf Schumacher's manager added to the pain with an alleged remark which was both widely reported and inaccurate.

Plenty of wing. The rear of a Jordan 198 in maximum downforce mode. The question was, which drivers would carry support from Benson and Hedges in 1999?

At 1900 hours, Eddie Jordan felt obliged to issue a brief media release in response. The statement said:

'Jordan Grand Prix refutes any allegations by Ralf Schumacher's manager Willi Weber that it has withdrawn from discussions over 1999. On the contrary, Jordan will vigorously defend the writ issued by Ralf Schumacher in the High Court in London. A hearing is expected in the next ten days.'

The show goes on. Spa was history.

In fact, things were moving very quickly. It was obvious that, come what might, Ralf had decided to leave. Regardless of whether or not the court would find in Jordan's favour, there would be no point in keeping a driver against his will. Eddie would have to take care of the legal dispute while at the same time checking the market for a replacement. It was already late in the season and the choice would be limited.

There was talk of signing Juan-Pablo Montoya, the brash young Colombian who was about to win the Formula 3000 championship. Montoya was also the test driver for Williams, and when it became apparent that he would be tied to Frank for another four years he was no longer an attractive option. Besides, Eddie Jordan had had enough of acting as a nanny for Formula 1 novices only to have them leave after his team had suffered the pain and expense of their inexperience.

Pedro Diniz, on the other hand, did have experience. He also had about $12m in sponsorship, a tidy sum which was tempting for any team. Diniz could best be described as a journeyman, a driver who would do a competent job but without setting the world on fire. Damon, who had driven alongside Diniz at Arrows in 1997, said the Brazilian was underrated. Either way, he was a likely candidate. Except for one thing.

If Jordan did sign Pedro Diniz, the media would immediately assume that Eddie had made the move purely to relieve an average driver of his considerable sponsorship. That, along with the nursery school image, was a perception which Eddie was keen to dispel. Strike Diniz from the list. For the time being.

Jordan switched his attention to Heinz-Harald Frentzen. Here was a driver with more than seventy Grands Prix and one victory to his credit. He had not enjoyed a happy two years with Williams, but Eddie felt he was the very man to help Frentzen rebuild his reputation.

Jordan knew him of old, Heinz-Harald having raced for Eddie Jordan Racing in Formula 3000. He was fast. He was also from Germany, a fact which would sit well with the marketing plans of Benson and Hedges. But he might not be available. The word was that Frentzen was going back to Sauber, the team which had given him his break in Formula 1 in 1994.

Jordan, meanwhile, was in the middle of hectic negotiations with Ralf thanks to the intervention of Bernie Ecclestone. The Formula 1 boss could see that the stand-off between Jordan and Schumacher was not to anyone's benefit, least of all the image of Formula 1. Ecclestone said he would broker a deal and both sides accepted his offer.

Jordan was with his lawyer on the Saturday afternoon following the Belgian weekend. Ecclestone called to say an offer was on the table: take it or leave it. Jordan said he would give the matter some thought. Ecclestone warned him not to delay unnecessarily.

EJ immediately phoned Frentzen's manager, Ortwin Podlech. He learned that the Sauber deal had not been finalized. One particular part in the contract was proving difficult for Sauber. Jordan assured Podlech that he would have no difficulty with the point in question. Clearly, there was still a chance that Frentzen could return to Jordan. Eddie rang Ecclestone and said he would accept the settlement on offer.

It took a further two days to prepare the legal documents for the Schumacher case, the judge granting an extension which allowed the matter to be sorted before it was due in court.

When he finally returned to his headquarters late the following Tuesday, Jordan had agreed terms with Frentzen. Now he had another matter to attend to.

Gary Anderson had finally decided to leave and a press release had to be prepared to their mutual agreement. On the one hand, Jordan had obvious regrets that such a long-standing partnership had finally come to an end. 'On the other,' he said, 'the time comes when you grow apart. Maybe it's a good thing for us both. But he takes our good wishes with him.'

On midday on Wednesday, yet another press release was issued, stating that Ralf would be leaving at the end of the season. Although Eddie would receive suitable financial recompense, he was quietly upset that Ralf was going in the first place. The statement was brief and to the point. Off the record, however, Jordan's remarks carried more substance.

'For a long time, it looked like Ralf would be staying, and everyone was happy about that,' said Eddie. 'But then Michael interfered – just as he seems to have been interfering in everything during the past few weeks. He made statements to the effect that Ralf should go to Williams. We were hurt that Michael, after a year and a half, should suddenly poke his nose into something that was really none of his business and certainly never bothered him before.

'We invested a small fortune in the car and made it competitive. Suddenly, Ralf's name is on everyone's lips and you have to ask what might have become of him if we had not made the investment in technology and improved the car.

'But that's the way life goes. I don't have a problem with it now. It's just that Ralf is one of the nicest people you could ever wish to have driving for you, but I'm not sure what's going to become of him if Michael is going to be forever whispering in his ear. Still, that's Ralf's problem now.'

All that remained was the announcement of Frentzen's signing and confirmation that Damon would be staying for a second season. That would be straightforward enough. Or so everyone believed.

The final release was due to be issued just after midnight on the Wednesday, an unhelpful time for publishing deadlines but one which was necessary from a legal standpoint so as not to appear on the same day as the Schumacher announcement. Pleased with progress, EJ took himself to Anfield to watch a midweek match between Liverpool and Coventry. Shortly before the start of the second half, his mobile phone rang. It was Ian Phillips. Trouble – serious trouble – was afoot in the Hill camp.

The relationship between Jordan Grand Prix and Damon Hill had been a strange one in certain respects. Following the difficulties over the credit card clash (see Chapter 8), Jordan had actually terminated Hill's contract. Damon was effectively working on a race-by-race, test-by-test basis.

On the Tuesday after the Belgian Grand Prix, Ian Phillips heard a whisper that British American Tobacco had been impressed by the media coverage given to Hill. Phillips' source said that an edict had been issued to 'get Damon Hill on board, whatever it costs'.

Phillips quickly withdrew Jordan's allegation of breach and reinstated Hill's contract, a move which would stop any hasty actions which Damon might later regret. Jordan's plan had been for continuity with Hill and, on paper, it seemed straightforward enough. Both sides had been willing to go ahead. But something was amiss.

Phillips's suspicions were aroused on the Wednesday before the Italian Grand Prix. Hill was not taking calls and his solicitor, Michael Breen, was unavailable.

Jordan gave their sponsors superb exposure in Belgium.

Phillips then passed on his concern to Jordan at Anfield. It was a major worry since the announcement was due to be made the next day at Monza.

Phillips and Jordan flew to Italy knowing that there was trouble afoot, but unable to say precisely what it would be. It soon became clear that Hill had been understandably unsettled by an absurd story – apparently from an 'unimpeachable source' within Formula 1 – that Jordan Grand Prix was in financial difficulties. The story was completely without foundation but Hill, as a precaution, said he would require some form of financial guarantee.

By now, further rumours had reached Phillips to the effect that British American Racing had already prepared a news release announcing that Damon Hill would be joining Jacques Villeneuve in 1999 – for a fee of $9.5 million with $3.5 million in bonus payments! As far as the new team was concerned, the deal was done. Or so they said.

As far as Jordan and Phillips were concerned, this was dangerous mischief-making by someone in the paddock. Nigel Northridge of Benson and Hedges was due to arrive that night in the expectation that his company's star performer had been confirmed. Jordan and Phillips remained confident that would happen. Nevertheless, thanks to the rumours, this was an anxious time for the team principals and their man Nigel Griffiths, whose principal role was sponsorship liaison with Benson and Hedges.

By a stroke of good fortune, the sales and marketing director for B&H had brought two guests who happened to be lawyers. Rather than enjoying a weekend off at the race, the legal experts found that their services were required by Northridge as assurances were hammered out. It took until 11 a.m. on Friday morning before Hill and Breen were satisfied. Damon would be staying for 1999 – just as he had confirmed at an FIA press conference the previous day. But it had been a close call, closer than anyone outside the Jordan enclosure had imagined.

Northridge's blood had run cold at the thought of Hill going elsewhere. The victory at Spa had merely served to underline Damon's popularity and his value to a sponsor, something which Benson and Hedges had begun to appreciate more fully at the launch of the car in January.

'Watching Damon at the launch was wonderful,' recalled Northridge. 'He did about forty interviews, and finding something different to say is a masterful skill. It was a fantastic day and when we sat in the Albert Hall I expected the team to win a race in 1998. I went into the season believing that because everyone kept telling me it was possible. It didn't take long to realize that finishing, never mind winning, was going to be a problem.'

Northridge knew all about the vagaries of motor racing thanks to an involvement, through the Silk Cut brand, with the Jaguar sportscar team in the 1980s. This had been a departure from the usual sporting sponsorship ethos of the parent company, Gallaher. The preferred method had been to support an event rather than a team; with the latter, you could be on the losing side more readily than being associated with the winner. Nonetheless, market research had shown clearly that few sports had the same reach among adult smokers as Formula 1. Having decided to move along that route, the question was: with which team?

'The problem with Silk Cut Jaguar was that we had been too successful, too soon,' said Northridge. 'We won the World Championship immediately. So, what do you do for an encore? It becomes very difficult. What you really want is a team that will go from fifth, to fourth, and so on, to first. You can't orchestrate something like that, but we felt Eddie Jordan would provide the best opportunity. He was on the cusp, banging on the door.'

The first year, 1996, had been spent understanding Formula 1 and appreciating how everything worked. Part of the learning process had been the realization that a gold colour scheme did not make the cars stand out. A change to bright yellow would not only solve that problem but also keep in line with a desire to make Jordan the most talked about team in 1997.

'One of the things Benson and Hedges has been noted for in any form of marketing we've done is an ability to stand out from the crowd,' said Northridge. 'We feel that novelty is very, very important. We were looking for innovative design and that's how the snake emblem came into being. Eddie didn't like it at first but he could soon see the value of the snake as pictures of the Jordan began to appear everywhere. We had encouraged that by working very closely with the drivers and developing relationships by bringing editors and top writers to the races.

'For 1998, we had Damon. There is no doubt that the man is idolized across the UK, added to which he's a really, really nice guy. When you've put together components like that, then there really is a good chance of success.'

The season had barely reached one-third distance when the team's expectations took their steepest dive at Monaco. Northridge admits he was as depressed about the situation as anyone else. 'The important thing was to sit down with Eddie and talk about why this had happened and try to ensure that we overcame

it as quickly as we could. It's very difficult for us to play a huge role in something like this, other than being always available to talk to Eddie when needed.

'The one thing we could say at that stage was that we had absolutely no thoughts about withdrawing. There was a lot of rumour at the time but Eddie knew that we understood the fundamental necessity that you've got to be in this game for the long haul; you have to work through those troubles.

'We did have our own concerns and I think that talking to Eddie about them was important because he needed to understand the pressure we were all under. But the one thing I could continue to do under the circumstances was give him even more support when he needed it most. I had to make sure he realized that there was no need to be concerned about Benson and Hedges making an instant decision which everyone would later regret.'

Northridge reported directly to his Chairman, Peter Wilson. Unlike spectators and the motor sport media, the sponsors were looking beyond mere results. The B&H sponsorship strategy was formed in association with M&C Saatchi, the advertising agency; it understood the culture of Gallaher and, through a Saatchi sponsorship director, Dave Marren, the intricacies of motor sport.

Six-footers both, Northridge and Marren made an imposing sight when on parade at the B&H motorhome. Northridge hailed from County Down, Marren from Dublin and the gentle Irish sense of humour could be called upon to provide relief in difficult times.

When discussing a proposed new scheme for the car earlier in the year, Marren had produced an official-looking set of spoof drawings with a World War II theme. Hill was depicted as the British chappie in a Spitfire, the nose of his Jordan bearing the spitting exhausts of the Merlin engine, a scarf painted on the side and streaming in the breeze from a cockpit with RAF roundels on the side. Ralf's car carried the German swastika and other trappings of the Luftwaffe. Hill's racing overalls were depicted as battle fatigues. Ralf wore a square crash helmet with a spike rising from the top.

When the subject of car livery came up at a formal meeting with Jordan, Marren, with a straight face, slid the drawings across the table and waited for Eddie's reaction. 'This is something really different,' said Marren. 'Never been done before. It's really good. We think you'll like it.'

As Northridge came close to chewing his fist in order to suppress laughter, Jordan examined the drawings, his expression a growing mixture of bewilderment and surprise. He said nothing as he sifted through the sheets. Then he came to the spike on Schumacher's helmet. 'That's the really clever bit,' said Marren, deadpan. 'That's the radio antenna.'

Jordan, for once in his life, was speechless as he worked out ways of asking his sponsors if they had lost their senses completely. Then came a volley of Irish abuse from EJ as Northridge and Marren could contain themselves no longer and collapsed in a heap.

Jordan had done a lot of laughing and talking since Spa. One way or another, it had been a hectic two weeks; the victory celebration followed by nonstop wheeling and dealing, all of which had gone his way. Jordan had been enervated by the intense bargaining almost as much as the success on the track. Perhaps more so, such was the thrill of chasing down 'the deal'.

He continued to be the centre of attention at the Jordan press breakfast on Friday morning at Monza, a healthy turnout of journalists indicating the team's newsworthiness as well as its relaxed mood. Those in the media unfamiliar with the ways of Formula 1 were surprised to see Ralf smiling and joshing with Jordan and Phillips as he passed their table.

'Never mind,' said Phillips to Schumacher, 'you've got three chances to win your first Grand Prix – in the next four years!' – a reference not to Schumacher's remaining three races with Jordan but to the fact that his new employers, Williams, might offer only a limited chance of winning in the seasons to come. As the banter continued, there was clearly no ill-feeling here despite the legal manoeuvrings of the past week.

'It was something both sides had to do, a formality really,' explained Phillips. 'It's cleared the air. Now everyone knows where they stand.'

Indeed, there had been talk of Jordan having the fabrication shop make an imitation Oscar which was to have been presented to whoever gave the best performance in the witness box in court. The settlement ruled that out, of course, but Phillips was deeply offended when Schumacher and Weber said the award should have gone to the team's Commercial Director.

'How can they say that?' asked Phillips. 'I've seen the documents prepared in evidence by Ralf and Willi and read the things they said. Bill Clinton couldn't have done a better job. They've got a bloody nerve!'

Regardless of which side was being more economical with the truth than the other, it was clear that an enormous weight had been lifted from Ralf's shoulders.

'Just watch him go,' said Jordan. 'He feels he has a point to prove after Spa. Damon's going to have to work hard this weekend.'

Full protection. Sparco flameproof overalls are proved for the pit crew, giving the sponsors even more coverage and a source of revenue for the mechanics at the season's end.

Both drivers were looking forward to trying out modifications to the side pods of the cars, this the latest work from Gascoyne in the wind tunnel. The fact that the revisions worked efficiently was evidenced by a strong performance, just as Jordan had predicted, from Ralf as he qualified sixth. Damon's fourteenth place on the grid – due to a mistake on his best lap – was not a fair reflection of his confidence in the car. Once again, Jordan Grand Prix was serious about a good result on race day.

No one was misguided enough to talk about winning but the aim now was to join the battle between Williams and Benetton for third place in the Constructors' Championship. With Villeneuve on the front row alongside Schumacher's pole-position Ferrari, that would be difficult. But at least the Benettons were stuck between Ralf and Damon on the grid.

The plan was for Hill to overtake Fisichella, Wurz, and anyone else he could manage, in the early stages of the race by employing the previously successful tactic of starting with a light load of fuel and making an early stop. The race scheme worked perfectly, Hill gaining places as the race went on.

Ralf had been in fifth place for most of the way, moving into fourth when Villeneuve spun out and then assuming third when Hakkinen dropped back with brake trouble. That made it two podiums in a row for Ralf and Jordan's day was complete when Damon's hard work rewarded him and the team with a valuable point for sixth place.

Here was proof – if it was needed – that Belgium had not been a fluke result. Jordan was indeed a force to be reckoned with. By the end of the season, fourth place for Hill in Japan would ensure that the team took fourth in the constructors' championship, their best result since starting Formula 1 eight seasons before. It marked a truly remarkable comeback. The Italian Grand Prix had been the sixth race in succession in which Jordan Mugen-Honda had scored points. Not two months before, it had celebrated a single solitary point at Silverstone as if it was the high point of the season. With the team on such a seemingly unstoppable charge, it was difficult to equate the two occasions.

If making a connection between two motor races was tricky, then drawing a comparison with events in the outside world was often an impossible task. It has been written that motor racing people are focused on their job and insulated from reality to such an extent that World War III could break out and no one in Formula 1 would notice. Images have been drawn of racing people, isolated from the horror of the real world, emerging from the paddock to express surprise at finding the surrounding countryside devastated and the nearest town reduced to a smouldering ruin.

That analogy was drawn in 1968. The advent of cable television means that every team now has the latest news from home beamed daily into the paddock. Sometimes the pictures are so shocking that the multimillion-pound business which surrounds those engaged in Formula 1 can seem shamefully irrelevant. Race morning in Hungary had been one such occasion.

The news of the Omagh bomb had stunned the Hungaroring paddock just as much as anywhere else in the world where decent people gathered and attempted to understand this latest atrocity. The sense of futility and helplessness was felt keenly at Jordan given the Irish presence within the team: Eddie Jordan, Gary Anderson, Mark Gallagher, Nigel Northridge, Dave Marren, Richard O'Driscoll. Added to which, Damon Hill lived near Dublin and Michael Breen came from Belfast. There was nothing that could be said. Nothing that could be done. Or so it seemed.

A few days later, Jordan received letters from the neighbour of a young boy, Alister Hall, and the surgeon who had operated on his appalling injuries. Alister had lost a leg but the first thing he wanted to know on his return to consciousness was how the Jordan team had got on during qualifying. It would help lift his spirits, they said, if Jordan could send a small memento.

EJ had a lump in his throat as he read the letters. He resolved to do far more than simply send an autographed cap.

Jordan's friendship with the Irish golfer Darren Clarke led to Eddie and Damon taking part in a charity VIP game on the Monday following the Italian Grand Prix. Thinking of the letters, EJ knew this was too good an opportunity to miss while in Ireland. A de Zille helicopter was arranged to fly Eddie and Damon from the golf course to the Altnagelvin Hospital, a major facility which overlooks the City of Derry and, perforce, has become expert at dealing with the victims of terrorism.

It was to be a low-key visit with strictly no publicity. It was also to be a surprise for Alister. Part of the car park was cleared to allow the helicopter to land. The entire place was buzzing since memories of Damon's victory at Spa were still fresh.

But this was not about Jordan Grand Prix or the exploits of the country's favourite Formula 1 driver. It was about those who were quietly battling in a harder and more private race. Hill and Jordan, family men both, left Altnagelvin deeply moved. What was a mere struggle for victory in motor sport compared to this?

Chapter Fourteen

A Tick in
the Box

'When you go into a sponsorship association with Eddie

Jordan, you get two opportunities. You get the car and

the character. And sometimes I think the car is easier to

run than the character . . . '

Nigel Northridge said those words at the end of a tricky season with the Jordan Mugen-Honda 198. But he was smiling as he spoke. Sign up with Eddie Jordan and you know that the association will not conform to the usual commercial relationship between sponsor and performer. Edmund Jordan is a law unto himself – and that's part of the deal.

It always was from the moment the boy from Bray in County Wicklow hit the streets and saw the world as a place to be used and enjoyed. He was into everything that might turn a reasonably honest shilling. You name it and Eddie could move it on for a small profit. But the trick was, his customers would believe he was doing it solely for their benefit.

It didn't matter about product knowledge. If there was a market, then Jordan was the master of his temporary trade. He would buy smoked salmon which had recently reached the end of its shelf-life, remove the sell-by date and flog the salmon to sloshed fans who were not quite at their sharpest after a soccer match or a rugby international at Lansdowne Road. When ordered to move on by the police, Jordan would do exactly as he was told and simply switch to another gate.

A job in the Camden Street branch of the Bank of Ireland in Dublin brought him into contact with customers looking for loans to buy second-hand cars. Not only would Jordan arrange the finance, he would have access – 'would you believe this for a piece of luck' – to the exact sort of car they were looking for. Or, at least, he would after a quick scan of the classifieds or a call to a few dealers, the motor – 'a lovely car, this; wouldn't mind keeping it meself' – then being transferred to the proud new owner.

On Sundays, he would switch to carpets. These were off-cuts for which the Dublin Carpet Mills had no further use. Jordan would sell them either from his car on the edge of the road or from a friend's stall in Dandelion Market. The boss of the carpet company was so impressed by Jordan's enterprise and success that he gave away the off-cuts for nothing. Typically, Jordan later tapped the man for sponsorship in Formula Ford.

By then, Jordan had been to Jersey and back, the result of a lull in banking business in Ireland due to a strike by officials. While he was there, he saw a kart race for the first time and was immediately attracted by this form of racing. Nothing would do but for him to have a go. And the rest, as they say, is history.

Jordan brought the motor sport bug back with him to Ireland, became champion in karting and began to move through Formula Ford, Formula 3 and into Formula

Atlantic. He was good enough to earn a test drive in a McLaren Formula 1 car. But that was as far as it went. He was competent rather than outstanding. Put another way, he was a potential champion in wheeling and dealing, but not in driving.

By the time he had decided to run drivers rather than race against them, Jordan had married and was living in England, the only place to be if motor sport was to become a career. It was a big step for Eddie and Marie in more than just the geographical sense. Their first child, Zoe, had been born. To help make ends meet, Marie had taken a job as a packer at a local factory. When they moved to a slightly larger house, there was room to take in lodgers, usually hopeful drivers wanting a roof over their heads while waiting to go racing at the weekends. Motor sport was now a vital part of the Jordan lifestyle.

Jordan formed his own team and won championships at every level as he moved up to Formula 3000, regarded as the final step to Grand Prix racing. When he won the Formula 3000 title with Jean Alesi in 1989, there was nowhere to go but up. Gambling hugely, Eddie laid plans for Jordan Grand Prix and entered Formula 1 in 1991.

That period seemed to belong to a different era as he sat in one of his motorhomes at the Nurburgring in September 1998 and reflected on one of the wildest and most emotional seasons of his life. Having hit rock bottom at Monaco, his team had scaled the absolute heights in Belgium. Jordan had never known anything like it.

'The launch of the new car was fantastic,' he said. 'The hype was massive, the team looked great, there was a lot of excitement.

'The initial feeling for the car was good but, by the second or third test, Damon said he wasn't so sure. It then became more and more obvious that there were some serious question marks.

'I have to admit that I became more and more depressed. My mind was some-what scrambled – although I didn't let on to many people. I couldn't. I had to keep the motivation of the team up and yet I knew there were some internal problems which needed sorting out.

'The competitiveness of the car was a real worry. Goodyear were not showing that well compared to Bridgestone but we didn't have any real clout because our car wasn't quick enough. Our relationship with Honda was in its early stages. Naturally, they wanted to see how good we were in terms of reliability and so on before they would push the boat out. So, all in all, this was hanging over me like a cloud.

'Monaco was the down side. On the other hand, you could also say it was the best thing that ever happened. It was so bad that I had to really roll up my sleeves and get stuck in. I had to say: "This has to happen and that has to happen. Sorry, but there can be no argument."

'One of the things I needed to change was the structure at the top end of the team. I'd like to think that we are a very democratic company. Some people might construe that as a ponderous way of going about things but, when a clear decision has to be made, then it's made. But I like to make sure that everyone has their say and everything is evaluated first.

'So, these were big decisions for me, not just from the commercial or financial point of view, but at a personal level. There is a strong human element within Jordan, and that makes it tough.

'Gary, for instance, didn't necessarily agree with the proposed structure. But it had to go ahead. Some people may have thought that we should have split earlier than we did. I feel comfortable that the time was absolutely right. The parting was very amicable indeed and we are back to the same level of friendship we had ten years ago – which is remarkable when you think about what we have been through this season.'

Jordan was fortunate that Marie had been present at Monaco. A former basketball player for Ireland, with a sharp mathematical mind to boot, Marie has the ideal credentials when it comes to understanding the thinking of her husband and the pressures of his business. Marie had lived the traumas with Eddie to the point of developing spots on her hands when he gambled everything by moving into Formula 1. The nadir of Monaco was just another battle to be won and Marie's firm but gentle authority and compassion was the perfect foil for a man whose seemingly inexhaustible enthusiasm was coming dangerously close to running dry.

'I said to Marie that I'd probably had enough,' recalls Eddie. 'I said that I'd tried my best. I'd won in every single formula I had contested, either as a driver or as an entrant, and I'd thought I could do it in Formula 1. I didn't think I'd failed because I had given it my best shot. But at that precise moment the light at the end of the tunnel had become very dim.

'We talked about taking on a partner to help give me the encouragement to carry on and move forward. I felt that maybe I was doing this wrong. I wondered why I didn't have investment from either an engine manufacturer or a financial partner to strengthen the structure of the company. After thirty years of taking the risk, the burden begins to grind you down.

'Of course, at times like that, you are supposed to sit back and think: "Life's not that bad, really. I wouldn't have had all of this working in a bank." But you don't think like that. When things aren't going right, you think of companies which you have seen crumble in the past, companies which were once strong but became victims of a recession or whatever. You think how that might affect you.

'Then I began to look at it in a more positive light and began thinking about what needed to be done. And you have seen the results since.

'But I do think that a partner inside Jordan can only make the team stronger. If we're going to win the championship then we are going to need a bit more financial muscle. That's not a reflection on our present sponsorship because there is no question we wouldn't be where we are today without Benson and Hedges. They have been massively supportive and shown the ultimate confidence in us by increasing their contract with Jordan by another two years.'

The flicker at the end of the tunnel may have become difficult to see but the vote of confidence by B&H helped strengthen its glow. Within three months, it would be a blinding light which would bathe the entire team as it emerged from the darkness after eight years. Eddie's only regret was that Marie had not been at Spa to see it.

'We've been married for twenty years and we were together for two years before that,' says Eddie. 'So Marie has been exposed to motor racing all that time. I don't know if she does it deliberately or not, but when I bring home discussion about business there always seems to be some mention of what's happening to the kids, or perhaps the latest curtain material she has bought. Marie will talk about a very wide choice of subjects. She won't dwell on motor racing for very long, not because she doesn't like it, but because she knows I'm exposed to it on a continual basis. We will talk about virtually everything else and I think that's nice. It keeps a sense of proportion.'

If Marie fails to keep Eddie's head straight then a call to Dublin at around eight o'clock every morning is guaranteed to keep his feet on the ground. Jordan rings his mother, Eileen, without fail. The call may be brief, lasting just long enough to ensure that 'me Ma' is OK. Or it might go on for half an hour. But it happens on a daily basis, from Melbourne to Monaco, from office to home to mobile phone.

Mrs Jordan takes no nonsense. She knows her boy well, since they are similar characters. Eddie's father, Paddy, was altogether different, an accountant with the Electricity Board who preferred a quiet pint and no fuss.

Eileen Jordan's sprightly presence and sharp mind belies the fact that she was born in 1916, a time when Ireland was about to enter just as much turmoil as it was to see several decades later. If Eddie has any views on the political and religious divide which has torn his country apart, he keeps them to himself. Working in such a cosmopolitan business, and with colleagues from both sides of the Irish border, he has always taken the wider view which, happily, has become the prevailing one in the corridors of power. All Jordan will say – loudly – is that he is Irish, and very proud of it.

Ireland is proud of him too. Eddie Jordan is the archetypal Irishman, a first-rate ambassador, an endearing mixture of infuriating habits and engaging charm. As Michael O'Carroll, an executive producer of sport for Irish television, put it so succinctly: 'He has the ability to shake your hand and at the same time tell you to fuck off.'

It's true. Jordan says it with a twinkle in his eye and it matters little who he is addressing. The fact is, he gets away with it and people seem to love him all the more. He is one of the boys, a David among the motor racing Goliaths.

When his team finished first and second at Spa, Eddie Jordan's place in Irish sporting history was secure. He is now mentioned in the same breath as Ron Delaney winning the 1,500 metres at the 1956 Olympics in Melbourne and Ireland defeating Italy in a round of the 1994 World Cup. That's how important the 1998 Belgian Grand Prix was to Jordan's home country.

'I was in the Czech Republic a few weeks later,' said Eddie. 'I was absolutely overwhelmed by the number of people who knew about that race. It's the same everywhere I go. Quite unbelievable.

'But the great thing is that we did it in style. That has always been Jordan's hallmark. I would have hated to have never got beyond everyone saying: "Jordan is only interested in the rock 'n' roll, the razzmatazz, girls on the grid, snakes on the car and stuff like that. Jordan's not serious." Well, now they know.

'We've had our imprimatur, if you like. A tick against the box which asks: "Have you won a Grand Prix?" That means everything to me. Trouble is, I won't stop now until I win the championship.'

So, more rock 'n' roll, then?

'Absolutely!'

Statistics

Compiled by Nick Henry

JORDAN GRAND PRIX RACING TEAM – STATISTICS 1991

		GRID	RESULT*
Round 1 – United States Grand Prix, Phoenix, Arizona			
10th March			
Bertrand Gachot	Jordan 191–Ford HB V8	14th	10th*
Andrea de Cesaris	Jordan 191–Ford HB V8	NPQ	–

* – classified but not running at the finish

		GRID	RESULT
Round 2 – Brazilian Grand Prix – Interlagos, São Paulo			
24th March			
Bertrand Gachot	Jordan 191–Ford HB V8	10th	13th*
Andrea de Cesaris	Jordan 191–Ford HB V8	13th	R

* – classified but not running at the finish

		GRID	RESULT
Round 3 – San Marino Grand Prix – Imola, Italy			
28th April			
Bertrand Gachot	Jordan 191–Ford HB V8	12th	R
Andrea de Cesaris	Jordan 191–Ford HB V8	11th	R

		GRID	RESULT
Round 4 – Monaco Grand Prix – Monte Carlo			
12th May			
Bertrand Gachot	Jordan 191–Ford HB V8	24th	8th
Andrea de Cesaris	Jordan 191–Ford HB V8	10th	R

*KEY: R=retired, NS=did not start, DQ=disqualified, NQ=did not qualify, NPQ=did not pre-qualify

Round 5 – Canadian Grand Prix – Montreal
2nd June

Bertrand Gachot	Jordan 191–Ford HB V8	14th	5th
Andrea de Cesaris	Jordan 191–Ford HB V8	11th	4th

Round 6 – Mexican Grand Prix – Mexico City
16th June

Bertrand Gachot	Jordan 191–Ford HB V8	20th	R
Andrea de Cesaris	Jordan 191–Ford HB V8	11th	4th

Round 7 – French Grand Prix – Magny-Cours
7th July

Bertrand Gachot	Jordan 191–Ford HB V8	19th	R
Andrea de Cesaris	Jordan 191–Ford HB V8	13th	6th

Round 8 – British Grand Prix – Silverstone
14th July

Bertrand Gachot	Jordan 191–Ford HB V8	17th	6th
Andrea de Cesaris	Jordan 191–Ford HB V8	13th	R

Round 9 – German Grand Prix – Hockenheim
28th July

Bertrand Gachot	Jordan 191–Ford HB V8	11th	6th
Andrea de Cesaris	Jordan 191–Ford HB V8	7th	5th

Round 10 – Hungarian Grand Prix – Hungaroring, Budapest
11th August

Bertrand Gachot	Jordan 191–Ford HB V8	16th	9th
Andrea de Cesaris	Jordan 191–Ford HB V8	17th	7th

Round 11 – Belgian Grand Prix – Spa-Francorchamps
25th August

Michael Schumacher	Jordan 191–Ford HB V8	7th	R
Andrea de Cesaris	Jordan 191–Ford HB V8	11th	13th*

* – classified but not running at the finish

Round 12 – Italian Grand Prix – Monza
8th September

| Roberto Moreno | Jordan 191–Ford HB V8 | 9th | R |
| Andrea de Cesaris | Jordan 191–Ford HB V8 | 14th | 7th |

Round 13 – Portuguese Grand Prix – Estoril
22nd September

| Roberto Moreno | Jordan 191–Ford HB V8 | 16th | 10th |
| Andrea de Cesaris | Jordan 191–Ford HB V8 | 14th | 8th |

Round 14 – Spanish Grand Prix – Barcelona
29th September

| Alessandro Zanardi | Jordan 191–Ford HB V8 | 20th | 9th |
| Andrea de Cesaris | Jordan 191–Ford HB V8 | 17th | R |

Round 15 – Japanese Grand Prix – Suzuka
20th October

| Alessandro Zanardi | Jordan 191–Ford HB V8 | 13th | R |
| Andrea de Cesaris | Jordan 191–Ford HB V8 | 11th | R |

Round 16 – Australian Grand Prix – Adelaide
3rd November

| Alessandro Zanardi | Jordan 191–Ford HB V8 | 16th | 9th |
| Andrea de Cesaris | Jordan 191–Ford HB V8 | 12th | 8th |

1991 Final Championship Positions
Drivers

| Andrea de Cesaris | 9 pts | 9th place |
| Bertrand Gachot | 4 pts | 12th= place |

Constructors

| Jordan | 13 pts | 5th place |

JORDAN GRAND PRIX RACING TEAM – STATISTICS 1992

Round 1 – South African Grand Prix – Kyalami
1st March

Stefano Modena	Jordan 192–Yamaha 0X99 V10	NQ	–
Mauricio Gugelmin	Jordan 192–Yamaha 0X99 V10	23rd	11th

Round 2 – Mexican Grand Prix – Mexico City
22nd March

Stefano Modena	Jordan 192–Yamaha 0X99 V10	15th*	R
Mauricio Gugelmin	Jordan 192–Yamaha 0X99 V10	8th	R

* – started from the pit lane

Round 3 – Brazilian Grand Prix – Interlagos, São Paulo
5th April

Stefano Modena	Jordan 192–Yamaha 0X99 V10	12th	R
Mauricio Gugelmin	Jordan 192–Yamaha 0X99 V10	21st	R

Round 4 – Spanish Grand Prix – Barcelona
3rd May

Stefano Modena	Jordan 192–Yamaha 0X99 V10	NQ	–
Mauricio Gugelmin	Jordan 192–Yamaha 0X99 V10	17th	R

Round 5 – San Marino Grand Prix – Imola, Italy
17th May

Stefano Modena	Jordan 192–Yamaha 0X99 V10	23rd*	R
Mauricio Gugelmin	Jordan 192–Yamaha 0X99 V10	18th	7th

* – started from the pit lane

Round 6 – Monaco Grand Prix – Monte Carlo
31st May

Stefano Modena	Jordan 192–Yamaha 0X99 V10	21st	R
Mauricio Gugelmin	Jordan 192–Yamaha 0X99 V10	13th	R

Round 7 – Canadian Grand Prix – Montreal
14th June

Stefano Modena	Jordan 192–Yamaha 0X99 V10	17th*	R
Mauricio Gugelmin	Jordan 192–Yamaha 0X99 V10	24th	R

* – started from the back of the grid

Round 8 – French Grand Prix – Magny-Cours
5th July

Stefano Modena	Jordan 192–Yamaha 0X99 V10	20th	R
Mauricio Gugelmin	Jordan 192–Yamaha 0X99 V10	24th	R

Round 9 – British Grand Prix – Silverstone
12th July

Stefano Modena	Jordan 192–Yamaha 0X99 V10	23rd	R
Mauricio Gugelmin	Jordan 192–Yamaha 0X99 V10	24th	R

Round 10 – German Grand Prix – Hockenheim
26th July

Stefano Modena	Jordan 192–Yamaha 0X99 V10	NQ	–
Mauricio Gugelmin	Jordan 192–Yamaha 0X99 V10	23rd	15th

Round 11 – Hungarian Grand Prix – Hungaroring, Budapest
16th August

Stefano Modena	Jordan 192–Yamaha 0X99 V10	24th	R
Mauricio Gugelmin	Jordan 192–Yamaha 0X99 V10	21st	10th

Round 12 – Belgian Grand Prix – Spa-Francorchamps
30th August

Stefano Modena	Jordan 192–Yamaha 0X99 V10	17th	15th
Mauricio Gugelmin	Jordan 192–Yamaha 0X99 V10	24th	14th

Round 13 – Italian Grand Prix – Monza
13th September

Stefano Modena	Jordan 192–Yamaha 0X99 V10	NQ	–
Mauricio Gugelmin	Jordan 192–Yamaha 0X99 V10	26th	R

Round 14 – Portuguese Grand Prix – Estoril
27th September

| Stefano Modena | Jordan 192–Yamaha 0X99 V10 | 24th | 13th |
| Mauricio Gugelmin | Jordan 192–Yamaha 0X99 V10 | 20th | R |

Round 15 – Japanese Grand Prix – Suzuka
25th October

| Stefano Modena | Jordan 192–Yamaha 0X99 V10 | 17th | 7th |
| Mauricio Gugelmin | Jordan 192–Yamaha 0X99 V10 | 25th | R |

Round 16 – Australian Grand Prix – Adelaide
8th November

| Stefano Modena | Jordan 192–Yamaha 0X99 V10 | 15th | 6th |
| Mauricio Gugelmin | Jordan 192–Yamaha 0X99 V10 | 20th | R |

1992 Final Championship Positions
Drivers

| Stefano Modena | 1 pt | 17th= place |

Constructors

| Jordan | 1 pt | 11th= place |

JORDAN GRAND PRIX RACING TEAM – STATISTICS 1993

Round 1 – South African Grand Prix – Kyalami
14th March

| Rubens Barrichello | Jordan 193–Hart 1035 V10 | 14th | R |
| Ivan Capelli | Jordan 193–Hart 1035 V10 | 18th | R |

Round 2 – Brazilian Grand Prix – Interlagos, São Paulo
28th March

| Rubens Barrichello | Jordan 193–Hart 1035 V10 | 14th | R |
| Ivan Capelli | Jordan 193–Hart 1035 V10 | NQ | – |

Round 3 – European Grand Prix – Donington Park, England
11th April

Rubens Barrichello	Jordan 193–Hart 1035 V10	12th	10*
Thierry Boutsen	Jordan 193–Hart 1035 V10	19th	R

* – classified but not running at finish

Round 4 – San Marino Grand Prix – Imola, Italy
25th April

Rubens Barrichello	Jordan 193–Hart 1035 V10	13th	R
Thierry Boutsen	Jordan 193–Hart 1035 V10	19th	R

Round 5 – Spanish Grand Prix – Barcelona
9th May

Rubens Barrichello	Jordan 193–Hart 1035 V10	17th	12th
Thierry Boutsen	Jordan 193–Hart 1035 V10	21st	11th

Round 6 – Monaco Grand Prix – Monte Carlo
23rd May

Rubens Barrichello	Jordan 193–Hart 1035 V10	16th	9th
Thierry Boutsen	Jordan 193–Hart 1035 V10	23rd	R

Round 7 – Canadian Grand Prix – Montreal
13th June

Rubens Barrichello	Jordan 193–Hart 1035 V10	14th	R
Thierry Boutsen	Jordan 193–Hart 1035 V10	24th	12th

Round 8 – French Grand Prix – Magny-Cours
4th July

Rubens Barrichello	Jordan 193–Hart 1035 V10	8th	7th
Thierry Boutsen	Jordan 193–Hart 1035 V10	20th	11th

Round 9 – British Grand Prix – Silverstone
11th July

Rubens Barrichello	Jordan 193–Hart 1035 V10	15th	10th
Thierry Boutsen	Jordan 193–Hart 1035 V10	23rd	R

Round 10 – German Grand Prix – Hockenheim
25th July

Rubens Barrichello	Jordan 193–Hart 1035 V10	17th	R
Thierry Boutsen	Jordan 193–Hart 1035 V10	24th	13th

Round 11 – Hungarian Grand Prix – Hungaroring, Budapest
15th August

Rubens Barrichello	Jordan 193–Hart 1035 V10	16th	R
Thierry Boutsen	Jordan 193–Hart 1035 V10	24th	9th

Round 12 – Belgian Grand Prix – Spa-Francorchamps
29th August

Rubens Barrichello	Jordan 193–Hart 1035 V10	13th	R
Thierry Boutsen	Jordan 193–Hart 1035 V10	20th	R

Round 13 – Italian Grand Prix – Monza
12th September

Rubens Barrichello	Jordan 193–Hart 1035 V10	19th	R
Marco Apicella	Jordan 193–Hart 1035 V10	23rd	R

Round 14 – Portuguese Grand Prix – Estoril
26th September

Rubens Barrichello	Jordan 193–Hart 1035 V10	15th	13th
Emanuele Naspetti	Jordan 193–Hart 1035 V10	23rd	R

Round 15 – Japanese Grand Prix – Suzuka
24th October

Rubens Barrichello	Jordan 193–Hart 1035 V10	12th	5th
Eddie Irvine	Jordan 193–Hart 1035 V10	8th	6th

Round 16 – Australian Grand Prix – Adelaide
7th November

Rubens Barrichello	Jordan 193–Hart 1035 V10	13th	11th
Eddie Irvine	Jordan 193–Hart 1035 V10	19th*	R

* – started from the back of the grid

1993 Final Championship Positions

Drivers

Rubens Barrichello	2 pts	17th= place
Eddie Irvine	1 pt	20th= place

Constructors

Jordan	3 pts	10th= place

JORDAN GRAND PRIX RACING TEAM – STATISTICS 1994

Round 1 – Brazilian Grand Prix – Interlagos, São Paulo
27th March

Rubens Barrichello	Jordan 194–Hart 1035 V10	14th	4th
Eddie Irvine	Jordan 194–Hart 1035 V10	16th	R

Round 2 – Pacific Grand Prix – TI Circuit, Aida, Japan
17th April

Rubens Barrichello	Jordan 194–Hart 1035 V10	8th	3rd
Aguri Suzuki	Jordan 194–Hart 1035 V10	20th	R

Round 3 – San Marino Grand Prix – Imola, Italy
1st May

Rubens Barrichello	Jordan 194–Hart 1035 V10	NQ	–
Andrea de Cesaris	Jordan 194–Hart 1035 V10	21st	R

Round 4 – Monaco Grand Prix – Monte Carlo
15th May

Rubens Barrichello	Jordan 194–Hart 1035 V10	15th	R
Andrea de Cesaris	Jordan 194–Hart 1035 V10	14th	4th

Round 5 – Spanish Grand Prix – Barcelona
29th May

Rubens Barrichello	Jordan 194–Hart 1035 V10	5th	R
Eddie Irvine	Jordan 194–Hart 1035 V10	13th	6th

Round 6 – Canadian Grand Prix – Montreal
12th June

Rubens Barrichello	Jordan 194–Hart 1035 V10	6th	7th
Eddie Irvine	Jordan 194–Hart 1035 V10	8th	R

Round 7 – French Grand Prix – Magny-Cours
3rd July

Rubens Barrichello	Jordan 194–Hart 1035 V10	7th	R
Eddie Irvine	Jordan 194–Hart 1035 V10	6th	R

Round 8 – British Grand Prix – Silverstone
10th July

Rubens Barrichello	Jordan 194–Hart 1035 V10	6th	4th*
Eddie Irvine	Jordan 194–Hart 1035 V10	12th	NS

* – after M. Schumacher's disqualification

Round 9 – German Grand Prix – Hockenheim
31st July

Rubens Barrichello	Jordan 194–Hart 1035 V10	11th	R
Eddie Irvine	Jordan 194–Hart 1035 V10	10th	R

Round 10 – Hungarian Grand Prix – Hungaroring, Budapest
14th August

Rubens Barrichello	Jordan 194–Hart 1035 V10	10th	R
Eddie Irvine	Jordan 194–Hart 1035 V10	7th	R

Round 11 – Belgian Grand Prix – Spa-Francorchamps
28th August

Rubens Barrichello	Jordan 194–Hart 1035 V10	1st	R
Eddie Irvine	Jordan 194–Hart 1035 V10	4th	13th*

* – classified but not running at finish

Round 12 – Italian Grand Prix – Monza
11th September

| Rubens Barrichello | Jordan 194–Hart 1035 V10 | 16th | 4th |
| Eddie Irvine | Jordan 194–Hart 1035 V10 | 9th | R |

Round 13 – Portuguese Grand Prix – Estoril
25th September

| Rubens Barrichello | Jordan 194–Hart 1035 V10 | 8th | 4th |
| Eddie Irvine | Jordan 194–Hart 1035 V10 | 13th | 7th |

Round 14 – European Grand Prix – Jerez, Spain
16th October

| Rubens Barrichello | Jordan 194–Hart 1035 V10 | 5th | 12th |
| Eddie Irvine | Jordan 194–Hart 1035 V10 | 10th | 4th |

Round 15 – Japanese Grand Prix – Suzuka
6th October

| Rubens Barrichello | Jordan 194–Hart 1035 V10 | 10th | R |
| Eddie Irvine | Jordan 194–Hart 1035 V10 | 6th | 5th |

Round 16 – Australian Grand Prix – Adelaide
13th November

| Rubens Barrichello | Jordan 194–Hart 1035 V10 | 5th | 4th |
| Eddie Irvine | Jordan 194–Hart 1035 V10 | 6th | R |

1994 Final Championship Positions
Drivers

Rubens Barrichello	19 pts	6th place
Eddie Irvine	6 pts	14th= place
Andrea de Cesaris	4 pts (3 pts for Jordan)	18th= place

Constructors

| Jordan | 28 pts | 5th place |

JORDAN GRAND PRIX RACING TEAM – STATISTICS 1995

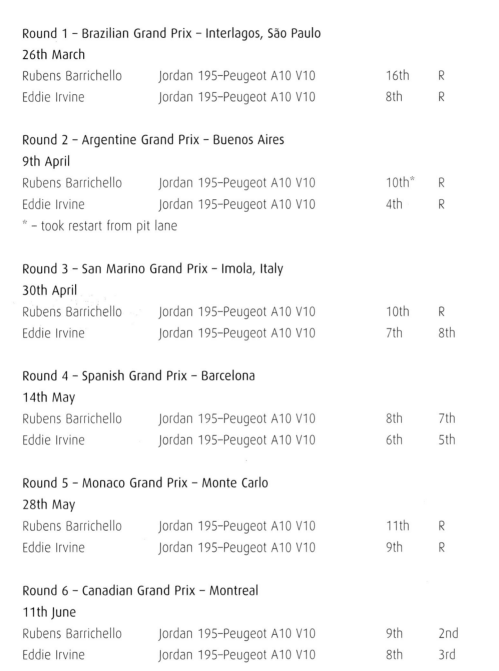

Round 1 – Brazilian Grand Prix – Interlagos, São Paulo
26th March

Rubens Barrichello	Jordan 195–Peugeot A10 V10	16th	R
Eddie Irvine	Jordan 195–Peugeot A10 V10	8th	R

Round 2 – Argentine Grand Prix – Buenos Aires
9th April

Rubens Barrichello	Jordan 195–Peugeot A10 V10	10th*	R
Eddie Irvine	Jordan 195–Peugeot A10 V10	4th	R

* – took restart from pit lane

Round 3 – San Marino Grand Prix – Imola, Italy
30th April

Rubens Barrichello	Jordan 195–Peugeot A10 V10	10th	R
Eddie Irvine	Jordan 195–Peugeot A10 V10	7th	8th

Round 4 – Spanish Grand Prix – Barcelona
14th May

Rubens Barrichello	Jordan 195–Peugeot A10 V10	8th	7th
Eddie Irvine	Jordan 195–Peugeot A10 V10	6th	5th

Round 5 – Monaco Grand Prix – Monte Carlo
28th May

Rubens Barrichello	Jordan 195–Peugeot A10 V10	11th	R
Eddie Irvine	Jordan 195–Peugeot A10 V10	9th	R

Round 6 – Canadian Grand Prix – Montreal
11th June

Rubens Barrichello	Jordan 195–Peugeot A10 V10	9th	2nd
Eddie Irvine	Jordan 195–Peugeot A10 V10	8th	3rd

Round 7 – French Grand Prix – Magny-Cours
2nd July

| Rubens Barrichello | Jordan 195–Peugeot A10 V10 | 5th | 6th |
| Eddie Irvine | Jordan 195–Peugeot A10 V10 | 11th | 9th |

Round 8 – British Grand Prix – Silverstone
16th July

| Rubens Barrichello | Jordan 195–Peugeot A10 V10 | 9th | 11th* |
| Eddie Irvine | Jordan 195–Peugeot A10 V10 | 7th | R |

* – classified but not running at the finish

Round 9 – German Grand Prix – Hockenheim
30th July

| Rubens Barrichello | Jordan 195–Peugeot A10 V10 | 5th | R |
| Eddie Irvine | Jordan 195–Peugeot A10 V10 | 6th | 9th* |

* – classified but not running at the finish

Round 10 – Hungarian Grand Prix – Hungaroring
13th August

| Rubens Barrichello | Jordan 195–Peugeot A10 V10 | 14th | 7th |
| Eddie Irvine | Jordan 195–Peugeot A10 V10 | 7th | 13th* |

* – classified but not running at the finish

Round 11 – Belgian Grand Prix – Spa-Francorchamps
27th August

| Rubens Barrichello | Jordan 195–Peugeot A10 V10 | 12th | 6th |
| Eddie Irvine | Jordan 195–Peugeot A10 V10 | 7th | R |

Round 12 – Italian Grand Prix – Monza
10th September

| Rubens Barrichello | Jordan 195–Peugeot A10 V10 | 6th | R |
| Eddie Irvine | Jordan 195–Peugeot A10 V10 | 12th | R |

Round 13 – Portuguese Grand Prix – Estoril
24th September

Rubens Barrichello	Jordan 195–Peugeot A10 V10	8th	11th
Eddie Irvine	Jordan 195–Peugeot A10 V10	10th	10th

Round 14 – European Grand Prix – Nurburgring, Germany
1st October

Rubens Barrichello	Jordan 195–Peugeot A10 V10	11th	4th
Eddie Irvine	Jordan 195–Peugeot A10 V10	5th	6th

Round 15 – Pacific Grand Prix – TI Circuit, Aida, Japan
22nd October

Rubens Barrichello	Jordan 195–Peugeot A10 V10	11th	R
Eddie Irvine	Jordan 195–Peugeot A10 V10	6th	11th

Round 16 – Japanese Grand Prix – Suzuka
29th October

Rubens Barrichello	Jordan 195–Peugeot A10 V10	10th	R
Eddie Irvine	Jordan 195–Peugeot A10 V10	7th	4th

Round 17 – Australian Grand Prix – Adelaide
12th November

Rubens Barrichello	Jordan 195–Peugeot A10 V10	7th	R
Eddie Irvine	Jordan 195–Peugeot A10 V10	9th	R

1995 Final Championship Positions
Drivers

Rubens Barrichello	11 pts	11th place
Eddie Irvine	10 pts	12th= place

Constructors

Jordan	21 pts	6th place

JORDAN GRAND PRIX RACING TEAM – STATISTICS 1996

Round 1 – Australian Grand Prix – Albert Park, Melbourne
10th March

Rubens Barrichello	Jordan 196–Peugeot A12EV5 V10	8th	R
Martin Brundle	Jordan 196–Peugeot A12EV5 V10	19th*	R

* – started from the pit lane

Round 2 – Brazilian Grand Prix – Interlagos, São Paulo
31st March

Rubens Barrichello	Jordan 196–Peugeot A12EV5 V10	2nd	R
Martin Brundle	Jordan 196–Peugeot A12EV5 V10	6th	12th*

* – classified but not running at the finish

Round 3 – Argentine Grand Prix – Buenos Aires
7th April

Rubens Barrichello	Jordan 196–Peugeot A12EV5 V10	6th	4th
Martin Brundle	Jordan 196–Peugeot A12EV5 V10	15th	R

Round 4 – European Grand Prix – Nurburgring, Germany
28th April

Rubens Barrichello	Jordan 196–Peugeot A12EV5 V10	5th	5th
Martin Brundle	Jordan 196–Peugeot A12EV5 V10	11th	6th

Round 5 – San Marino Grand Prix – Imola, Italy
5th May

Rubens Barrichello	Jordan 196–Peugeot A12EV5 V10	9th	5th
Martin Brundle	Jordan 196–Peugeot A12EV5 V10	12th	R

Round 6 – Monaco Grand Prix – Monte Carlo
19th May

Rubens Barrichello	Jordan 196–Peugeot A12EV5 V10	6th	R
Martin Brundle	Jordan 196–Peugeot A12EV5 V10	16th	R

Round 7 – Spanish Grand Prix – Barcelona
2nd June

Rubens Barrichello	Jordan 196–Peugeot A12EV5 V10	7th	R
Martin Brundle	Jordan 196–Peugeot A12EV5 V10	15th	R

Round 8 – Canadian Grand Prix – Montreal
16th June

Rubens Barrichello	Jordan 196–Peugeot A12EV5 V10	8th	R
Martin Brundle	Jordan 196–Peugeot A12EV5 V10	9th	6th

Round 9 – French Grand Prix – Magny-Cours
30th June

Rubens Barrichello	Jordan 196–Peugeot A12EV5 V10	11th	9th
Martin Brundle	Jordan 196–Peugeot A12EV5 V10	8th	8th

Round 10 – British Grand Prix – Silverstone
14th July

Rubens Barrichello	Jordan 196–Peugeot A12EV5 V10	6th	4th
Martin Brundle	Jordan 196–Peugeot A12EV5 V10	8th	6th

Round 11 – German Grand Prix – Hockenheim
28th July

Rubens Barrichello	Jordan 196–Peugeot A12EV5 V10	9th	6th
Martin Brundle	Jordan 196–Peugeot A12EV5 V10	10th	10th

Round 12 – Hungarian Grand Prix – Hungaroring, Budapest
11th August

Rubens Barrichello	Jordan 196–Peugeot A12EV5 V10	13th	6th
Martin Brundle	Jordan 196–Peugeot A12EV5 V10	12th	R

Round 13 – Belgian Grand Prix – Spa-Francorchamps
25th August

Rubens Barrichello	Jordan 196–Peugeot A12EV5 V10	10th	R
Martin Brundle	Jordan 196–Peugeot A12EV5 V10	8th	R

Round 14 – Italian Grand Prix – Monza
8th September

Rubens Barrichello	Jordan 196–Peugeot A12EV5 V10	10th	5th
Martin Brundle	Jordan 196–Peugeot A12EV5 V10	9th	4th

Round 15 – Portuguese Grand Prix – Estoril
22nd September

Rubens Barrichello	Jordan 196–Peugeot A12EV5 V10	9th	R
Martin Brundle	Jordan 196–Peugeot A12EV5 V10	10th	9th

Round 16 – Japanese Grand Prix – Suzuka
13th October

Rubens Barrichello	Jordan 196–Peugeot A12EV5 V10	11th	9th
Martin Brundle	Jordan 196–Peugeot A12EV5 V10	10th	5th

1996 Final Championship Positions
Drivers

Rubens Barrichello	14 pts	8th place
Martin Brundle	8 pts	11th place

Constructors

Jordan	22 pts	5th place

JORDAN GRAND PRIX RACING TEAM – STATISTICS 1997

Round 1 – Australian Grand Prix – Melbourne
9th March

Ralf Schumacher	Jordan 197–Peugeot A14 V10	12th	R
Giancarlo Fisichella	Jordan 197–Peugeot A14 V10	14th	R

Round 2 – Brazilian Grand Prix – Interlagos, São Paulo
30th March

Ralf Schumacher	Jordan 197–Peugeot A14 V10	10th	R
Giancarlo Fisichella	Jordan 197–Peugeot A14 V10	7th	8th

Round 3 – Argentine Grand Prix – Buenos Aires
13th April

Ralf Schumacher	Jordan 197–Peugeot A14 V10	6th	3rd
Giancarlo Fisichella	Jordan 197–Peugeot A14 V10	9th	R

Round 4 – San Marino Grand Prix – Imola, Italy
27th April

Ralf Schumacher	Jordan 197–Peugeot A14 V10	5th	R
Giancarlo Fisichella	Jordan 197–Peugeot A14 V10	6th	4th

Round 5 – Monaco Grand Prix – Monte Carlo
11th May

Ralf Schumacher	Jordan 197–Peugeot A14 V10	6th	R
Giancarlo Fisichella	Jordan 197–Peugeot A14 V10	4th	6th

Round 6 – Spanish Grand Prix – Barcelona
25th May

Ralf Schumacher	Jordan 197–Peugeot A14 V10	9th*	R
Giancarlo Fisichella	Jordan 197–Peugeot A14 V10	8th	9th

* – started from the back of the grid

Round 7 – Canadian Grand Prix – Montreal
15th June

Ralf Schumacher	Jordan 197–Peugeot A14 V10	7th	R
Giancarlo Fisichella	Jordan 197–Peugeot A14 V10	6th	3rd

Round 8 – French Grand Prix – Magny-Cours
29th June

Ralf Schumacher	Jordan 197–Peugeot A14 V10	3rd	6th
Giancarlo Fisichella	Jordan 197–Peugeot A14 V10	11th	9th

Round 9 – British Grand Prix – Silverstone
13th July

Ralf Schumacher	Jordan 197–Peugeot A14 V10	5th	5th
Giancarlo Fisichella	Jordan 197–Peugeot A14 V10	10th	7th

Round 10 – German Grand Prix – Hockenheim
27th July

Ralf Schumacher	Jordan 197–Peugeot A14 V10	7th	5th
Giancarlo Fisichella	Jordan 197–Peugeot A14 V10	2nd	11th*

* – classified but not running at the finish

Round 11 – Hungarian Grand Prix – Hungaroring, Budapest
10th August

Ralf Schumacher	Jordan 197–Peugeot A14 V10	14th	5th
Giancarlo Fisichella	Jordan 197–Peugeot A14 V10	13th	R

Round 12 – Belgian Grand Prix – Spa-Francorchamps
24th August

Ralf Schumacher	Jordan 197–Peugeot A14 V10	6th*	R
Giancarlo Fisichella	Jordan 197–Peugeot A14 V10	4th	2nd

* – started from the pit lane

Round 13 – Italian Grand Prix – Monza
7th September

Ralf Schumacher	Jordan 197–Peugeot A14 V10	8th	R
Giancarlo Fisichella	Jordan 197–Peugeot A14 V10	3rd	4th

Round 14 – Austrian Grand Prix – A1 Ring, Zeltweg
21st September

Ralf Schumacher	Jordan 197–Peugeot A14 V10	11th	5th
Giancarlo Fisichella	Jordan 197–Peugeot A14 V10	14th	4th

Round 15 – Luxembourg Grand Prix – Nurburgring, Germany
28th September

Ralf Schumacher	Jordan 197–Peugeot A14 V10	8th	R
Giancarlo Fisichella	Jordan 197–Peugeot A14 V10	4th	R

Round 16 – Japanese Grand Prix – Suzuka
12th October

Ralf Schumacher	Jordan 197–Peugeot A14 V10	13th	9th
Giancarlo Fisichella	Jordan 197–Peugeot A14 V10	9th	7th

Round 17 – European Grand Prix – Jerez, Spain
26th October

Ralf Schumacher	Jordan 197–Peugeot A14 V10	16th	R
Giancarlo Fisichella	Jordan 197–Peugeot A14 V10	17th	11th

1997 Final Championship Positions
Drivers

Giancarlo Fisichella	20 pts	8th place
Ralf Schumacher	13 pts	11th place

Constructors

Jordan	33 pts	5th place

JORDAN GRAND PRIX RACING TEAM – STATISTICS 1998

Round 1 – Australian Grand Prix – Melbourne
8th March

Damon Hill	Jordan 198–Mugen-Honda MF301C V10	9th	8th
Ralf Schumacher	Jordan 198–Mugen-Honda MF301C V10	10th	R

Round 2 – Brazilian Grand Prix – Interlagos, São Paulo
29th March

Damon Hill	Jordan 198–Mugen-Honda MF301C V10	11th	DQ
Ralf Schumacher	Jordan 198–Mugen-Honda MF301C V10	8th	R

Round 3 – Argentine Grand Prix – Buenos Aires
12th April

Damon Hill	Jordan 198–Mugen-Honda MF301C V10	9th	8th
Ralf Schumacher	Jordan 198–Mugen-Honda MF301C V10	5th	R

Round 4 – San Marino Grand Prix – Imola, Italy
26th April

| Damon Hill | Jordan 198–Mugen-Honda MF301C V10 | 7th | 10th* |
| Ralf Schumacher | Jordan 198–Mugen-Honda MF301C V10 | 9th | 7th |

Round 5 – Spanish Grand Prix – Barcelona
10th May

| Damon Hill | Jordan 198–Mugen-Honda MF301C V10 | 8th | R |
| Ralf Schumacher | Jordan 198–Mugen-Honda MF301C V10 | 11th | 11th |

Round 6 – Monaco Grand Prix – Monte Carlo
24th May

| Damon Hill | Jordan 198–Mugen-Honda MF301C V10 | 15th | 8th |
| Ralf Schumacher | Jordan 198–Mugen-Honda MF301C V10 | 16th | R |

Round 7 – Canadian Grand Prix – Montreal
7th June

| Damon Hill | Jordan 198–Mugen-Honda MF301C V10 | 10th | R |
| Ralf Schumacher | Jordan 198–Mugen-Honda MF301C V10 | 5th | R |

Round 8 – French Grand Prix – Magny-Cours
28th June

| Damon Hill | Jordan 198–Mugen-Honda MF301C V10 | 7th | R |
| Ralf Schumacher | Jordan 198–Mugen-Honda MF301C V10 | 6th | 16th |

Round 9 – British Grand Prix – Silverstone
12th July

| Damon Hill | Jordan 198–Mugen-Honda MF301C V10 | 7th | R |
| Ralf Schumacher | Jordan 198–Mugen-Honda MF301C V10 | 21st* | 6th |

* – qualifying times disallowed

Round 10 – Austrian Grand Prix – A1 Ring, Zeltweg
26th July

Damon Hill	Jordan 198–Mugen-Honda MF301C V10	15th	7th
Ralf Schumacher	Jordan 198–Mugen-Honda MF301C V10	9th	5th

Round 11 – German Grand Prix – Hockenheim
2th August

Damon Hill	Jordan 198–Mugen-Honda MF301C V10	5th	4th
Ralf Schumacher	Jordan 198–Mugen-Honda MF301C V10	4th	6th

Round 12 – Hungarian Grand Prix – Hungaroring, Budapest
16th August

Damon Hill	Jordan 198–Mugen-Honda MF301C V10	4th	4th
Ralf Schumacher	Jordan 198–Mugen-Honda MF301C V10	10th	9th

Round 13 – Belgian Grand Prix – Spa-Francorchamps
30th August

Damon Hill	Jordan 198–Mugen-Honda MF301C V10	3rd	1st
Ralf Schumacher	Jordan 198–Mugen-Honda MF301C V10	8th	2nd

Round 14 – Italian Grand Prix – Monza
13th September

Damon Hill	Jordan 198–Mugen-Honda MF301C V10	14th	6th
Ralf Schumacher	Jordan 198–Mugen-Honda MF301C V10	6th	3rd

Round 15 – Luxembourg Grand Prix – Nurburgring, Germany
27th September

Damon Hill	Jordan 198–Mugen-Honda MF301C V10	10th	9th
Ralf Schumacher	Jordan 198–Mugen-Honda MF301C V10	6th	R

Round 16 – Japanese Grand Prix – Suzuka
1st November

Damon Hill	Jordan 198–Mugen-Honda MF301C V10	8th	4th
Ralf Schumacher	Jordan 198–Mugen-Honda MF301C V10	7th	R

1998 Final Championship Positions

Drivers

| Damon Hill | 20 pts | 6th place |
| Ralf Schumacher | 14 pts | 10th place |

Constructors

| Jordan | 34 points | 4th place |

Jordan Grand Prix 1998

COMMERCIAL
Eddie Jordan
Ian Phillips
Lindsay Haylett
Giselle Davies
Mark Gallagher
Trudie Edwards
Claire Walker
Tony Laszlo
Nigel Griffiths
Emma Owens

FINANCE
Richard O'Driscoll
Karen Wingrove
Denise Williams
Tina Warnes

DRAWING OFFICE
Gary Anderson
Mike Gascoyne
Keith Barclay
Marc Logan
Bruce Eddington
John McQilliam

Mark Smith
John Iley
Simon Phillips
Doug Reeves
James Pocock
Ian Hall
John Davis
Tim Holloway
Dino Toso
Sam Michael
Chris Warner
James Key
Stephen Hollis
William Grey
Stephen Norris
Phillip Thomas
Paul Nixon
Paul Foster
Simon Gardener

ELECTRONICS/SOFTWARE
Mike Wroe
Paul Snow
John Matless
Barry Hayes
Rob Worner

Marc Donovan
Hari Roberts
Andrew Jones

**RESEARCH &
DEVELOPMENT**
Simon Smart
Paul Thompson
Mark Turner
Gary North
Richard Frith

RACE TEAM
Trevor Foster
Jim Vale
Tim Edwards
Sophie Ashley-Carter
Nick Burrows
Darren Beacroft
Dave Perrott
Andy Stevenson
Patrick Grandidier
Phil Howell
Mark Shurety
Darren Burton

Ian Michell
Martin Bishop
Stuart Collins
Julian Clarke
Gerrard O'Reilly
Dave Coates
Warwick Pugh
Ian Marchant
Ged Robb
Leigh Pettifer
Paul Pinney

HYDRAULICS
Wayne Greedy
Craig Spencer
Gary Taylor
Alan Yeates

SUB ASSEMBLY
Marek Sobas
Barry Burgess
Mark Rosling
Andy Lovell
Paul Bennett
Stuart McNally
Tim Gulland
Nick Caceres
Marcus Fenning
Greg Borril

INSPECTION
Phil Gilbert

Pete Laye
Steve Harvey
Graham Smith

STORES
Michael Gomme
Andy Glover
Andy Beacroft
Matt Lecoche
Roy Henderson
Graham Pratt
Carl Scarlett

MAINTENANCE
Roy Summerfield
Tony Daly
Richard Lawson

FABRICATION
Mick Carter
Dave Gledhill
Andy Thomas
Dave Alcock
Arne Jonnson

MACHINE SHOP
Trevor Lecoche
Christian Knight
Kevin Coles
Gerry Wayman

COMPOSITES
Tom Anderson
Tisa Bolton
Simon Shinkins
Pete Richardson
Paul Moore
Jason Back
Gary Parker
Tony Wright
Nigel Johnson
Domonic Mirto
Ben Leatherland
Matthew Thom
Chris Duddley
Barry Newman
Rob Tween
Stephen Sharpe

PURCHASING
Paul Hicks
Tony Merry
Patrick Pedersen

PRODUCTION CONTROL
Bob Halliwell
Steve Cochrane
Ben Mullens
Sukhi Bhogal

INFORMATION
TECHNOLOGY
Aubrey Mitchell

Mark Cormican
Adrian Collinson

**FACTORY
MANAGEMENT**
Adrian Rowland
Dorthy Graham

TEST TEAM
Phil Spencer
Matt Deane
Danny Slater
Mark Hicks
David O'Neill

Jimmy Waddell
Dave Burr
Rick Wiltshire
Dave Fogden
Darren Jeffs

MODEL SHOP
Adrian Smith
Keith Austin
James Best
Simon Page
Des Boyles
Mark Laitte
Chris Goddard

PATTERN SHOP
Neil Shadbolt
Ian George
Stephen Edwards

WIND TUNNEL
Simon Belcher
Michael Ewin
Brian Riordan
Tony Lisence

RECEPTION
Jaime Taylor

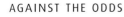

Acknowledgements

Maurice Hamilton

It took courage of a special kind to allow this book to happen during such a difficult year. I am not only indebted to Eddie Jordan for granting full access to his team but I am also grateful for his continued approval despite the inevitable path the story had to follow.

The book, however, could not have been written without the unstinting help of Ian Phillips and Trevor Foster, both of whom provided detail and encouragement, even when times were tough. I can have no complaints whatsoever about the level of assistance from within the team and any mistakes are mine, not theirs. I can't thank them enough for their time and patience.

Thanks, also, to Damon Hill, Ralf Schumacher, Nigel Northridge, Dave Marren, Marie Jordan, Lindsay Haylett, Giselle Davies, Mark Gallagher, Nigel Griffiths, Richard O'Driscoll, Gary Anderson, Mike Gascoyne, Jim Vale, Tim Edwards, Sophie Ashley–Carter, Nick Burrows, Andy Stevenson, Dave Perrott, Phil Howell, Gerrard O'Reilly, Dave Coates, Warwick Pugh and John Matless for their support in various ways. And not forgetting Trudie Edwards for the welcome cups of tea.

Finally, my gratitude to everyone at Macmillan for their full support throughout. I'd like to think their faith has been rewarded.

Jon Nicholson

Thanks to Olympus Optical and Metro Photographic. I'm also grateful to all at Jordan for allowing me to go about my job, even when times were difficult.